The Comprehensive and Acclaimed
Program for Making a Life-defining Decision

Motherhood
Is It For Me?

Your Step-by-Step Guide to Clarity

Denise L. Carlini & Ann Davidman

Foreword by Mardy S. Ireland

Published by:
Transformation Books
211 Pauline Drive #513
York, PA 17402
www.TransformationBooks.com

ISBN # 9781945252167
Library of Congress Control No: 2016959637

Printed in the United States of America

Motherhood
Is It For Me?

Your Step-by-Step Guide to Clarity

In Praise of *Motherhood – Is It For Me?*
Your Step-by-Step Guide to Clarity

"Most women struggling to decide whether or not to have a child make this choice alone, rarely sharing their doubts and fears with anybody because of the shame and anxiety involved in even considering motherhood an option rather than an imperative. Now, they will find the wise, thoughtful and non-judgmental advice they need in *Motherhood – Is It For Me?*, the systematic program designed to guide any woman to the life choice that is right for her."

~ **Jeanne Safer, PhD,** author of *Beyond Motherhood:*
Choosing a Life without Children

"Welcome to a contemporary guide for the contemporary woman! No longer is it to be assumed that there is a 'maternal instinct' in a framework of moral judgment. In this book conflict and ambivalence are accepted as a normalized rite of passage to self-acceptance. From a neutral and nurturing point of view regarding the choice, the authors provide a graceful, twelve-week encounter a woman can make with herself. The writing is accessible and the techniques relevant, all with the goal to help a woman gradually uncover hidden, unconscious parts of herself – echoes from the past – that when integrated into her sense of herself can move her forward regarding a choice about motherhood. This book provides a well recommended journey for the questioning woman."

~ **Phyllis Tobin, PhD,** author of *Motherhood Optional:*
A Psychological Journey

"Motherhood – Is It For Me? is a book that will help so many women to find their way to peace around whether to have children or not. It is much needed as it addresses one of the core social taboos that make having a frank dialogue about this so difficult – ambivalence. Many involuntarily childless women who seek the support of Gateway Women often come to the painful realization that one of the reasons they didn't pursue motherhood more actively was because of unexplored ambivalence, often stemming from childhood experiences that left them confused about what motherhood 'meant.' I believe that ambivalence is quite normal, yet the prevailing view of society's pronatalism is that women 'just know'; a belief that fails to recognize that modern women's lives and opportunities, including access to birth control, have created choices that make 'just knowing' a thing of the past, if ever it truly existed. As a society, we're only just beginning to create a space and a language for how to navigate these choices, and this thorough, intelligent, empathic, non-judgmental book takes us a big step forward. Whether you wish to explore and be sure of your reasons for choosing to live childfree, or to understand what's blocking you from actively pursuing the path to motherhood, this book will be your friend and guide. I know many women who will wish it had been around twenty years ago, and I am grateful to Denise and Ann for making it available to the generations of daughters that come after us."

  ~ **Jody Day,** founder of Gateway Women and author of
*Living the Life Unexpected: 12 Weeks to Your Plan B for a
Meaningful and Fulfilling Life without Children*
www.gateway-women.com

"When I became a father 35 years ago I made a list of pros and cons of becoming a parent. Although *Motherhood – Is It For Me?* is written for women, I wish I had this book when I was trying to decide if having a child was for me. This is 'the book' for a couple that wants to explore all the 'normal' ambivalence that every woman (or man) struggles with in making this life-changing decision to become a parent. The open-hearted, non-judgmental approach Ann and Denise have developed offers the most intimate path to your own deepest feelings to discover whether being or not being a parent is right for you. If you read this book you'll know, for the rest of your life, you seriously answered the question for yourself... is being a parent for me?"

> ~ **Bruce Linton, PhD,** founder of the Fathers' Forum,
> author of *Finding Time for Fatherhood:*
> *Men's Concerns as Parents* and *Becoming a Dad:*
> *How Fatherhood Changes Men*

"Becoming a mother is a radical transformation. If you are called to it, if you know you must have a child, then by all means do it. Raising a child is one of the most creative endeavors you could possibly engage in. But if you're not sure that motherhood is your path, this book – filled with wisdom and compassion – is a sure guide to clarity. The stories and exercises are inviting and inspiring in their depth of understanding. Every word of this carefully constructed program lights your way to the life that is right for you and yours."

> ~ **Shoshana Alexander,** author of *In Praise of Single Parents*
> and co-author with James Baraz of *Awakening Joy:*
> *10 Steps to Happiness*

"*Motherhood – Is It For Me?* is the first of its kind! It offers an inward focused, self-directed process designed to put aside outside influences, tend to places inside that may be in the way of inner knowing, and reveal your true desires about whether you want to become a parent. Denise L. Carlini and Ann Davidman's valuable tool will skillfully help you uncover the roots of your ambivalence and guide you on your unique path to clarity."

~ **Laura Carroll,** author of *Families of Two* and *The Baby Matrix*

"In *Motherhood – Is It For Me?* I've encountered one of the best examples of what a serious piece of process work can look like. You get this occasionally in many psychology books, but I've never encountered anything so thorough or providing such containment. It reminds me of a book I've used on how to work with dreams, except this book has so much 'holding power' for the feminine reality."

~ **Carol Shoopman, MFT,** psychotherapist

"As parenthood moves from an assumption to a decision, it's important to give yourself some reflective time, away from all the external chatter, to examine your motives, stories, and history and decide for yourself whether being a birth parent or adoptive parent is an appropriate role for you. *Motherhood – Is It For Me?* is your invitation to be an independent decision maker and the creator of your rich experience of life as you make the choice to be a parent or to remain contentedly childfree."

~ **Laura S. Scott,** author of *Two Is Enough:*
A Couple's Guide to Living Childless by Choice, and director of the Childless by Choice Project

"This insightful and invaluable book helps women decide what is possibly the biggest decision of their life. I am forever grateful to Denise and Ann for guiding all the women who read this in a way that is thoughtful and very user-friendly."

~ **Henriette Mantel,** actress, filmmaker, and author/editor of
No Kidding: Women Writers on Bypassing Parenthood

"I'm delighted to see such a fine program in print. I've been aware of this program since it was developed over twenty years ago and I know how much it has helped others. My ex-partner and I consciously chose to adopt an infant girl over two decades ago and today I'm a proud grandfather of two. I worked for many years in child protective services and had direct contact with families, often witnessing the pain that comes from neglect and abuse. I've also seen parents who lacked skill become more capable as they developed resources to better care for their children. *Motherhood – Is It For Me?* is a valuable contribution toward a better future for all. Thank you Denise and Ann!"

~ **Peter Barrett, MFT,** retired CPS manager, father and grandfather

"I heartily recommend the wise and well-paced approach of *Motherhood – Is It For Me?* The authors respectfully explore the many layers and angles of ambivalence about choosing to become a mother; readers are treated to exercises that are accessible and truly helpful; the personal stories open the heart as well as bring clarity to the mind. A real gem."

~ **Linda Graham, MFT,** author of *Bouncing Back: Rewiring Your Brain for Maximum Resilience and Well-Being*

Participants of the Motherhood-Is it for me?™ program acclaim:

"Motherhood-Is it for me? helped me realize that what was holding me back from seeing what I wanted had nothing to do with the question of whether I wanted children or not. Once I was freed of that paralyzing thought pattern I was able to seek out what was true for me amidst all the clutter, an experience that changed my life for the better and helped me gain clarity on many levels."

"The program helped me understand what had shaped my hesitation throughout my life. Meeting other women struggling with the same issue was comforting, since I always felt very alone with this before. My partner told me that I became much calmer during the program, which I regarded as the first step of a process."

"The program was a powerful reminder of who I am amid all of life's uncertainty and complications. Instead of being overly focused on what I can't control, I have found that I am really enjoying shaping my life and being grateful for the gifts it brings. I am not at the mercy of my feelings, because I have new tools for understanding, sharing, and moving towards what I want."

"After going through the program, I had a very clear internal sense of direction. I particularly appreciated the approach, which recognized that we had all tried an analytical, 'pros and cons' problem-solving approach to answering the question and that hadn't worked. This process was extremely valuable to help me uncover – and overcome – fears I didn't even know I had about becoming a mother."

"I gained invaluable self-awareness and insight and started on a road to self-healing that went far beyond the decision around whether to become a mother. I realized that my ambivalence and doubt is rooted deeply in issues of self-esteem and confidence, which was a revelation."

"The biggest revelation/blessing I received was the understanding that deep down, I really DID know the answer. It was just that there were some blocks in my life that I had to work through in order to get to the clarity and wisdom that was already there."

"I was 50/50 and just couldn't decide. The 12-week program helped heal childhood wounds and identify my true desires amid a confusing array of societal expectations, hopes, fears, wants and needs. My decision feels right and good, and it has freed up tons of energy that was going into a daily see-saw over this."

"I went on a personalized, nourishing and spiritual journey to not only discover my true feelings about motherhood but also who I am as a woman at a deeper level."

~ for all women

The Road Not Taken

Two roads diverged in a yellow wood,
And sorry I could not travel both
And be one traveler, long I stood
And looked down one as far as I could
To where it bent in the undergrowth;

Then took the other, as just as fair,
And having perhaps the better claim,
Because it was grassy and wanted wear;
Though as for that the passing there
Had worn them really about the same,

And both that morning equally lay
In leaves no step had trodden black.
Oh, I kept the first for another day!
Yet knowing how way leads on to way,
I doubted if I should ever come back.

I shall be telling this with a sigh
Somewhere ages and ages hence:
Two roads diverged in a wood, and I–
I took the one less traveled by,
And that has made all the difference.

—Robert Frost[1]

Table of Contents

Foreword by Mardy S. Ireland 1

Introduction 5

How to Use *Motherhood – Is It For Me?* 9

   The Different Ways to Work This Program 9

   How to Get the Most from the Program 12

   What to Expect Each Week 18

The Twelve-Week Program 23

Week 1: Preparing for Your Journey 25

   What Happens in Week 1 26

      Your Journal 27

      Your Family Map 29

      Creating Your Family Map 32

      Meet Four Women 40

      A Little More about the Externals 42

   Working with Guided Visualizations 43

   Week 1 First Guided Visualization 44

   Be Curious: Assignments for Week 1 47

   Week 1 Second Guided Visualization 53

   What to Hold Inside This Week 57

   Self-Care 57

Week 2: Your Journey Begins – Getting Packed and Ready to Go.. 61

Week 2 Guided Visualization 63

What Happens in Week 2... 66

The Mantra 66

Big Project, Not Big Effort 72

Be Curious: Assignments for Week 2 72

What to Hold Inside This Week 76

Self-Care 77

You Are Not Alone 78

Week 3: A Surprise Encounter 87

Week 3 Guided Visualization 88

What Happens in Week 3... 94

It's Never Too Late to Heal................................... 95

Inner Freedom 96

Be Curious: Assignments for Week 3 97

What to Hold Inside This Week 103

Self-Care 105

You Are Not Alone 105

Week 4: Getting Your Bearings and Calibrating Your Compass 119

Week 4 Guided Visualization 121

What Happens in Week 4... 126

Feeling Yes 126

Saying No... 128

The Consequences of Not Being Able to Say No.... 129

Handling Disappointment 130

Making Decisions as a Two-Step Process 131

Be Curious: Assignments for Week 4 134

What to Hold Inside This Week 140

Self-Care 141

You Are Not Alone 142

Week 5: The Dialogue **151**

Week 5 Guided Visualization 152

What Happens in Week 5 159

Revisiting Unresolved Issues 160

Understanding Needs Frozen in Time 161

Generational Inheritance 163

Be Curious: Assignments for Week 5 165

What to Hold Inside This Week 172

Self-Care 173

You Are Not Alone 174

Week 6: Your Mother – How Well Do You Know Her? **185**

Week 6 Guided Visualization 186

What Happens in Week 6 191

Generational Inheritance Revisited 193

Internalized Messages 194

Attachment Wounds 195

Personal Boundaries 198

A Woman's Rite of Passage 201

Changing Your Story 202

Be Curious: Assignments for Week 6 203

What to Hold Inside This Week 207

Self-Care 208

You Are Not Alone 209

Week 7: Yes ~ No ~ Maybe **219**

Week 7 Guided Visualization 221

What Happens in Week 7 224

Making a Decision 225

Understanding the Role of Ambivalence 226

Pressure or Judgment from Self or Others 227

Be Curious: Assignments for Week 7 228

What to Hold Inside This Week 236

Self-Care 238

You Are Not Alone 240

Week 8: Being Decisive **251**

Week 8 Guided Visualization 252

What Happens in Week 8 255

More on Making a Decision 256

Celebrating a Decision 257

More on the Role of Ambivalence 258

Choice Invites Loss 260

Be Curious: Assignments for Week 8 262

What to Hold Inside This Week 266

Self-Care 267

You Are Not Alone 268

TABLE OF CONTENTS

Week 9: Gaining Perspective **275**

Week 9 Guided Visualization 276

What Happens in Week 9.. 281

    Gaining Perspective.. 282

    Uncharted Territory 283

    Reframing Perceptions.................................... 284

Be Curious: Assignments for Week 9 287

What to Hold Inside This Week 296

Self-Care 297

You Are Not Alone.. 298

Week 10: Wise Woman **309**

Week 10 Guided Visualization 310

What Happens in Week 10.. 315

    Wise Women 315

    The Impulse to Thrive 316

    Cultivating Resilience..................................... 317

    Be on the Lookout – Shame and Self-Sabotage 319

Be Curious: Assignments for Week 10 321

What to Hold Inside This Week 327

Self-Care 328

You Are Not Alone.. 329

Week 11: Anticipating Arrival **343**

Week 11 Guided Visualization 344

What Happens in Week 11.. 350

    Revisiting Your Externals 350

    Fears... 354

The Pulse of Your Desire.. 359

Closing One Chapter to Open Another 361

Be Curious: Assignments for Week 11 364

What to Hold Inside This Week 370

Self-Care 371

You Are Not Alone 372

Week 12: Arriving.. **383**

Week 12 Guided Visualization 385

What Happens in Week 12.................................... 389

Refining Your Current Story 390

Your Totem 394

Wrapping It All Up 394

Be Curious: Assignments for Week 12 406

What to Hold Inside Your Sweet Self as You Go Forth 414

Acknowledgments.. 417

Appendix I: Tools for Sharing the Process 421

A. A Letter to Your Partner Clarifying Recommendations
of the Program 421

B. Templates for Sharing Your Experience
with Your Partner 426

Appendix II: "I Still Don't Know!?" – Next Steps............ 431

References... 437

Resources.. 439

About the Authors.. 445

Index 447

Foreword

As a woman there are very few things in your life that, if *they happen* or *they don't happen*, profoundly shape and color your adulthood. I believe that first among these "few things" is the staking out your territory and relationship to "motherhood." Regardless if you make motherhood happen – or you don't – the arc of your life will be significantly etched by this decision. This decision is such a "big deal" that some women simply deny it and pretend it's not something they have to deal with and external circumstances will decide for them. Yet there is no escaping this decision's life-orienting effects because "motherhood" – to this very 21st century day – still remains a defining feature of how society understands what a woman is – and so a woman will have to answer for her decision or non-decision sooner or later. The bottom line is that as a woman you can take this decision up *actively* or *passively*, but you cannot avoid the life-shaping influence of this thing called "motherhood" – whether it is a yes or a no. And that is why this book is so vital for you if you have not staked out your territory and relationship to motherhood! Let me tell you why.

Foremost is that you, the reader, are not going to feel like you are having to make such a huge decision completely alone, even if you do read this book unaccompanied by others. The authors, who are both therapists, have spent over two decades of work creating this program. They have woven a web of emotional holding into the content of everything that is important to consider in making this decision for yourself. While they are guiding you step by step through the very salient topics in each of the chapters, you feel their presence with you.

The program topics are organized so they – and you – evolve over twelve weeks such that by its very structure, important time is built in for the unfolding of your personal truth. In each chapter the authors help you learn to trust your own process of unfolding and to honor it, starting with the first chapter, in creating your psychic working space, drawing your family map, and constructing a reliable "comfort place" for yourself to be used throughout the rest of the book. This book is not a simple analysis and list of the crucial elements when considering motherhood – yes or no. In each chapter you *experience yourself*; you don't just think your way through something. Through guided visualizations, slowly, you plumb your deeper self and then gather that experience into your net by writing about it (and I would offer writing the old fashioned way versus a computer will gather it better!).

Self-care is also a crucial element tended to in each of the chapters' topics – from the little girl in you (Week 3) and her concerns – to meeting and talking with your mother and father (Weeks 5 and 6) looking for things transmitted across the generational line. Thus, you learn from cumulative experiential processes, a series of writings, and art projects, where your initial yes or no may be coming from inside. You "try on" each decision fully, living with it for a while, and in doing so discover where the fault lines may be in your understandings of motherhood and yourself. By Week 10, the building of your experiences across the ten weeks of work allows the "wise woman" inside you to be more accessible and more ready to speak. And maybe you thought you didn't have a "wise woman" in there!

If you can read this book with others it will certainly augment your discoveries and emotional experiences, but it is not necessary to do so. You can experience this journey fully because the authors in their writing, and how they guide you through their program, have created a thoughtful, sensitive, and empathic sojourn toward one of the most important decisions you, as a woman, will ever make. I recommend this book to any – and every – woman who has yet to face this decision!

Mardy S. Ireland

Introduction

There are few places women can go to explore their ambivalence about motherhood without being judged or told what to do. Do *you* want to be a mom? It's a simple enough question, unless it's not. If you're ambivalent about this choice, the reason is multilayered, and it can be a lonely struggle with indecision.

Are you struggling with not knowing if you want to have children? Does it seem like everyone else *just knows,* and you don't? Do you need the answer yesterday, if not yesteryear? Or do you simply want to clarify once and for all whether becoming a mother is your calling in life?

If you answered yes to any of these questions, *Motherhood – Is It For Me?* is written for you. We offer this book as your oasis, your sanctuary – a place for you to explore, discover, and know your deepest truth. You might be single, partnered, or married, and of any age, cultural background, or sexual orientation. You might be struggling with conceiving. You might be considering adopting or becoming a biological parent, single parent, part-time parent, co-parent, or step-parent. You – or your partner – might already be a parent and you're considering having another child. Perhaps you've already decided but have mixed feelings that you want to explore.

What if you don't have to figure this one out alone? What if you could know the answer and be at peace? What if you could make your decision without having to impress anyone or make anyone else happy?

Whatever the circumstances that brought you to be standing somewhere between *yes* and *no* on the question of motherhood, we've learned that your uncertainty is complex and likely accompanied by powerful feelings such as fear, ambivalence, doubt, confusion, sadness, and shame. Experience has taught us that a deep *knowing* of what you truly *want* must precede making a clear and informed decision.

We're confident that through the step-by-step approach delineated in this book, you'll arrive at the other side of ambivalence just as numerous women already have with the Motherhood-Is it for me?™ program.

You've likely heard someone say, "How can you not know?" with a tone of incredulity that leaves you feeling badly about yourself or just plain angry. But deciding whether or not to have a child is a complex issue; most societies hold strong collective views regarding motherhood, and women who question or reject this path can be subjected to strong judgments. It's very possible that as you explore your fears and wishes about motherhood, someone close to you is finding it hard to understand your need for resolution.

Rest assured that there isn't one place in *Motherhood – Is It For Me?* that you'll be told what you should or shouldn't do. We have no agenda other than helping you find the clarity you seek. *Only you can know what is true for you.* You are the definer of you. You are the expert on you.

We advocate conscious choice because we believe it is the basis of personal freedom. We want you to have the internal freedom that comes with true knowing while offering you the confidence to explore and make discoveries without pressure or judgment. This one-of-a-kind program provides you with a haven for the in-depth exploration of all your feelings associated with the choices around motherhood. Every step of the way we want you to feel validated and safe.

We present our program in an easy-to-follow format. You'll find pertinent explanations and tried-and-true guidance in addition to fun, creative exercises designed to stir up whatever is inside you that's been blocking your path to clarity. If you want valuable tools to help you heal and enhance your life, this book is for you. If you want guidance through your ambivalence and confusion to find the clarity that has eluded you, this book is for you.

With an open heart and a lucid mind, it will be much easier to make the life-defining decisions you want to be able to make. So no matter where you are on the *yes-no continuum*, we wish you a fruitful journey.

How to Use *Motherhood – Is It For Me?*

You're about to embark on a unique process that will almost certainly transform your life. It promises to be a gradual unfolding rather than a process of digging around or overthinking to get what you need; of slowing down internally to catch up emotionally; of allowing the pertinent information to fall into place like the pieces of a puzzle. It's supportive and gently asks you to take risks. The program is based on the premise that your clarity is already there; it's just buried. We're confident of this. *Trusting your process is key.* We know from experience that you can't do it wrong.

The Different Ways to Work This Program

Working on Your Own

The majority of readers will work through the program on their own, and it's designed especially for you to do so. You can go at your own pace, in the safety and comfort of your home. If you've done some introspective work or have had counseling or therapy at some point in your life, you might find that helps here; but it's by no means necessary.

Working One to One

Sharing your discoveries with another woman who also wants to do this work can be very powerful. When considering your choice, make it someone who'll allow you to explore without judgment and give you the space you need when you need it. Will she respect that you have your own path to travel? Is she a reasonably good listener? It can be someone you know, but you might feel less constrained working with someone you don't know or don't know well. Mostly you want to be able to have your *own* uncensored process.

Working with a Group of Women

Many women feel isolated as they struggle with not knowing whether they want a child or children. Working the program with a circle of women who are all exploring this issue can provide invaluable support. If you're fortunate enough to be able to gather together a small group of like-minded women (three to six works best), you can meet weekly in a self-facilitated group.

Working with a Professional

If you're already working with a counselor, psychologist, or psychotherapist, you can take this book to your regular sessions and ask for guidance with the weekly material. It can be very healing to be witnessed and supported through the program by someone who's already earned your trust and wants what's best for you.

Some women who aren't already working with a professional feel, as they progress through the program, that this is the time to find one. Even though the program is designed to provide an ample "container" with its step-by-step guidance, it's possible to become flooded with emotions or experience a higher-than-anticipated level of distress. If this happens, we recommend that you consider finding a competent professional for support as you complete the program.

Working with Your Spouse or Partner: Not Recommended

If you're partnered, it might occur to you to work the program together, especially if you're both uncertain whether or not you want to become parents. But sharing the details of what you learn with your intimate partner can make the experience more complicated than it needs to be. Discovering your true desire is a deeply personal experience, and it's so very easy to censor yourself unconsciously in the face of your partner's opinions or fears.

What can work is this: Each of you work the program separately but simultaneously, *not* sharing the details with each other as you go along. After both of you complete the program, use the guidelines in Appendix I to help you share how the experience unfolded for each of you. Please note that this book is written for women, so if your partner is male, he'll have to adapt the exercises to fit a male perspective.

To avoid repeating "spouse or partner" each time we refer to your significant other, we use the word *partner* throughout the book to mean the person you are intimately sharing your life with.

Other Special Circumstances

While the majority of women who've used this program over the years were trying to figure out whether or not they wanted children, women with a variety of personal circumstances have found it to be beneficial in decision-making. The program is so adaptable that you can use it even if you're already well on your path of choice. If you feel unresolved about this path or what led to it, this process is an efficient and gentle way to consider and identify what still needs to be resolved. If you've already become a mother, you can use the program to look back and consider whether your personal desire matched the decision you made. You can also use it to help decide if you want to have a second or third child. If you're going to become a mother and it wasn't your first choice, this program can help you get on board. Honestly!

How to Get the Most from the Program

A Body-Mind Approach to Discovery and Healing

The Motherhood-Is it for me? program uses an experiential body-mind approach to the discovery and healing that occur as the weeks go by. The program is *experiential* in that your embodied experience might elicit a thought in your mind, or a thought in your mind might evoke emotion (we use the words *emotion* and *feeling* interchangeably). Some emotions feel big while others feel small or subtle; either way, emotions are felt through all the cells of your body. Each of the exercises in these pages is designed to help you get in touch with your felt experience of *thoughts and emotions* to access the crucial information you might not otherwise discover. You cannot solely *think* your way to clarity, but you will be able to *feel* your way, step by step, toward knowing your true desire. When you isolate your *desire* first, and then weigh it carefully against your personal circumstances, it's easier to make your *decision*.

Distinguishing between thoughts and feelings can be confusing, and you might have trouble finding the right label for what you feel. If you're new to naming your feelings, think about using the acronym

MeGSS, which stands for Mad, Glad, Sad, or Scared (the *e* is for emotion). These four feelings cover the broadest categories and can, of course, be expanded on. But if labeling feelings is new to you, this shortcut can help.

If you've had a difficult personal history, some emotions can feel dangerous or scary. You may hold a belief that if you let a little emotion out, it will just keep coming, overwhelming you. While this fear is common, it is not what happens. In fact the opposite is true: Constructively releasing pent-up emotions helps you feel more at ease in your body, more emotionally and cognitively receptive and responsive, and less reactive.

"Having Children" and "Becoming a Mother"

We use the expressions *having children* and *becoming a mother* interchangeably throughout the program. It's important that you know what we mean by them. The short answer is this: anything you can think of. The long answer includes adoption, surrogacy, becoming a step-parent or co-parent, and conceiving through reproductive medical intervention. For the purposes of this book, "having children" and "becoming a mother" are not limited to their narrowest meanings.

The Externals

To help focus exclusively on your internal process, we ask that you temporarily set aside all of life's current external circumstances that seem intertwined with your decision. You will receive precise guidance to help you do this. Some of you are thinking about finances, career, relationships, health issues, family pressures, cultural messages, and more. Whatever your *externals* are, they're real and not to be discounted or minimized. However, for the time it takes to complete the program, you'll need to put them aside and pretend to the best of your ability that they don't exist. Even though this can feel like an impossible task, we ask that you try to do it anyway. Your externals don't play a part in the first step, which is discovering what you truly want for yourself. Thoughtfully and realistically considering your externals is part of step two – making your decision, which comes at the very end of the process.

Containing Your Process

Containing your experience of the program within a specified period of time and space offers you the same feelings of predictability, support, and safety that we'd be cultivating if you were doing this introspective work in person with us. We recommend setting aside the same day and time each week to complete your reading and the related exercises. Pick a physical space for this work that's quiet and free from outside distractions, and set aside at least thirty to forty-five minutes for each time you sit with this book or your journal. You'll benefit if you spend more time than that, even if you use the additional time just to rest. You and your psyche will become accustomed to this regularity, and the rhythm will support you.

There's another aspect of optimal containment that's an extremely important one. We ask that for the entire duration of the program, you refrain from discussing with anyone – especially your partner if you have one – the specifics of what's happening for you. You can of course let others know you're engaged in a program to help you better understand what you want for yourself; just be sure to clarify that you'll be happy to share specifics *after* you finish. We call this aspect of containment *honoring your process*. If you're working with a group, this means respecting the privacy of the others by not discussing their process with them or others outside the group meeting.

Why do we ask you to contain your experience? The most important reason is that you're engaging in a process that stirs up sensitive and intimate aspects of your inner life. These deserve and need to be protected, especially in the early stages. Sometimes an important piece of information needs time to completely unfold, and sharing it prematurely can disrupt the unfolding. Also, even the most well-intentioned feedback from others can disturb the feeling of safety you've been creating for yourself and push you off track.

If you feel that keeping things from your partner will be difficult for you, ask them to help you keep up the *containment wall*. If you'd like extra support on how to do this, we've included a template in Appendix I that you can use to structure this conversation. You can certainly choose to share all the details once you've completed the program, but for now you're entitled to protect your privacy.

Encouragement When the Going Gets Rough

We just talked about the benefits of not sharing the details of your process while you're in it. That doesn't mean you can't share with a trusted friend or your partner that you're feeling anxious or sad because of something that came up during an exercise. We certainly don't want you to feel isolated. It's always best to ask for support when overwhelmed by uncomfortable feelings. It's when you share specific details that there's room for another person's feelings of concern or unintentional judgment to get in the way of what's unfolding for you. Staying vague about the feelings you're having even while you're seeking emotional support allows for connection without interference.

As you journey along, there will most likely be some bumps in the road. It's quite natural to feel anxious, scared that an answer won't come, discouraged, bored, sad, heartbroken, hopeless, angry, hopeful, or delighted – and everything else in between. It's also natural, at times, to feel more physically tired than you otherwise would. Allow more time for sleeping at night and resting during the day if you can. Remember to make time for nourishment. Use the self-care suggestions presented at the end of each week.

You might also experience what some people describe as *big feelings*. These could surprise you in their intensity, which is often in proportion to how much they've been hidden or pushed down. Try to the best of your ability to let these feelings come forth when you can. Give yourself dedicated time, in a safe place, just to *feel*. If feelings arise when you are at work or tending to important life concerns, even a five-minute private time-out to feel whatever's asking to be felt can be sufficient. You can more carefully tend to your feelings when you have more time.

About three-quarters of the way through this process, some women find themselves with a sense of knowing less than when they started. We've witnessed it over and over again. Each week a significant amount of exploration occurs. By the time you've completed Weeks 8, 9, and 10, so much has been stirred up that you can feel there is too much to fully resolve, leaving you a bit unsettled and wondering if clarity will ever come. If this happens, hang in there. If it doesn't happen, that's perfectly natural too. You're still sorting out all the puzzle pieces that you turned over. You *are* making progress. You *will* resolve the issues that surface and can trust that clarity is on its way. We'll remind you of this when it's appropriate.

For some it becomes too overwhelming to get through the twelve weeks without the help of a professional counselor or psychotherapist. Seeking help does not mean you have failed – quite the contrary. Asking for help can be the most self-caring and wisest choice if you feel you're having trouble with what is emerging. It's natural and normal for intense feelings to arise. If you happen to find yourself repeatedly flooded with feelings or experience constant high levels of distress that do not ebb and flow, we suggest finding a competent counselor or psychotherapist in your area for support as you continue through the program.

Setting the Pace

This program was carefully designed to take at least twelve weeks, and can easily take a few weeks longer. The passage of time is necessary to support the process. It just doesn't work to try and move it along more quickly. Think of yourself at the start as a tight bud that over time and under the right conditions opens to a full and glorious flower. The beauty of that unfolding should never be rushed.

We ask that you put on hold any decisions about the circumstances of your life for the entire time you're engaged in this program. Slowing down may indeed feel uncomfortable at first, but we've learned that allowing yourself time and space to examine and accurately perceive the various aspects of your life is far more effective than generating those pros-and-cons lists that only seem to keep you stuck in an endless loop of indecision. The payoff for slowing down is big: clarity!

Even though the presentation of the program is highly structured, your internal experience will most likely not take a linear path. You can find yourself all over the map with all kinds of feelings and thoughts as the weeks go by. But however circuitous your process seems, it *is* realistic to expect that at the end of the program you'll know more than you do now. Though the end may not seem grand like a fireworks finale (though it is possible), at the very least you will have embraced many subtle internal shifts that over time add up to something sizeable.

Our Agenda: Your Clarity!

Our only agenda is to help you move from confusion to clarity, from exhaustion to ease, from internal struggle to internal softness. We're not taking a stand on whether or not you should have children or become a mother or participate in raising the next generation. Only you can figure out and finally know what is right for you.

What to Expect Each Week

Except for Week 1, each week is structured similarly. We begin with a brief check-in to help you get grounded and prepared for the week's activities.

Next we ask you to partake in an experiential activity by either reading a guided visualization or recording it so you can listen to it later with your eyes closed. The other option is to have someone you trust read it to you or record it for you. The guided visualizations are the backbone of the program. Their element of surprise is so important to the process that we don't provide a lot of explanation beforehand. Some will feel more valuable to you than others; your response to one might feel flat while another feels so powerful that it's a "game changer." Over the course of the program they assemble a more complete picture than you have now.

Then we ask you to write. The writing exercises allow for greater integration of your experience. If your emotional state feels unmanageable after a writing exercise, we direct you through easy-to-follow steps that help reconnect you to the present moment while grounding you.

Next we discuss specific topics relevant to the week's activities, followed by additional assignments, many of them writing exercises. Some prefer to do their assignments right after completing the guided visualization, and others like to wait until later that week. What's important about the writing assignments is that you *actually write*, and longhand is preferable to using an electronic device, though for additional journaling and organizing your work, feel free to use an electronic device if you prefer. This doesn't mean you will miss something if you use your computer or tablet, and if that's less physically demanding for you by all means do so, but the intimacy with your words that comes from handwriting can add a dimension to your experience. You can even experiment with using your less-dominant hand – yet another dimension to explore.

Over the years we've heard, "Oh, I didn't do the writing, but I gave it a lot of thought." Thinking is good, of course, but so much more happens when you write. The writing itself takes twists and turns in a way that thought processes can't, creating a fertile environment for more and more to emerge. We cannot count the times we've heard women say, "I had no idea I was going to write *that*."

If you find yourself resistant to doing the writing assignments, you might think you're not doing the program correctly or even that you're failing in general. This is not the case. If a writing assignment seems to want to open you up to a feeling you're not quite ready for, write about that – how it is to be in *that* place. Write from where you are and give yourself permission to be exactly where you are at that moment in time. As you let yourself go with the writing, it will begin to flow more easily.

Following the assignments, there's a section to help you explore what you discovered in more depth. This section starts with reading what you wrote, and we strongly recommend that you do this out loud, slowly, noticing any and all changes in your bodily sensations – physical and emotional. Check in with yourself to see which phrase, sentence, or section feels loaded, juicy, or weighty, or has the most energy. Reading your writing out loud truly takes the experience to another level; you'll know what we mean when you try it.

Next we offer optional exercises to meet your particular level of curiosity. Many of these activities are fun, and they take you deeper into your feelings, but you'll still get the benefits of the program if you don't do any of them. We also suggest something to think about or hold inside for the week, such as "notice how you feel whenever you say no to someone." These suggestions help you set your intention.

Last, but not least, we remind you to do some self-care that week, and provide some suggestions just in case you need a little help remembering what brings you pleasure, joy, and ease.

Working with the tools we provide in each chapter – guided visualizations combined with writing and other creative exercises – helps unlock unconscious messages and deeply buried feelings to which you don't have everyday access. Keeping a journal readily at hand will benefit you greatly because the more you write, the more thoughts and feelings come to you, revealing more pieces to the puzzle.

At times you may wonder what a particular exercise has to do with deciding whether or not to have children. We ask you to suspend judgment and trust that there's a method to our madness. Every single activity of this program offers up an essential piece to the puzzle, and each one builds on what's gone before. There's something useful in every reaction or response you have, even when an exercise is hard or seems to fall flat. Bring intention to your process while you suspend judgment, and trust that on a deeper level something is happening. Over time every effort you make serves your path to clarity.

Weeks 2 through 11 end with the stories of two women who struggled in their quests to make a decision. They completed lengthy questionnaires to let you know you're not alone. Reading the stories can feel very validating and comforting; or they might feel like a distraction from your journey, in which case you can choose to go back and read them after you've completed Week 12. You decide how to make them most helpful and useful to you.

This program works! We understand it can be really difficult at times and that it requires ongoing courage. While we refer to it as a passive process – one that requires you only to follow the guide – you have to stay actively engaged to allow and witness the unfolding as it occurs. It's a little like bringing focused attention to relaxing: On the one hand it can seem like not a lot is going on; but on the other, a whole different state is emerging, and you can miss the nuances of it if you aren't paying attention! The more intentionally engaged you can be and the more you show up for yourself, the more you'll discover.

Good luck, and let the journey begin!

The

Twelve-Week

Program

Week 1

Preparing for Your Journey

"At the center of your being you have the answer;
you know who you are and you know what you want."
–Lao Tzu[2]

Welcome! You've decided this tried-and-tested program is for you. The introduction described in detail how to get the most out of this program. Refer to it anytime you need to. Let's jump right in after highlighting these important reminders:

- Trust your process; you'll get more out of it if you do. Let half-clues and stray puzzle pieces exist even if you don't understand what they mean. Sometimes their meaning isn't clear until the very end.
- Pace is important. The program is deliberately designed to take a minimum of twelve weeks. Percolation time is built into it. Your psyche and your heart need this time. If you try to speed things up, it will work against you. You might lose ground rather than

gaining time. You can decide to take longer than twelve weeks, which works just fine.

- Try to the best of your ability to be open to uncertainty. Let yourself be okay with not knowing what you will ultimately decide. Most women find that once they grant themselves permission to *not know*, they feel less fatigue and have more energy for exploring. You'll read more about this during Week 2.

- Remember the importance of not sharing the details with others until you complete the program. While this sounds unusual and perhaps not what you're accustomed to, it is for your protection. Containing your process inside yourself, as best you can, reaps greater rewards. If you have a partner, it is especially important to wait until the end to share your experience to avoid clashing with their feelings or agenda about this topic. These could be disruptive to your process or steer you in a direction that is more about them than you.

- At times during the program the content overlaps. It's all intentional, as well as unavoidable. We want to be sure everything is covered in depth so you gain the clarity you want to make a decision you'll feel good about!

What Happens in Week 1

This opening week lays things out in preparation for a successful and fruitful journey. It presents essential information you'll need in the weeks that follow. It's in a slightly different order than subsequent weeks. For example, this "What Happens" section is presented first for orientation. If you feel that two weeks is a more realistic time frame to complete the groundwork of Week 1, by all means take the time. It's more important that you feel in step with yourself rather than driven by the calendar.

First we talk about your journal and why you need one. Then you'll be directed to create a family map. We introduce four women whose life stories serve as examples. And we invite you to identify what we call the *externals* in your life. Every week we include a guided visualization, and in this first week there are two specially designed to ensure that your initial experience of moving through the process is as gentle as possible. Assignments and writing prompts follow the guided visualizations. In this first week, the writing helps you identify any fears that might be getting in the way of making a decision.

Your Journal

Find a notebook to write in. Or embark on a more purposeful ritual of shopping for and selecting a special journal. Give yourself permission to indulge a bit here. Maybe you'll find something that's already perfect, or choose a journal with a blank cover you can embellish with images and words that speak to you personally. Of course you can't beat the convenience of a laptop or tablet if that's what you prefer.

You'll use your journal in a variety of ways in the coming weeks. Each week we ask you to write after guided visualizations and to complete core writing assignments. We ask you to create a section in your journal called "Things to Revisit Later." No doubt issues will surface and not get fully processed when they arise. They will likely need your attention at another time. We invite you to review such sections later on, so it makes for an easy reference to have one place to look. Keep your journal nearby to record thoughts and feelings that come to you unexpectedly throughout the day.

While the program uses a combination of listening, feeling, experiencing, and writing activities to create the internal stirring that leads to clarity, the approach is weighted toward writing. We have no doubt that much is discovered through thinking things through, but it doesn't compare to what you can access when you're writing in your journal or typing on your computer. When we think, our thoughts can be circular. When we write, new information tends to come forward. The more you write down, the more fresh material emerges.

In addition to using a journal for writing, you can draw pictures, scribble, rant, rave, or record dreams and even daytime fantasies. Pay special attention not only to the storylines of your dreams but also to their feeling and tone. Besides writing, you can work three-dimensionally by making collages, drawings, paintings, cartoons, or doodles. There are no limits except your time and inclination. Use your imagination and give yourself access to images, crayons, paints, pencils, and paper. If you are new to working this way, remember that every child is an artist, and deep inside we all have a child yearning to play. Through writing, creative play, and working with images, more pieces of the puzzle reveal themselves. Whether you write or draw, make sure you use your journal to record your experiences in a physical and concrete way rather than merely thinking, imagining, or meditating.

You might be surprised by the insights that come to you as you fill the pages of your journal. We often hear women say, "I had no idea I was going to write this – it's not what I set out to say." The insights you access can feel like they're coming out of nowhere. They're not – they're coming from your wellspring at the source of your personal desire. At the end of the program you might find it interesting, enlightening, and helpful to revisit your entire process, from the bubbling up of initial thoughts and feelings to the eventual emergence of clarity. Your journal will help you do this.

Your Family Map

We know from experience that creating a family map will bring you immense benefits, and we strongly recommend that you complete this project using the instructions below *before* engaging in the following weeks. Your family map is a *genogram* – a family tree with additional details – that includes psychological and emotional attributes of your family members. There are plenty of resources available on the internet about family maps if you decide you want to delve deeper than the instructions we provide here.

When your map is complete, you'll have a complex, in-depth picture of your family of origin, one that reveals the web between family members and their possible influences on you. Seeing your family's dynamics represented on paper can help you appreciate just how many people are involved, on both a conscious and unconscious level, in your deciding whether or not to have children. Over the coming weeks you'll likely discover more influences, so you might add to your family map later as well.

Set aside anywhere from forty-five to sixty minutes to create your map, depending on family size and complexity. The larger the paper you use, the easier it will be, especially if you have a large family or many extended family members to include.

The instructions direct you to create a map of your family of origin. If you find you're foggy on some details, just include what you can, noticing what you do and don't know about your family's history. The questions are meant to expand your knowledge about the members of your family.

Refer to the sample illustration on the next page before getting started. It's Sue's family, and she is one of the four women we reference throughout the book. You'll be introduced to her shortly.

Sue's family map is just one way a family map can look. You can see that Sue is forty-two. Her parents divorced when she was ten years old. She is the second of four siblings, just like her mother, Betty. And just like her mother she has an older brother, a younger brother, and a younger sister (squares are males; circles are females). Betty had a miscarriage when Sue was three years old (the small circle with the M in it), and was very depressed for about nine months. Four years after the miscarriage, Betty gave birth to Frank. About two years later, Sue's sister Sally was conceived in hopes of saving the marriage, but shortly after Sally's birth Sue's parents divorced (hash marks between Betty and Wesley signify the divorce). Sue added a list of where her mother and siblings currently live. (Diagonal lines through squares and circles indicate that those people have died.)

There are other details that Sue could have included in her family map. For example, names and ages of her aunts and uncles and their offspring, and whether or not they have children. The more details you add to your map, the more likely you will uncover emotions that could factor into your decision-making process. The goal is not to get stirred up for no reason, but rather to see if any emotions remain unresolved so you can tend to them and begin healing. Creating your family map might uncover something that has obstructed your clarity, or you might become aware of connections you hadn't discerned previously.

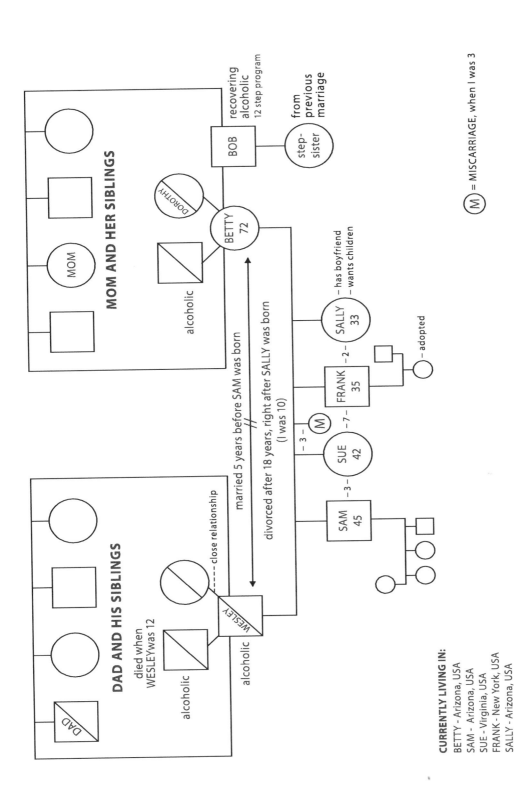

SUE'S FAMILY MAP

MOM AND HER SIBLINGS

DAD AND HIS SIBLINGS
died when WESLEY was 12

BOB — recovering alcoholic — 12 step program

step-sister — from previous marriage

DOROTHY

BETTY 72

alcoholic

WESLEY — alcoholic

----- close relationship

married 5 years before SAM was born

divorced after 18 years, right after SALLY was born (I was 10)

SAM 45

SUE 42

FRANK 35

SALLY 33 — has boyfriend — wants children

– 3 –

– 7 –

(M)

– 3 –

– 2 –

alcoholic

– adopted

(M) = MISCARRIAGE, when I was 3

CURRENTLY LIVING IN:
BETTY - Arizona, USA
SAM - Arizona, USA
SUE - Virginia, USA
FRANK - New York, USA
SALLY - Arizona, USA

Creating Your Family Map

1. Drawing yourself and any siblings you have (using Sue's family map as a template)
    - Begin by placing your piece of paper in landscape orientation.
    - Draw a horizontal line across the page one-quarter of the way up from the bottom of the page.
    - Under this line, on the far left, write the name and age of the first-born among you and your siblings. If you are an only child, simply write your name in the middle of the page below the line. Continue adding the names and current ages of your siblings, from left to right, following birth order from oldest to youngest. Include any step-siblings and half-siblings. Do this in a way that makes sense to you.
    - Now draw circles around the females and squares around the males. When the map is complete, these circles and squares will help you identify patterns.

    Note: The common symbol for females is a circle and a square for males, but notate sexuality in any way that makes sense to you. If you or anyone in your family is questioning their gender, in transition, or transgender, reflect that on your map. Possibilities for designating transgender are to draw a circle in a square or a square in a circle. Remember that this map is for your benefit and it only needs to make sense to you. Be consistent so you can identify patterns.

    - If someone is deceased, draw a diagonal line through the circle or square. Write down the year of their death or their age at death, as well as the cause of death, if known.

- Are/were you married or do you have a partner or significant other? Draw a circle (for a female) or a square (for a male) beside your name for that person and do the same for your siblings. Add any children of this generation. Notice on Sue's map that her brother Frank is married to his male partner and her brother Sam is married to his female partner.
- Draw short vertical lines connecting the circles and squares to the horizontal line.

2. Drawing your parents

Above the horizontal line, write your parents' names and current ages. Traditionally the male is on the left and the female is on the right. Write these at the far ends of the line to provide space for what's to come. Since there are many different types of families – for example, same-sex parents, single parent, blended, foster, and adoptive families with many parents involved – draw your family configuration in a way that works for you. Draw circles around females and squares around males. Indicate anyone who is deceased. Draw connecting lines as needed following Sue's example.

3. Drawing grandparents
   - Write the names of each set of grandparents above each of your parents' names. Again, draw circles around females and squares around males and indicate anyone who is deceased.
   - Draw lines to connect your grandparents to your parents.

4. Drawing aunts and uncles

- Draw horizontal lines above each of your grandparents' names, about one-quarter of the way from the top of the page. This is where you'll add the names of your parents and their siblings.

- Under that line, on the far left, write the name and age of your father's oldest sibling (if you drew your father to the left of your mother as suggested above). If your father is an only child, simply write his name under the middle of the line.

- Continue adding the names and current ages of your father's siblings, from left to right, following birth order from oldest to youngest. Include any step-siblings and half-siblings.

- Repeat these directions with your mother and/or other parent(s) and her siblings. Repeat as many times as needed for each person you identify as a parent.

- Draw circles around females, squares around males, indicate anyone who is deceased, and draw connecting lines as on Sue's map.

5. Adding details to yourself and any siblings

Beneath your name and your siblings' names, write the names of their children and their current ages, from left to right, following birth order from oldest to youngest. Include any step-siblings and half-siblings. Draw circles around females, squares around males, indicate anyone who is deceased, and draw lines connecting the children with their parents. If it's important to you, write the name of the place where each sibling resides. You may want to list these details to the side as Sue did. Perhaps geography plays a part in your family dynamics. You can also acknowledge sexuality where it's relevant.

6. Adding other important details
   - If your mother had any other pregnancies, note on the line connecting you with your siblings what occurred (miscarriage, terminated pregnancy, stillborn birth, etc.) and when.
   - Add the same information about pregnancies for yourself, your sister(s), your grandmothers, and your mother's sister(s).
   - Note any surprise children or unplanned pregnancies.

Now take an overall look at your map so far. As you do, you might notice emotional sensations beginning to bubble up to the surface or you might make a thoughtful connection with something in your map that you hadn't realized before. This is a good time to record either in your journal.

Answering the following questions is helpful to further develop your family map. They facilitate inquiry and introspection and help you paint a more in-depth picture of your family of origin. Add to your map as much information as you can while exploring the questions, notating details in a way that makes sense to you. Use Sue's map as an example, and use your journal to record your answers. Some of these questions are not relevant if a single parent or parents of the same sex raised you.

1. Looking more closely at your parents:
   - Were they married to each other? Are they still married? How would you rate the quality of their marriage/partnership/relationship?
   - Was there a death, divorce, or separation, and if so, how old were you when it happened? Did anyone remarry or re-partner?

- If your parents divorced/separated, how did this impact you and each of your siblings?

2. Looking more closely at yourself and any siblings:
   - If you have siblings, do you have the same parents?
   - If your siblings are in relationships, how would you rate these relationships? Consider how having children or not impacts these relationships.
   - Are you aware of any opinions your siblings have about whether or not you should have children?
   - Which of your siblings are you closest to? Which siblings are you not close to? Are any of your other siblings close to each other?
   - Do you have any memories of life before the sibling directly younger than you was born?

3. Looking more closely at your mother:
   - How old was your mother when you were born? If your mother is postmenopausal, and her symptoms have subsided, how old was she when they did?
   - Which of her siblings was/is she closest to? Who was she close to when you were young? Where do her siblings live? Does or did your mother play an important aunt role in her nieces' and/or nephews' lives?
   - Did you know your mother's siblings while growing up? Did you like each of them? If you know them now, has your regard for them changed?

- Did or do you like your mother's parents? Did or does your mother like her parents? Is there anything special, either negative or positive, about those relationships that you want to write down?
- Did your mother have more or fewer children than she wanted? In your opinion, were there consequences of this?

4. Looking more closely at your father:
   - Did you know your father's siblings while growing up? Did you like each of them? If you know them now, has your regard for them changed?
   - Does or did your father play an important uncle role in his nieces' and nephews' lives?
   - Did or do you like your father's parents? Did or does your father like his parents? Is there anything special, either negative or positive, about those relationships that you want to write down?
   - Did your father have more or fewer children than he wanted? In your opinion, were there consequences of this?

5. Looking at family influences and patterns:
   - Were you close with any of your first or second cousins on either side of your family?
   - Was your family of origin religious? What are your current religious beliefs or practices and how do these compare with those of other family members?
   - Who on your family map has/had the greatest positive influence on you? And the greatest negative influence?

- Was/is there drug or alcohol use in your family? Was anyone identified as being an addict or having a drinking problem? Do you consider yourself an adult child of an alcoholic? Do you use or abuse alcohol or drugs for recreation or to self-medicate?
- Are you aware of any emotional, physical, or sexual abuse in your family while you were growing up, or in the generations before you?
- Is there anything that has not yet been asked or that has not been included in the family map that would make it more complete for your situation, such as important accomplishments, big career changes, physical and learning disabilities, diseases and hospitalizations, socioeconomic struggles, education anomalies, homophobia in the family, suicides or attempted suicides, mental illnesses and hospitalizations for such, institutionalized family members, hysterectomies, post-partum depressions, family secrets, sudden deaths, injuries, major accidents, jobs or professions you deem significant? Think about these topics and write about anything that pertains to your family.

Congratulations! You've made it through the lengthy instructions for creating your family map.

How do you feel now? Your map is a valuable tool, though it can bring up a lot of emotions and even be a bit overwhelming. If that feels true for you, take a deep breath now and place one hand on your heart and the other on your stomach. Close your eyes and feel your body's movements as you breathe. Relax for as long as you want to before proceeding.

Now it's time to take an overall look at your completed map. What stands out? Do you see any patterns? Does anything surprise you? Does something make you proud? Are there any buried emotions beginning to arise? Does something bring up sadness? What other thoughts and feelings surface? Are you getting in touch with things that feel good? Are you aware of any anger – brand new or forgotten until now?

Here's a sampling of some additional themes and trends you can observe: Notice the number of siblings and the birth order of each generation. Notice the ages of the mothers at the time their first children were born. Notice if relationships changed after negative or positive big events. Look for repetitions of particular behaviors across generations. Look for anything else that you might not have been aware of previously. Are there relationships that you wish were better than they were or are, either your own or those of other people?

Stay as open as you can with yourself and the family information represented on your map. Sometimes by looking at your family represented this way you can glean information that wasn't obvious before. For example, as you can see in Sue's map, she realized that each of her parents had a total of four children in their family. That possibly contributed to their choice to have their fourth child, Sue's younger sister, Sally. Sue also saw a generational pattern of alcohol dependency on both sides of her family in a way she hadn't before. She also remembered learning that her mother's sister had an abortion (illegal at the time) at a young age.

Don't be surprised if you feel caught off guard with your feelings or thoughts. Use your journal to record them. It's perfectly normal to feel a sense of heightened emotion or sensitivity after creating a family map. If it feels overwhelming, do your best to absorb your findings incrementally by putting the map aside for now and referring to it again later.

As you progress through the activities of this program and discover new information about your family, revisit your map. Over time you may have insights or notice new patterns or influences that you want to add to it. Keep your map with your program paperwork so it can be easily referenced.

Meet Four Women

Now we introduce four women who are composites of the characteristics of women we've worked with over the years. As Sue's family of origin helped demonstrate the construction of a family map, at times we also refer to the experiences of Samantha, Birgit, and Holly to help you understand certain themes or activities.

Sue, at forty-two, single and heterosexual, is leaning toward not having children. She is happy and well adjusted, without any major life issues. She spent some time gaining personal insight through 12-step programs and individual psychotherapy. From her map we know that alcoholism existed in her family, and she identifies as an adult child of an alcoholic. She is the second of four children, and her parents divorced when she was ten years old.

Samantha is forty-four, in a same-sex relationship, and leaning toward wanting to have a child. She and her partner, Elise, who is forty-five, have been in a stable and committed relationship for nine years. Samantha is feeling a bit of time pressure on deciding. She has one older brother she isn't emotionally close to. Both her parents are deceased. Her mother was bipolar, but the condition had not been diagnosed while she and her brother were growing up, so she was not taking medication that could have tempered her mood swings. Samantha experienced her father as being emotionally unavailable. For Samantha, a saving grace in her family of origin is her Aunt Bea, who has always loved Samantha dearly and treated her as a beloved child. Samantha's partner, Elise, also worked the Motherhood-Is it for me? program, a little after Samantha did.

Birgit is thirty-three, heterosexual, and in a stable marriage of six years. Her husband, Jeff, says he'll go either way on the decision and wants Birgit to decide what's important to her. He says he is happy to father their two Labrador retrievers. Birgit has focused on developing her career and is leaning toward not having children. She was treated successfully for breast cancer at age thirty-one. She has two siblings, one older and one younger, neither of whom have children. Birgit's parents live near her home and haven't kept it a secret that they would like to become grandparents. Birgit and her husband both feel some pressure as a result.

Holly is thirty-seven, single, heterosexual, and still looking for lasting love. She is leaning toward wanting to have children, but she wants to share that experience with a partner rather than being a single mom. Holly is the only child of parents who were older than average when they had her. Her father died when she was a young teen, but her mother is still living. Alcoholism was present on both sides of the family in her grandparents' generation. Holly's aloof mother might have had a personality disorder that made it difficult to see her daughter as a separate being with separate needs and desires.

A Little More about the Externals

The current circumstances of your life – finances, health, age, relationship status, and so on – are what we call the *externals*. For this process to work well, it's important that you try to the best of your ability to mentally put these factors aside for the time you're engaged in the program. As much as possible, we want you to pretend your externals simply don't exist.

Of course we're asking you to do the impossible as you face the daily realities of your life. Setting the externals aside can feel counterintuitive because financial woes, lack of a relationship or one in conflict, lifestyle challenges, health concerns, age, career, or fears of all kinds can be perceived as the very reason you can't decide if you want to have children.

We're not saying your externals are unimportant; rather they're unimportant right now. What needs to be known first is what you want for yourself *regardless of the circumstances of your life.* When what you want becomes clear, and it's time to think about your decision going forward, some of the details of your life will be relevant and others will no longer play an active part in your decision. In the meantime, trying to make a decision based on your internal emotions and the externals in your life at the same time creates all kinds of pressure. Another way this can be said is that trying to figure out your *desire* and your *decision* at the same time creates gridlock.

At this point, please stop reading, have a heart-to-heart chat with yourself, and get your journal or whatever you're using for writing. Make a list of all the externals in your life that feel worrisome or about which you feel conflicted. They might not be clear-cut; that's fine. Just write down the ones that keep swirling around in your head. Then put this list aside for now. You'll be asked to refer to it later this week in an assignment.

Throughout the weeks ahead, keep pushing the current circumstances of your life to the outskirts of your mind. You'll likely find that you have to make frequent, conscious efforts to do this. Even though it does get easier as the weeks go on, we'll offer you tools this week and in Week 2 to help with this seemingly impossible task.

Working with Guided Visualizations

A guided visualization is presented each week, and no previous experience is needed to receive its benefit. All that's required is allowing whatever occurs to happen. Trust that your attentive mind will go where it needs to and that you will become aware of the information that needs to surface. We recommend having someone read the guided visualizations to you so you can benefit from the element of surprise; or have them record them for you. If that's not possible, record them yourself so you can listen with eyes closed to deepen the experience of where the exercise takes you. Closing your eyes engages a part of your brain that isn't easily accessed when your eyes are open. If you read the visualizations to yourself, read silently and very slowly, and at the very least close your eyes every few sentences to take in the experience. All of this said, there's no wrong way to do them. What's most important is that you do what works best for you.

If after experiencing a guided visualization you feel nothing has happened for you, this might not, in fact, be true. The mind is very powerful. With time and a little percolation, something will surface

– if not this week, then the next or the week after. Even if you don't experience anything right away, trust both yourself and the process. Some guided visualizations feel more powerful than others, but each one is important.

Week 1 has two visualizations, both important for establishing support as you begin your journey of discovery. The first, "Creating Comfort Within," helps you create an environment in which you feel safe, protected, and nourished – one that you can choose to return to over and over again. As you cultivate the practice of returning to this place, you strengthen your inner resources and resilience.

The second visualization, "Creating Your Circle of Support," allows you, in your imagination, to invite others for support as you need it. They'll be your consultants and comfort, always there for you in the background. They'll support you and perhaps, at times, offer very active advice. Call on them anytime, or simply rest in the knowledge that you have reinforcements who care deeply about you and who want only the best for you.

WEEK 1 FIRST GUIDED VISUALIZATION

These visualizations are like jewels, and their function is to bring into awareness information from your unconscious that will ultimately help you on your journey of discovery.

With all of the guided visualizations, there are two things to remember: the experience you have is what matters most; and there's no wrong way to do them. Have your journal and writing tool nearby so you can record your impressions and images immediately.

To prepare, choose a quiet place where people and noise won't disturb or distract you, and a time when there's nothing else for you to do and no one who needs your attention; this time is solely for your benefit. Either sit comfortably in a chair or, if you prefer, lie down on the floor.

Creating Comfort Within

Now that you're ready, become conscious of your breathing. Let your eyes close gently as you take a deep breath and exhale. Inhale and hold your breath for five counts. Then exhale until most of the air has left your lungs. Inhale again and slowly exhale, letting out an audible sigh through your mouth while you count silently from ten to one. Continue breathing slowly and deeply. As you breathe, you relax. Allow your natural breath to bring a deep sense of peace and well-being. Feel your body relax and let your mind free-associate. B-r-e-a-t-h-e.

Now's the perfect time to create a place in your mind that feels safe and protected, and where you can be completely yourself. Here you feel uninhibited, completely at ease, and, most of all, free from all judgments – your own and those of others. This is a place to visit anytime you need or want to rest, renew, regroup, or receive deep nourishment.

Visualize your place now. It can be a place you've been before or one you invent in your imagination. This place touches your heart and soul. It might be a warm beach, a sunny meadow in springtime, a beautiful mountain, or something else entirely. See what presents to you and trust it. This is a place where you can say, "Yes, yes. This is where my heart and soul can rest."

Using all of your senses, explore your place and discover it completely. If you're on a beach, listen to the waves. If in a field of flowers, absorb their delicate scent through your nose. Find a spot to settle in for a while if you wish. Whether you continue to explore or settle in one spot, keep enjoying a deep state of relaxation and well-being. Allow all the pleasant sensations to permeate your being. Embrace the serenity that is generated.

Say to yourself, "I am open to establishing a safe place, my comfort zone within. I can return to it whenever I wish." With each new breath, take these words deep into your heart, your mind, and your body. Pause now for as long as you desire to enjoy the place and the opportunity to soak in every drop of nourishment available to you. There is no hurry.

Then say good-bye to your nourishing *comfort within,* and remember that it is available to you anytime.

Keep your eyes closed while you slowly return to your present environment, allowing a few moments to be with your emotional and physical sensations. B-r-e-a-t-h-e.

When you're ready, slowly open your eyes and begin to write in your journal. Record your immediate thoughts, feelings, insights, and anything else you want to about your experience.

Immediate Writing after the Guided Visualization

Writing immediately after a guided visualization is important because it helps concretize your experience. Document everything – uncensored – that comes to you from the experience, whether or not it makes sense. This program facilitates a process that unfolds over time, and pieces of information that come to you don't always stand alone with meaning.

This is why nothing should get swept under the rug or dismissed as unimportant as you go along. Write it all down! Take as long as you wish. When you finish journaling, continue reading. If you continue reading without having written at all, part of your experience will fade away and not be available to you later, as happens when you awaken in the morning from a dream and get up too quickly before recording it. The dream content and its essence evaporate and are irretrievable.

Did an image of a location come to you right away, or not at all? Were you surprised by your thoughts, images, or feelings? If there was abundant detail, did you describe it? If there were no clear images for you during this initial visualization, don't be surprised or disappointed. We believe they will come. In the meantime, simply describe what occurred for you. The purpose of the visualizations is to stir up memories, thoughts, and feelings.

Be Curious: Assignments for Week 1

Your first writing assignment is designed to help you identify the fears that live inside you. The second is designed to help you access the assumptions you live with about your future. As you write, let your mind free-associate. The writing doesn't necessarily have to make sense, be linear, or even be in complete sentences. Yours may look more like pictures or diagrams. This stream-of-consciousness writing allows your unconscious to be unleashed. There is no wrong way to do the writing assignments. Not only that, you will be surprised by what surfaces as you answer the questions we present to you.

We provide a detailed explanation of each assignment. What you do with them is your choice. If you need to tweak the exercise to get more drawn into it, please do so, although we encourage you to try the suggested assignment first. When there are multiple writing assignments, we ask that you follow the order in which they are presented. When you begin to write, let your writing flow uncensored.

1. It is helpful to recognize fears because they often run the show from behind the scenes when they haven't been identified. The question below is intentionally vague. Interpret it the way you need to. Trust that. There are no appropriate or inappropriate fears. There are only the fears that live inside you for good reason. This is your time to give a voice to what they are and let them out. Write from any point in time in your life. Resist the urge to second-guess what we are asking.

   As you face making this decision, what is your biggest fear in deciding?

   When you finish writing your answer, continue.

2a. Consider the next question from the perspective of any time in your life. You might think about it from several points of time as your views change. Notice what comes to mind first. There is no wrong way to do this.

   I always thought that by now my life would look like...

   After you've answered question 2a, walk away from it. Take anywhere from an hour to a day or two, then reread what you wrote and go on to 2b.

2b. How does it feel to read what you wrote? The writing prompt in 2a is about your thoughts. Now pay attention to your feelings and write about them.

   As I read what I wrote, my feelings about this are...

3. Begin to collect words and images from various sources like magazines or the Internet. You may be drawn to them either because they make you feel good or because they elicit uncomfortable feelings. Either way, don't think too much about it. Trust that they caught your eye for a reason. Start by cutting out words and images and putting them in a box or folder. If you are so inclined, carry around a small camera and take pictures of things that move you, either positively or negatively. These will all be used later in the program for other exercises.

Further Exploration and Discovery

This is the section where we help you take what you've written to the next level, digging deeper into the meaning of what you wrote. Read your written responses out loud. It might feel funny or awkward when no one is around to listen, but try doing it regardless. Reading your writing aloud can give it new meaning. It can also connect you emotionally to the content. When we work with women one on one or in a group, we have them read their writing out loud. Another suggestion is to record and then listen to your written words. As you listen you might hear something you didn't notice while you were recording.

Your Checklist for Reflection (below) consists of questions designed to help you consider more carefully what you've written. Use this checklist throughout the program as a guide only. Don't stop at these questions, especially if you're inspired by your own.

❖ *Your Checklist for Reflection:*
   ☐ What do I feel as I read out loud what I wrote?
   ☐ Does anything that I wrote surprise me? What new information has come to me?
   ☐ Is there anything I wrote that I want to write about some more? (If so, by all means go ahead!)
   ☐ When I reread slowly what I wrote, do I notice emotional and physical sensations or changes in my body? Which phrase(s) and sentence(s) feel loaded, feel juicier or weightier than others, or have more energy than others?
   ☐ Is there something that doesn't make sense to me that might make more sense later?
   ☐ Do I feel shame from anything I wrote?
   ☐ Is there something that I've not thought about for a long time?
   ☐ Is there anything I might want to discuss with a psychotherapist, counselor, coach, mentor, spiritual advisor, or supportive friend?

If you struggle with a specific assignment, be gentle with yourself. Don't add additional pressure to push through it if it feels extremely difficult. Your discomfort could be related to a forgotten experience that might surface later in the process. Being patient and compassionate with yourself is the best way forward. That said, at times you might want to motivate yourself to push through a bit of resistance to access feelings on the other side. Ideally we want you to strike a balance between challenging yourself and creatively reworking an exercise when that's the only way you can complete it.

Now let's look more closely at your first writing assignment: your biggest fears in deciding. Humans don't carry around fear for the fun of it. You can assume that your fears exist for some reason. They are usually reactions to something that happened long ago. They can linger on or persist because at the time they initially arose, no one was there to help you make sense of what happened and the incident went underground into your subconscious.

People tend to believe their fears are rational and reasonable. Fears certainly feel real, so it might not occur to you to question or examine them. "Of course I feel afraid of making the wrong decision and regretting it," you might declare. "Who doesn't?" Or, "Of course I'm afraid I won't be a good enough mother. I have every reason to feel that way." Most of us are under the impression that we need to live with our fears and the best we can hope for is to manage or cope with them.

The reality is that fear is a feeling. Fears are not facts. Feelings and fears will continue to get stirred up each week during this process. This is natural. Instead of trying to figure out how not to have your fears, or how to manage them, for now just notice what it's like to have them. See if you can breathe into them and feel they exist. Bask in them if you can. See if you feel any sadness or anger about having them. Do your best to notice them without judgment.

Below are some common fears we've heard repeatedly. Do any sound familiar?

"I fear time will slip by without my having made a conscious decision."

"I fear I'll resent my partner if I go along with what they want."

"I fear I'll say yes (or no) to motherhood without fully knowing why, and later realize it was for the wrong reason."

"I fear my free time will evaporate."

"I'm so afraid of pregnancy and giving birth that I fear my desire to be a mother won't prevail."

"I love my dog more than anything. This love is spontaneous. I fear that loving my child won't come naturally."

"I fear being perceived as non-feminine and non-maternal if I decide not to have children. I don't want to be socially ostracized."

Now add all the fears that came up to your list of externals. Now that you've identified your fears, we want you to do your best not to acknowledge them for the duration of the program. Various activities in the program will help you work through your fears, especially those standing in the way of deciding about motherhood. By the end of the program you'll likely find that you've moved through and greatly minimized your greatest fears.

Here's a suggestion that will help you keep your fears and the externals you don't want to think about right now a little bit further away. Find a jar with a very tight lid in your kitchen, or buy one and decorate it for this purpose. Have fun with it. Write one fear on a strip of paper and place it in the jar. Continue doing this with each fear, and then with each external. Include everything you want to put aside for now. Then close that lid and put the jar away out of sight. Feel free to add to the jar during this process, putting it away and out of sight each time. This physical activity helps you move forward less encumbered.

Now take a closer look at your responses to 2a and 2b, *I always thought that by now my life would look like...* and *My feelings about this are....* Was envisioning the life you thought you'd have easy, or was it challenging? Some women find that they've never thought about their future. Others feel that all their ducks are in a row except for the decision about children. Sometimes doing this exercise drives home that your life isn't at all what you thought it was going to be – for better or worse. It's really important not to evaluate yourself, but to simply notice how you feel. Be curious, without judgment about what or how much you wrote. You might find yourself feeling sad or discouraged. Each week we want you to get more and more comfortable with unearthing all your feelings. Hang in there! Answers will come, and your load will lighten.

WEEK 1 SECOND GUIDED VISUALIZATION

This is another opportunity to get in touch with your inner resources, which will help you feel grounded throughout this process-oriented program.

As already mentioned, there are two things to remember: the experience *you* have is what matters most; and there's no wrong way to do the visualization. Have your journal and writing tool nearby so you can record your impressions and images immediately.

To prepare, choose a quiet place where people and noise won't disturb or distract you, and a time when there's nothing else for you to do and no one who needs your attention; this time is solely for your benefit. Either sit comfortably in a chair or, if you prefer, lie down on the floor.

Creating Your Circle of Support

Now that you're ready, become conscious of your breathing. Let your eyes close gently as you take a deep breath and exhale. Inhale and hold your breath for five counts. Then exhale until most of the air has left your lungs. Inhale again and slowly exhale, letting out an audible sigh through your mouth while you count silently from ten to one. Continue breathing slowly and deeply. As you breathe, you relax. Allow your natural breath to bring a deep sense of peace and well-being. Feel your body relax and let your mind free-associate. B-r-e-a-t-h-e.

Picture yourself situated in a cozy, peaceful place, real or imagined, that is different from the one you created in the previous visualization – your comfort within place – as that place is yours only. You will be inviting others to join you in this new place.

Once you have your place in mind, let yourself enjoy the sensations of calm and comfort before you invite others to join you. These others can be human, animal, real, imagined, fictional, mythical, living, dead, young, or old. You get to choose exactly who and how many get invited. Invite those who will add value as you move through your exploration. Who will accept and support you without question? Who will give you the space to find your truth? Who will encourage you to be true to yourself always?

How many guests you invite is ultimately your choice. You can even decide to stay solo in your place. Take a few minutes to invite exactly whom you want to be with you.

This is your *circle of support*. Allow yourself to bask in their presence. Imagine each member of your circle of support telling you what they appreciate about you, or sit quietly and simply enjoy their silent company. If you chose to be alone, feel the support you have for yourself as you embark on this journey.

The sole purpose of this exercise is to feel that you are supported with care, respect, and love. You can call on your circle of support at any time throughout this process. It's always there in the background offering encouragement. You can return at any point along the way to add or dismiss members.

Keep your eyes closed while you slowly return to your present environment, allowing a few moments to be with your emotional and physical sensations. Breathe.

When you're ready, slowly open your eyes and begin to write in your journal. Record your immediate thoughts, feelings, insights, and anything else you want to about your experience.

Immediate Writing after the Guided Visualization

Write as much as you can right now to help internalize the experience you just had so you can reach for it when you want to. Do this now, before you continue reading.

Notice if you're surprised by who showed up in your circle of support – or who didn't show up. Even though the visualization is over, you can add or remove your invitees or re-create anything about your circle of support until it feels just right for you. The point of your circle of support is to have an internal resource when you need it. Anytime you feel alone or need help, you can conjure it up in your mind. Again, it doesn't have to be rational or make sense; if it feels good and is helpful, it's right.

Be Even More Curious: Optional Exercises

If you stop here, you'll have completed the core activities for Week 1. However, if you have the time and you feel moved to do more, below are some additional assignments to help you get even more out of the first week. You can do these any time in the program.

1. Scan your life from birth until now and create a timeline of the significant events. Include births, deaths, divorces, separations, marriages, relationship beginnings and endings, moves, career changes, successes (emotional and physical), pregnancies, abortions, miscarriages, etc. As you chart this timeline, write in your journal about where there are emotional charges.

2. Make a timeline of only the most wonderful highlights of your life, and keep it in an accessible place. When you're feeling a little challenged, stuck, or hopeless, this timeline can be used to redirect your attention to when things have been good.

3. Use your journal to describe your dreams. Paying attention to them can be another powerful tool for unearthing what you're allowing to happen. You might notice your dreams changing as you work through this process.

4. Look at what you wrote regarding your biggest fears. Is there anything there you can draw or turn into an image? Draw or paint your fear(s).

What to Hold Inside This Week

Be curious and interested in all your thoughts and feelings, no matter what they are. Don't assume anything. Do trust that plenty is happening internally. A small amount of writing doesn't mean little progress. This approach has proven to be effective over and over again. We trust this, and you can also. Everything that's percolating inside you will reveal itself in time.

Notice what it's like not to share the details of your journey with others. It's important to have your own contained, private, and uncensored process.

Pay attention to your thoughts and feelings about your family map. Add any new information as it comes to you.

Keep your journal nearby to write the thoughts and feelings that arise throughout the week. Don't underestimate what has already taken place and how much has been stirred up. Be gentle with yourself.

If you find yourself not thinking about any of this at all until you sit down to begin the activities for Week 2, that's completely all right. It can even prove to be beneficial. Forgetting about the exercises after you complete them is just fine. There is no wrong way to do this process.

Self-Care

Self-care is a practice that most of us need to teach ourselves and cultivate over time until it becomes habitual. Few people, especially women, come naturally to this. Women are culturally trained to think of others first, and they often care for themselves last, if at all. What's more, difficulty giving yourself *permission* to care for yourself is a recurring theme for many women. Cultivating good, regular self-care is as important as brushing your teeth. Really! Each week there are recommendations and ideas about how to take extra good care of yourself.

Carving out even a few minutes from a busy day to slow down, tune in, and reconnect with yourself goes a long way in supporting you through this process. Good self-care helps maintain overall mental and physical health while nourishing your soul. At the very least, embrace the self-care suggestions offered – everything from a few stolen moments of breathing with awareness to a day out in nature or at a spa. Work toward a commitment to carve out "me-time" *every* day. It helps to schedule it at the same time each day, when you'll be less likely to bump it; perhaps when you first arise in the morning or the very last thing before bed. How much time you spend is not as important initially as making the switch from the external world to your internal world. Me-time is *not* selfish; rather it is essential to sustaining relationships and staying engaged in spite of the challenges of a busy life. Build a repertoire of personal self-care practices that speak to you and benefit your exploration while enhancing your regular daily activities.

Why not make your favorite meal one evening this week and eat it by candlelight? Enjoy.

The self-care I did for myself this week was...

Whether you take our suggestion or come up with something more to your liking, record your weekly self-care rituals in your journal. You may end up with a lovely list by the end of the twelve weeks.

Congratulations! You've come to the end of Week 1.

Check in with what's happening for you right now. How do you feel as you embark on this journey solely focused on you? Open up your journal and write down a few sentences about this right now. You might find it interesting to reread your initial thoughts and feelings at the end of the program.

Good luck with all the discoveries that are about to unfold as you come to *your* truth that only *you* can know.

Week 2

Your Journey Begins –
Getting Packed and
Ready to Go!

❧ You're on the road to discovering your truth. ❧

Take a nice long breath. Notice what's gone well for you in the last week as you stepped out of your routine and into this process. Name one way you felt good about yourself. Was there a particular success? On the other hand, did anything happen that was particularly challenging? Sometimes you can feel like something is off but not be able to identify the source. Periodically checking in with yourself helps keep your attention focused in a balanced way. Jot down your discoveries in your journal.

In Week 1 you created a family map to identify the people who populate your psyche and who may also play a part in your decision-making. As new information comes to you, feel free to add to it.

You also identified the externals in your life. Remember to put them aside for now. We make the point about your externals again here because it's important. Finding a solution while you're stuck in externals is very difficult. When you finish the program and have turned over more stones than you thought possible, your externals will look and feel different even though they haven't changed. *You* will be different.

We recommended that you avoid sharing any details with others for now – especially with your partner if you have one. How is that request going for you? You examined your fears, then put them aside along with your externals. You also conjured up an image of how you thought your life would look by this time. You might have had some feelings come up as you completed those exercises.

You experienced your first two guided visualizations. Hopefully those two places you created in your mind – your comfort within and your circle of support – have popped up now and then and been meaningful for you. Your mind is powerful! If at any time you need to retreat to a peaceful place or consult with your circle of support, you can close your eyes, take a few breaths, and call up those images.

You started your journal to record feelings, images, thoughts, and insights. They're worth writing down immediately because they carry useful information and can disappear as fast as they arise. Be like a curious detective and capture these clues in your journal even if you don't yet comprehend their meaning.

Again, we invite you to trust that your mind and body are offering you information worth paying attention to.

WEEK 2 GUIDED VISUALIZATION

As we mentioned last week, trust that your attentive mind will go where it needs to go. When your eyes are closed, you engage the part of your brain that isn't as easily accessed when your eyes are open. Have someone read the visualization to you or record it for you so you can listen while your eyes are closed, as its power also lies in the element of surprise. If that's not possible, make a recording yourself so you can listen with eyes closed to deepen the experience of where the visualization takes you. If you read the visualization to yourself, read it silently and slowly to give yourself time to savor the experience. Close your eyes now and then to open to the power of your imagination.

Remember that the experience you have is what matters most, and there's no wrong way to do it. Have your journal and writing tool nearby so you can record your impressions and images immediately.

To prepare, choose a quiet place where people and noise won't disturb or distract you, and a time when there's nothing else for you to do and no one who needs your attention; this time is solely for your benefit. Either sit comfortably in a chair or, if you prefer, lie down on the floor.

The Journey Begins

Now that you're ready, become conscious of your breathing. Let your eyes close gently as you take a deep breath and exhale. Inhale and hold your breath for five counts. Then exhale until most of the air has left your lungs. Inhale again and slowly exhale, letting out an audible sigh through your mouth while you count silently from ten to one. Continue breathing slowly and deeply. As you breathe, you relax. Allow your natural breath to bring a deep sense of peace and well-being. Feel your body relax and let your mind free-associate. B-r-e-a-t-h-e.

Imagine you're preparing for a trip. You're beginning a journey that involves travel to a place where your desires about motherhood or having children will become clearer. Picture yourself in the environment where you'll begin this journey. It can be a place you already know. It can be real or imagined, current or from long ago, nearby or far away. Picture yourself now in the place from which you'll embark on your journey. Notice all the surrounding details of this place. Take your time. There is no need to hurry.

What do you see? What feelings are you having right now? Are you feeling excited? Fearful? Confused? Annoyed? Overwhelmed? Restless? Sad? Hopeful? Impatient? Eager? Curious? Bored? Scared? Doubtful? Peaceful? Or any other feeling not mentioned? Now is the time to take note of any and all feelings even if they are conflicting. There is room to experience all of them. Notice these feelings and welcome them without any judgment. B-r-e-a-t-h-e.

Now turn your attention back to the details of your surroundings. Take your time as you consider each of the following questions: Where are you? What is important to you about this particular setting? Are you alone or is someone there with you? What do you think or feel is important to manage before taking off on your journey? Is there something you want to take with you? How do you want to travel; what mode of transportation will you use? What do you hope to discover on this trip? Check in with yourself to notice what emotions are present.

What physical sensations are you experiencing in your body? Do you feel open or constricted? Breathe. Whatever you are noticing is just as it should be.

Take care to note this place of beginning, including all of the feelings you have had. Say good-bye to it for now. You'll revisit this place later in the program.

Keep your eyes closed while you slowly return to your present environment, allowing a few moments to be with your emotional and physical sensations. Breathe.

When you're ready, slowly open your eyes and begin to write in your journal. Record your immediate thoughts, feelings, insights, and anything else you want to about your experience.

Immediate Writing after the Guided Visualization

Writing immediately helps you actualize the experience of the guided visualization.

If you're having trouble with what to write, think about the following: Where did your mind go? What happened for you overall? You might want to describe where you started or identify feelings that came to you during the guided visualization. What needs tending before you begin your journey? Is there anything significant about the mode of transportation you chose? Was anyone with you? Since you'll come back to this particular guided visualization at a later date, it's useful to record as much of your internal experience as you can right now; you might not be able to retrieve it all later. Write for as long as you wish with as many details as you can recall.

Once you've written your immediate response, the guided visualization has served its purpose – to stir up memories, thoughts, and feelings.

What Happens in Week 2

This week your conscious journey begins in earnest. You're on the road to discovering your truth. We'll be your guides and introduce you to The Mantra©, a tool we hope will provide you with immediate relief and continued support on your journey in the weeks to come. This big project of figuring out what you want does not necessarily require a big effort. It simply requires that you stay engaged with the process and leave the navigating to us. You'll also begin to define and redefine motherhood, and you'll be asked to take a brief look back to remember your experiences with adults when you were a young person.

Beginning now and in each subsequent week through the eleventh week of the program, at the end of each chapter we share stories of two women speaking to you in their voices. Everything is real except their names. The stories are compiled from an in-depth questionnaire we created for this purpose. We hope the words of these women help you recognize that you're not alone but rather part of a larger community of women who've been in your shoes. We hope they inspire you to relax and trust that your answers will come. You might feel that reading the stories in the order in which they are presented will influence you or get in the way of your process; if so, feel free to wait until you've completed the program to read them. You decide what's best for you. Use the stories in the way that will help you the most.

The Mantra

We invite you to read, breathe, and live this mantra throughout the program. Its purpose is to bring immediate relief from any pressure you feel about your uncertainty.

I don't know.
I don't know why I don't know.
It's not my fault that I don't know.
It's okay that I don't know.
I have had clarity before about many things.
My true desire matters and no one can know it better than I.
I am the definer of me.
The answers will come because they never left.
Only I can know what's true for me… It's all within me.

I don't know. The mantra begins with *I don't know* because it is right there on the surface of your consciousness – the foremost thought causing you distress. We have good news for you: Throughout the program you have total permission not to know. In fact it's essential that you *choose* not to know, with intention, for the process to work its magic.

We frequently hear women say, "One minute I can see how I want to be a mom and the next minute I don't see how I possibly can." Human nature compels us to seek answers actively. It can feel excruciating not to know, and fluctuating between answers creates the perpetual illusion that any moment the answer will come and provide relief. In fact, making a case for *yes* and then making a case for *no* doesn't help you get any closer to getting off the fence; it only serves to temporarily soothe anxiety, nothing more.

When you find yourself swinging in one direction or the other, guide your thoughts back to the center – the *I don't know*. It can be helpful to imagine yourself traveling on the trajectory of a horizontal figure eight, or infinity sign, with *I don't know* as the center point. As you slide toward either direction, let yourself easily slide back to that center point. Keep in mind that this is fluid and gentle rather than rigid; there's no need to hold on tightly.

It might take a few weeks to sink comfortably into the state of actively not knowing. It might feel painful, hopeless, or scary at times. If you're already leaning in one direction or the other, returning to *I don't know* can feel like you're backsliding. Rest assured that *not knowing* is risk-free. You can't lose your true desire. Your truth will only become clear as you allow yourself further exploration, pressure-free.

We invite you to frame your experience of *I don't know* as being liberating. Letting your shoulders drop an inch or two, taking a few deep breaths, and being able to say *I don't know* without any judgment can feel like a reprieve that allows you to be more present and more available to receive authentic answers.

I don't know why I don't know. Many women believe that if they only knew *why* they don't know, they would automatically arrive at the clarity and all would be well. But all is well right now. Even if you have an inkling about why you don't yet know, trust that you don't have access to all the pieces that are playing parts in your truth, and that you don't need to. For right now you simply don't know. The details of *why* are unimportant at this point, and trying to figure them out prematurely only distracts you from your goal of achieving clarity.

You can be sure of one thing: *The reason you don't know is a good reason.* It might be due to any number of things, including societal pressure, unresolved childhood problems or other hurts, the belief that you don't matter, a general feeling of shame, or possibly a combination of factors. The pain or discomfort you experience when you're not aligned with your true self disconnects you further from your knowing.

It's not my fault that I don't know. We all have personal struggles, and while we are accountable for our actions, we are not to be blamed for our struggles. If something hurtful happened in your childhood and the outcome has turned into a personal struggle, you're not to be blamed for that. If you internalized an inaccurate belief about yourself due to earlier events, you are not to blame. It is true that it's up to you to heal the injury that caused the struggle or difficulty; however, that is different from blaming yourself for the struggle that has kept you stuck. We hope you can let go of self-blame while you allow your journey to unfold.

It's okay that I don't know. This statement is meant to help you soften internally and experience more ease. We want you to feel spaciousness around not knowing.

Society at large wants you to know whether or not you'll be a mom, but the reality is that you don't know. Your internal life doesn't match the expectations imposed by your external life. And that feels bad. Your self-judgment – the critical inner voice that insists you *should* know – can compound your discomfort.

The statement *It's okay that I don't know* helps you step back a bit. Give yourself permission to be exactly where you are, without self-judgment. When you relax into self-acceptance, the result is spaciousness. From there you can more easily gain access to the answers that are already there. Try to feel at peace. Be kind to yourself.

I have had clarity before about many things. This reminds you of what is true: You have known and still know many things. You have felt clarity before. And as you've experienced it before, you'll most certainly experience it again.

The knowing will come in time. You don't have to look for it. As you complete the weekly "Be Curious" sections, you'll find yourself immersed in an unfolding process that brings you information and ultimately personal clarity.

Make a list of three precise times in your life when you had complete clarity, and read it whenever you want to recapture that wonderful sensation of knowing. Trust that you will experience the same complete clarity regarding the question of motherhood.

My true desire matters, and no one can know it better than I. This truth is very important to embrace. Society, family, and friends all want to tell you how to think and feel, particularly when it comes to this decision. Women are bombarded with judgmental messages regarding motherhood:

> "Of course you should have a child; it's the most rewarding thing."
> "How selfish of you if you don't [or do] have a child."
> "You don't have what it takes to have a child."

The endless comments actually reveal more about the people speaking them than they do about you. You cannot look to anyone to tell you what is best for you.

We're confident that as you do the exercises in these pages, the assurance *My true desire matters, and no one can know it better than I* will take on new meaning and become more and more accurate.

I am the definer of me. You must own this! You know you better than anyone else.

If you grew up in a dysfunctional environment with the message that you shouldn't or couldn't trust your thoughts or feelings, it might be difficult to know and accept the message *I am the definer of me.* When you are either taught intentionally or inadvertently (without malice) to focus on the needs of others instead of your own, it's easy to merge where you end and another begins. Personal boundaries become blurry. How can you possibly know that you're the definer of you without feeling a clear connection to exactly who you are?

If you work this program in the way it is presented, you'll be able to fully embrace the truth of *I am the definer of me.*

The answers will come because they never left. This statement confirms why this program is *not* a strategy for thinking your way through to an answer that does not currently exist. It's not about your career, your bank account, your partner, or what you might lack. You know internally what you desire; however, you don't have access to it because layers of hurt, ambivalence, and confusion are sitting on top of it.

Only I can know what's true for me… It's all within me. It's time to look inward. This is why we ask you to stop making pros-and-cons lists and to put aside the external details of your life as you're working through the twelve weeks. This is why we recommend not sharing your process with others until you complete the program. The depth of anxiety many women feel about not knowing is in part due to focusing on external circumstances and influences, most of which are out of their control. Everything you need to access your truth can be found right inside you.

Repeat The Mantra as often as necessary over the coming weeks to help you relax into *I don't know*:

I don't know.

I don't know why I don't know.

It's not my fault that I don't know.

It's okay that I don't know.

I have had clarity before about many things.

My true desire matters and no one can know it better than I.

I am the definer of me.

The answers will come because they never left.

Only I can know what's true for me… It's all within me.

Big Project, Not Big Effort

The Motherhood-Is it for me? program is a relatively passive journey. We want you to do the guided visualizations and weekly assignments to the best of your ability, complete the optional exercises if you are so moved, and even be inspired to create additional ones of your own; but not much else needs to happen. The point is to invite information to come to you instead of chasing after it. Each activity is designed to tease out and release unconscious material. This will happen without forcing it.

Be Curious: Assignments for Week 2

Remember that the only agenda is to let your mind free-associate and notice what comes to you. In these assignments you might write about things you haven't thought about in a long time.

WEEK 2

1. Redefining Motherhood

The role of motherhood is constantly changing. It is impacted by current fashion, the evolution of our collective consciousness, and women's continuing emancipation and fluctuating economics, among other things. Some women are afraid of motherhood because they assume it can only look a certain way that is narrowly defined by current social norms. It is not uncommon to feel that there is only one way you can be a mother.

In this exercise you'll explore your view of motherhood today, imagine how your mother would have defined it, and entertain your fantasy interpretation. Delineating motherhood is a subjective task, and everyone answers the questions below differently. There are no correct or incorrect answers; there is only your perception and your experience.

Be Curious:
a. Define *motherhood* in your words. Describe not what you think it should be or is supposed to be, but rather what it looks like from where you stand today as you look around.
b. How do you imagine your mother defines or would have defined motherhood? Base your response on what you witnessed and experienced while you were growing up. In other words, this question is not about your mother's definition of her experience, but rather about your guess or intuition as to what her experience was. If your mother is still living and available for a conversation, at some point you may want to talk to her about her definition of motherhood – but not for this writing assignment.

c. If you were the definer of motherhood or had the last word on how it should be defined, how would you like it to be defined today? What would you want it to look and feel like? How does this differ from how you defined it in question 1a?

2. Your Youth

Your experiences as a youngster were instrumental in forming your ideas about how the world works and how other people behave. It can be fruitful to "unpack the bags" of these early years and see what you find.

Be Curious:

a. What did you like about your childhood or being young?

b. What was challenging about your childhood or being young?

c. What did you like about adults? What did you enjoy about hanging out with them?

d. What didn't you like about adults? What was difficult about hanging out with them?

Further Exploration and Discovery

Go through the questions in "Your Checklist for Reflection" on page 50 to further explore what you wrote in this week's assignments. Take the time to write more as you move through the checklist. While you do this each week, you'll notice themes emerge and reemerge. Continue to be relentlessly curious.

When you read your definitions of motherhood aloud, did you gain additional information or meaning? Did it offer you an increased emotional connection to what you wrote?

Notice what beliefs you hold about motherhood and ask yourself whether they are true for most women or only for you. Where do these beliefs come from – a deep knowing, instinct, your mother, or someone else? Have you always thought this way without questioning? Be curious about preconceptions about motherhood that you might have internalized through no fault of your own.

If you found the checklist questions or those directly above difficult to answer, appreciate that you're not alone. The questions are important to ponder even if you don't yet know exactly what you want to say about each of them.

As you read aloud your responses to the questions about being young, was it comfortable or uncomfortable walking down memory lane? Some women feel it was so long ago that they don't want to think about it. There is also a tendency to make snap assumptions about how it was back then. Did slowing down to write the answers allow you to think about things differently?

This is a good time to take a quick look at your family map and see if you perceive it differently now, or if there's anything you want to add to it.

Be Even More Curious: Optional Exercises

If you want to keep exploring, read on for some ideas. These exercises are completely optional and aren't necessary to get the program's full benefits.

1. Continue to collect pictures, words, and images. You'll have the opportunity to use them for an activity toward the end of the program.

2. Keep noticing and writing down your dreams. If a particular image makes itself known, write specifically about it. What might it be saying to you? Draw the image.

3. Make a list of things that nourish or recharge you. Refer to this list at a later time, particularly if you get loaded down with more feelings than you can handle.

What to Hold Inside This Week

The key is not to try to *think* your way through, but instead focus on welcoming and inviting information to come to you without your working hard to find it. You're not conducting an archeological dig. Place your effort in *allowing* each activity to percolate. Trying too hard to make something happen impedes discovery.

There might be times when you have uncomfortable feelings. Expect this. Do your best to breathe, appreciate your courage, and let the program "happen" to you. Stay engaged with it. Be gentle with yourself and trust that your mind and body will work well for you.

Always have your journal handy to record thoughts and feelings that arise during the week.

Use The Mantra regularly, especially when you notice yourself making a case for yes or no. Gently steer yourself back to *I don't know*.

Continue choosing to keep your internal thoughts and feelings to yourself. If you find them difficult to contain, use your journal to write about the challenges.

Don't underestimate what has already taken place, even in this very short time.

Take time for yourself to just be. Give yourself permission to open more space inside you for new feelings.

Self-Care

Stirring up emotions can feel exhausting at times, and good self-care matters during these twelve weeks and beyond. This week's self-care suggestion is to take time out from your usual routine to enjoy a tea break, treating it as a ritual. Rituals are sacred forms of self-care because they help transcend the mundane in order to connect with the divine in each present moment. Rituals create an elixir effect.

Create a pot of tea in your favorite teapot or your favorite cup. Move slowly as you do this with intention, as if it's a sacred ritual. You'll be rewarded. Sip gently. Quiet your mind. As you enjoy your tea, think about your glorious self and feel proud that you are on the road to discovering your true desire, which will lead you to making a conscious choice.

The self-care I did for myself this week was…

If you didn't take our suggestion, write down what you did.

You Are Not Alone

As mentioned earlier, beginning this week and continuing through Week 11, we include two stories of real women who generously took the time to share their journey to clarity with the intention of helping other women who are struggling to find their truth. Only their names have been changed to protect their privacy.

Be mindful of your emotions while reading the following stories. If you sense a connection to yourself (or them), and it feels supportive to hear their experiences, read on. However, if you feel crowded in any way or distracted from your process, we encourage you to save these stories for later.

Lesley's Story

Although I always assumed I would someday have at least one child, a couple of years into my starter marriage (I was in my mid-twenties) I recognized having a child with this husband would be an absolute disaster. I watched my husband interacting with my young nephew, the only child from the siblings in my family. It was clear my husband didn't like competition, no matter how cute the child was. He grew up as the center of the universe, as the only child of parents who were themselves only children, and wasn't about to share the spotlight with a child intruder.

Looking back, it was a wise decision not to have a child with that husband. By the time I extricated myself from that marriage and started dating my present husband, I was in my late thirties. He is ten years older than I and the father of a grown son twelve years my junior; a second family wasn't an option. So by my early forties I needed to make a choice to either stay or move on to someone who was interested in having a child.

Going into my relationship with my current husband, I was aware that I was choosing not to be a mom. Was I disappointed? Yes and no. I think I would have enjoyed being a mother, but I don't think I had that killer drive to have children at any cost. The cost would have been to lose a relationship I cherished.

Having made the decision, I didn't feel emotionally tortured or desperately unhappy or terribly regretful. There is a degree of sadness and regret, but it's not something I struggle with by any stretch. I did feel and still feel that my husband's life, as well as my own, would have been enhanced in different ways if we'd had a child.

I am a third-generation Asian American. I would describe my family as culturally Asian. It's a loving and extremely loyal family, but reserved – not very demonstrative by traditional touchy-feely American standards. I remember *being comforted by my mom when I was hurt, but I don't remember cuddling up to her as a young child. I always felt loved by my mom and always knew she'd give her life for my siblings or me, but there was a level of reserve always in place. It's just the family pattern and not uncommon in Asian families, despite the families' having been in this country for generations. If I were a mother, I hopefully would be more touchy-feely.*

I think my mom was better able to relate to her kids as adults than as children. In some ways, as she aged she seemed to take down some of the filters and express herself, really tell us what she thought. My mom is now in her mid-eighties, and at times is in floundering health. Her condition has taken down even more of her reserve persona. She's much more open to her kids than ever before.

I think my decision can best be described as thought through as opposed to felt through. It was a gradual process – no Aha! moment that I can pinpoint as an absolute decision time.

I love my relationship with my husband. Would that have changed in a variety of ways had we become parents? We have our own time, and we have the independence that I don't think we would have had if there were a child.

Lesley is in her early fifties, works as a freelance professional in media, and is happily married. The youngest of three children, she was born to an extremely bright, highly educated woman who Lesley believes would have been more fulfilled had she worked outside the home, even at a part-time job. The children could see their mother's boredom and frustration. While not all women of her mom's generation were stay-at-home mothers, the majority were. Her mother clearly wanted to provide her children with every opportunity possible, and went about making that happen.

Lesley's father is also intelligent and well educated, and had a successful career. While Lesley was growing up he fulfilled the role of the breadwinner. Although he didn't have energy during the week, as he was tired after working a full day, on weekends he had all kinds of time for projects with his children. He was the fun one; he left the role of disciplinarian to Lesley's mother.

The family plan was to have a total of four children, with the first two and the second two reasonably close in age. But they stopped after Lesley was born. She does not have the younger sibling she might have had and suspects her mother had had enough by then. Of her two siblings, only her brother has a son. This is a family that has shrunk considerably in four generations.

Lesley loves the relationship she and her husband share. That said, there are times when their personal freedom is overshadowed by the needs of her husband's adult son, who has struggled for nearly two decades with the developmental steps sometimes referred to as launching into adulthood. The son is likable, smart, and funny. He has had more than one long-term girlfriend, but lacks the confidence, drive, and self-regard he needs to gain traction and move forward in life. His struggles weigh heavily on Lesley's husband and, consequently of course, on her.

She is quite involved, providing support – practical and emotional – to both. Might she also be frustrated at times? It would be natural to feel this when faced with a sense of powerlessness to help a loved one who seemingly cannot or will not help himself.

For friendship, Lesley gravitated toward women who didn't have children. Many school friends, including those she met at university, pursued careers first. Some of those women had children later, but many remain childless today. Virtually all of her most recent friends are without children. In addition to her personal friends, Lesley shares many friends from her husband's wide social circle. The couple spends time doing family things with her husband's son, who now lives in the area; her sister and brother and his family; and other family members. Lesley's parents live a fair distance away, but now that her mother's health is diminishing they make more frequent visits to see them. There is no shortage of personal and familial support in Lesley's life.

Lea's Story

I do not remember ever thinking about my choice! I knew from a young age, when I was a teenager, that I had contracts with souls to have them as my kids and to be their mother. I simply said yes to what my soul had already decided. Knowing I would have kids was, as far as I can tell, unrelated to my spouse. I do not remember thinking about having kids before the time we were together. My husband and I became a couple with my knowing already in place. It was similar for him. I knew he was my man for this lifetime and was to be the father of my kids.

To have kids was expected. To have them exactly when I wanted them was another issue. Yet as far as I was concerned, I was going to give birth to my kids when I wanted to and not a moment earlier.

My spouse and I probably spoke about our wish to have kids. I don't remember now what brought it up. It may have been around the time someone asked me how my kid was doing, way before I had any, or when I was told that I was self-centered and probably because of that didn't want to have children. At that time, when my spouse and I were in our early twenties, most young people, especially if they had partners, got married and had kids at a very young age, like my sister and brother did. Although I knew I would have kids, I was not in a rush. This was unusual and difficult for people in my extended family to understand.

I remember thinking that having kids might not be a good idea in the world as I knew it (and for sure as I know it now) and in the specific country – Israel – we live in, where the kids go into the army or some other civil service. These were thoughts, but they never really touched the knowing in my heart.

Perhaps my case is not very common, and I am not clear if it can help anyone else. I know that if my inner knowing had been that I would not have children, it would have been harder to follow. The perception in my family was that a woman is not a woman if she does not have children. I am lucky that I was clear about having children and that what I had to protect myself from was only the pressure about time. Compared to my friends and people my age in Israel, I gave birth late, after age thirty. This is common today, but it wasn't then. So I am very lucky and can only wish for more people, especially women, to be lucky and have the strength to follow what is right for them no matter what.

Lea is as busy as ever at this stage of her life (her early sixties), sharing her teaching and training vocation with students all over the world. She is talented and hardworking, and finds deep fulfillment in her work. Her supportive husband and partner of over forty years maintains their home base while she travels extensively for work. They have two grown children, a son and a daughter, both married and settled into their adult lives.

Lea's father died before she gave birth to her children. She described her relationship with him as very loving when she was growing up. She has two older siblings, a sister and a brother. Lea knows that she was a wanted child when her parents conceived her, as her mother aborted other pregnancies when she chose to. Lea's relationship with her mother isn't traditional at all. When Lea was fourteen, the two switched emotional roles, her mother becoming the child and Lea the adult. Lea shared that her mother is fun to be around – the kind of fun of someone who is perpetually young at heart. The extended family enjoys her mom's youthful point of view, and they have come to accept that she cannot give what she does not have: the qualities that make someone dependable; the qualities one would hope for in a mother. Lea says that her grown children are more emotionally mature than their grandmother. Her mother encouraged Lea to follow her dreams and to be independent. Lea loves her mother and has compassion for her.

Lea wishes that as a young person she had appreciated just how fortunate she was that she knew very clearly what she wanted for these two life-defining choices: her choice of mate and her decision to be a mother. Experiencing this clarity told her she would marry and become a mother to two children. She acknowledges that her greatest struggles come when she doesn't clearly hear her *knowingness*, something she calls more a feeling than a thought. Could we also call it intuition – the guidance that allows a person to follow clearly what is true for them at any given moment? To a woman who is facing the question of becoming a mother or not, Lea said, "I'd support her in listening to her heart and soul and following what she hears no matter what."

Week 3

A Surprise Encounter

"I am no bird; and no net ensnares me:
I am a free human being with an independent will."
–Charlotte Brontë[3]

Welcome to Week 3! Are you aware of any new insights since last week? When you look at a situation with fresh eyes or a fresh mind, the subtle change in perspective can have a not-so-subtle impact. Does anything come to mind?

Last week you began exploring definitions of motherhood. No matter where that writing assignment took you, chances are you're looking at the world around you more keenly. You may be watching mothers interact with their young ones. You may be remembering more about your mother. You also revisited memories of good and challenging times from childhood. This is all grist for the mill and food for thought.

You've been trying to hang out more with not knowing, and this suspension of certainty can arouse emotions. If it does, you needn't do anything about them now except notice. Remember to use your journal as soon as possible when thoughts, images, feelings, or insights come to you.

Week 3 Guided Visualization

(Adapted from "Walking Along the Shore of the Beach" by John O. Stevens in *Awareness: Exploring, Experimenting, Experiencing.* Boulder, Colorado: Real People Press, 1971.)

This week's visualization is a bit different because it has two parts. Halfway through you'll be asked to stop and write about your experience. Then you'll be invited to continue.

Trust that your attentive mind will go where it needs to go. When your eyes are closed, you engage the part of your brain that isn't as easily accessed when your eyes are open. Have someone read the visualization to you or record it for you so you can listen while your eyes are closed, as its power also lies in the element of surprise. If that's not possible, make a recording yourself so you can listen with eyes closed to deepen the experience of where the visualization takes you. If you read the visualization to yourself, read it silently and slowly to give yourself time to savor the experience. Close your eyes now and then to open to the power of your imagination.

Remember that the experience you have is what matters most, and there's no wrong way to do it. Have your journal and writing tool nearby so you can record your impressions and images immediately.

To prepare, choose a quiet place where people and noise won't disturb or distract you, and a time when there's nothing else for you to do and no one who needs your attention; this time is solely for your benefit. Either sit comfortably in a chair or, if you prefer, lie down on the floor.

A Surprise Encounter

Now that you're ready, become conscious of your breathing. Let your eyes close gently as you take a deep breath and exhale. Inhale and hold your breath for five counts. Then exhale until most of the air has left your lungs. Inhale again and slowly exhale, letting out an audible sigh through your mouth while you count silently from ten to one. Continue breathing slowly and deeply. As you breathe, you relax. Allow your natural breath to bring a deep sense of peace and well-being. Feel your body relax and let your mind free-associate. B-r-e-a-t-h-e.

Imagine yourself on the most beautiful beach with the softest sand and the clearest water. Maybe you see some rock formations and stunning seashells, perhaps birds reveling in their capacity for flight. You're in one of the most exquisite places you've ever been. Settle in. If unwanted thoughts come into your mind, let them move on like clouds overhead in the sky. With your next breath, breathe in tranquility and serenity. As you exhale, let go of any remaining body tension and mental energy. You're quiet and peaceful. You're enjoying the environment. B-r-e-a-t-h-e.

Bring your attention to your heart and breathe in deeply. Remember a time when you felt unconditional love from another person or a beloved animal. Breathe into the feeling of love in your heart. Accept this unconditional love and notice your heart opening more. Be aware of the emotional and physical sensations in your body as you experience the sensation of being loved. B-r-e-a-t-h-e.

Now remember a time when you felt unconditional love *for* another person or an animal. Again, sense your heart expand with the memory. Maybe it was yesterday, or a long time ago. What matters is experiencing that kind of love for someone else. Notice the emotional and physical sensations in your body. B-r-e-a-t-h-e.

Bring your attention back to your beach. See yourself walking along your private shoreline. While strolling along the sand, feel the warm sun on your skin and the gentle breeze kissing your face. Listen to the seagulls flying above. Take in the smell of the water. Hear the sound of the waves and feel them lapping at your feet. The air temperature and the warmth of the water are just as you would like them. Even the angle of the sun is perfect. Take in the beauty and calmness around you.

In the distance you see a young girl playing in the sand, building sand castles. She appears to be about three or four years old. As you approach, she notices you, gets excited, and jumps up. She runs toward you. Upon closer look, this girl is you, when you were her age! You observe immediately her innocence and vulnerability. Her welcoming eyes meet yours. She is glad to see you. You can tell that this little girl means no harm to anyone. All she wants is to love and be loved in return, to play and to have fun. Notice what your immediate feelings are. What sensations are in your heart? Do you want to hug her, hold her hand, or pick her up? Do you want to keep your distance? Go ahead and notice all the feelings you have about her, whatever they may be.

Gently take her hand and together walk over to a nearby rock where you both can sit. As you're sitting next to each other, feel her energy beside you. Is her energy restless, quiet, peaceful, exuberant, worried, or calm? How is her energy for you? Ask this little girl the following questions: "What do you need?" "What do you want?" How does she answer? What does she say to you?

Pause now for a few moments. Open your eyes and use your journal to record what's occurred so far. Keep writing until you feel you've expressed all your feelings and thoughts.

Now close your eyes and continue with the guided visualization.

Return your imagination to the spot on the rock where the two of you are hanging out together. Reconnect with the young girl. You are about to read slowly or listen to a list of messages that every young person needs to hear to feel secure and connected with others. These messages are universal to all children no matter their cultural background. As you hear these words of love and care, imagine saying them to this little girl. Notice how it feels to say them to her. Notice which words you received when you were young, and which ones you didn't.

My Child, You Matter, and You Matter to Me!

I love you very much, and I'll always love you.

You are wanted.

I see you, and I hear you.

You don't have to perform or jump through hoops for my love.

I love you for who you are and not for what you do.

I'll take care of you.

I love you, and I give you complete permission to be different from me.

You can trust me.

You can trust your inner voice.

You don't have to be perfect; I give you permission to make mistakes.

Your thoughts and feelings are important to me.

When you're ready, you get to make your own choices,

and I'll support you.

You don't have to be like anyone else.

Sometimes I'll tell you no and set limits, because I love you.

If you feel afraid or alone, I want to know about it.

If you fall, I'll help you get up.

I'll listen to your joys, your hurts, and your tears.
You make a difference in the world by just being here.
You can go after your biggest dreams.
I give you permission to be the same as I am, and permission to soar
beyond anything I've become.
I give you permission to be your own person.
You matter, and you matter to me.

How did it feel to say these messages to this young girl? Did you hear these messages while you were growing up? Perhaps sometimes you heard the words without experiencing the behavior to back them up; or perhaps the behavior was there without the words. Ideally words and behavior match. This allows a person to feel secure and connected. Breathe.

It's time now to take the little girl's hand and walk her back to the sand castle she was building. While you walk together, notice what it feels like to have heard those messages. How was it to say them to her? Once she is settled back at her sand castle, let her know that you'll be back to play with her another time, but for now you have to say good-bye.

Keep your eyes closed while you slowly return to your present environment, allowing a few moments to be with your emotional and physical sensations. B-r-e-a-t-h-e.

When you're ready, slowly open your eyes and begin to write in your journal. Record your immediate thoughts, feelings, insights, and anything else you want to about your experience.

Immediate Writing after the Guided Visualization

Write as much as you can before reading on. If you feel like nothing much happened for you, journal about that. If you're still not sure what to write, think about the feelings that first came to you when you noticed the young girl. Did you feel positive, negative, or neutral? What was it like to be with her? What did she want? How did it feel to express the messages of love to her? Were these the messages she heard growing up? Did any feelings arise when it was time to say good-bye? Writing immediately helps settle the guided visualization more deeply in your body and mind. Trust that there's meaning in your writing even if you don't yet see it. Continue journaling right now if there's more you'd like to express.

Now tune in to your feelings by scanning your body from head to toe. If you don't feel anything, or if you felt numb during the guided visualization, please don't judge yourself. Numbness is information. Just because you feel nothing doesn't mean nothing is happening – or that you did it wrong (remember that there's no wrong way). Some visualizations will feel fruitful, really impacting you and setting you on a new course of thinking and feeling. Others won't. Sometimes the gentle stirring won't register until later. Either way, you gain information. You're unique, and your experiences are also unique. Take it all in your stride and keep going.

When your writing feels complete, check in with your emotional state. Are your feelings manageable? If you feel overwhelmed, follow these instructions:

Take a deep breath, then exhale as slowly as possible, letting all the air escape your lungs. Allow your body to take in a breath on its own. Continue this several times until you notice a sense of calm. Then tap your feet on the floor. Follow that by tapping the tops of your thighs with your hands. Then tap your arms with your hands. Clench your fists and then release them. These actions help reconnect you to the present and ground you. Doing this is especially important when the emotions you experience feel overwhelming or just too much for you to manage. If you need to take further action to feel reconnected or grounded in the present, stand up and stamp your feet. Then reach your hands up in the air and stretch.

Look around the room and notice objects that bring a gentle smile to your face. Is your focus where you want it to be? Are your emotions manageable? Before you continue, make sure your attention is where you need it to be.

What Happens in Week 3

This week we invite you to examine your early childhood. Visiting the past in a variety of ways helps you discover what might still be causing an emotional blockage, and can provide an essential key to clarity.

The experiences you've had thus far, along with this week's activities, could cause you to start feeling that you're "all over the place." At some point this week you might feel overwhelming grief, sadness, anger, worry, or frustration, and then relief, peace, and calm. You could feel one, some, or all of these emotions. The process stirs up a different mix for everyone.

Keep considering that your mind and body are offering up information for you to observe. The deep recesses of your psyche are at work, but the details that get dredged up might not have obvious inherent meaning. Trust that what arises is useful. Trust the process and remember that it is not necessarily a linear one. By the end of the program most or all of the puzzle pieces will have come together. For some women this happens along the way; for others it happens at the very end.

It's Never Too Late to Heal

Young children have a complex array of physical, emotional, and psychological needs. Sometimes not all of these needs are adequately met. When an unmet need goes hungry, it can confound emotional and psychological development. If you didn't identify your unmet needs and work through them when you were young, they can impact you later in life. You try to get them satisfied over and over again in adulthood, constructing endless familiar scenarios, and end up disappointed over and over again.

If you are fortunate to attain the necessary insight, you can realize that the opportunity to address these needs has passed and come to understand that *no one* can meet them. That does not mean that nothing can be done to address the missing fulfillment. Your unmet needs *can* be worked through. Recovery and healing occur when you face and grieve your losses. This program is designed to support you through this. For example, when you work on the assignments this week, sadness might surface. Hold this sadness gently and be curious. See if you can identify an unmet need.

When listening to the statements from "My Child, You Matter, and You Matter to Me!" many women realize that while they received the stated messages verbally, there was no matching loving behavior. This inconsistency can be very confusing to a young person. If you didn't receive the essence of these wonderful messages when you were young, it isn't too late to experience them now. As you grieve what didn't happen for your younger self, you nurture her. This brings about the healing that wants to happen. When you fully reconcile and reclaim the spirit of these nurturing messages, it's as if you *did* originally receive them.

If you've done inner-child work in the past, you may be excited about this week's activities because you'll be able to take the work to the next level. Or you may feel like you've "been there, done that" and there's no need to revisit the past. If you're grumbling or feeling resistant, we ask you to entertain the possibility that like layers of an onion, there is another deeper layer asking for your attention – the same hurt feelings perhaps, but a bit closer to the core. There might be just a tiny bit more work to do that could make all the difference. If you feel a sense of foreboding at all, don't worry; this week's activities will gently and respectfully guide you to where you need to go. Work you've previously done on yourself does matter; it will contribute to your success here and now.

Inner Freedom

When you're able to heal from suffering, energy is freed up and becomes available to use as you choose. Emotional healing, in particular, allows you to respond more authentically to others and to the environment in the here and now rather than reacting out of a habit based on a past unhealed event.

One way to notice if you're harboring old hurts is to pay attention to your *reactions* and *responses* to others and events. A reaction to something or someone, whether verbal or physical, is automatic, without thought. It comes quickly, without rational consideration and often without awareness of your body. It can *feel* real, but your clue that it's a reaction is the activated energy in your body combined with behavior that doesn't match what is happening in the here and now. Your heart might race, or your body might feel hot. Reactions are based on remnants of old, unmet needs or unresolved pain. If you're unaware of an old, unmet need that you're carrying around, you can be reactive (or triggered) in certain situations. When you *respond*, on the other hand, there's an embodied sense of *Yes, this is my personal truth.* You're aware of your body sensations and they feel aligned with your thoughts and words. There's a sense of calm. You feel present.

As you heal, you find yourself replacing *reactions* with *responses*. You feel an inner freedom – a freedom that is your birthright. This week's suggested assignments can help facilitate this healing.

Be Curious: Assignments for Week 3

1. The first assignment this week involves writing a letter to the little girl you met on the beach in the guided visualization. Can you imagine what it would have been like to have someone like you in your life when you were as young as she? You know best what's going to come her way; here's your opportunity to prepare her. What do you want to tell her? What do you want her to know? What do you want her to remember about who she is? What do you want her never to forget about herself? Go ahead and write your letter. It's a fantasy letter. It doesn't have to make sense or be linear. That little girl needed to hear certain things back then, and it's not too late for her to hear them now. Reach for her in this letter if you can.

Be Curious: Start your letter with "Dear Young One..." and continue it in your own words. For example, here is how two of the women introduced in Week 1 started their letters:

Dear precious Sue,

You're only four years old now and so very precious, full of love to give, and you just want to be loved in return. I want to share some thoughts with you that I wish you'd known back then. There are also a few things that I don't want you ever to forget about who you are. You're very sweet and smart. I can tell you're worried that your mom hasn't acted like herself lately. Don't worry – it isn't about you at all. She is hurt and brokenhearted, and doesn't know how to be there for you now. It's not your job to make her happy. It really isn't. This is not a reflection of anything about you. You are good and wonderful. Don't let your parents' confusion or pain be about who you are. You are totally loveable, and you'll find the love in your life that you deserve and want. In the years ahead, it will seem like it's expected of you to take on caring for others in your family. This isn't your responsibility. It doesn't have to be the role for you. You get to decide what you want for yourself, and I'm here to help you...

Dear young Samantha,

You are such a dear little girl, with your clear, sweet, brown eyes. I love you so very much. You are strong and smart, too. Your intelligence will help you through the chaos. Remember always how special you truly are. I know you are struggling. It is so confusing with the ups and downs at home. You don't know what to expect moment to moment. All of this confusion has nothing at all to do with you. You are not causing any of it. You can trust that. It's just too bad that you have to see and feel it. I'm so sorry this is happening to you. You deserve to feel safe and cared about always. I am aware of some things that will help you as you develop, and I'd like to share them with you now…

2. The second assignment relates to the list of messages entitled "My Child, You Matter, and You Matter to Me!" that you read or heard during the guided visualization. Reading them can provide you with different insights than hearing them, so this is one instance in which we encourage you to read them if you haven't already.

   These messages are universal. Every child needs the words they hear to be consistent with the behavior they experience. If you did not receive these messages one way or another when you were young, it's not too late to give them to yourself now as an adult.

   Be Curious: Read the list of messages from the visualization. Does your body relax, or tense up when you read certain ones? You can feel good that you received certain messages because they made such a difference in your life, or you can feel a longing for messages you didn't hear. Select two or three messages that feel emotionally charged (positive or negative) and write about them.

3. You can begin this activity now and embellish it as the weeks go by.

   Be Curious: Find some old pictures of yourself and lay them out in front of you. What feelings are evoked as you look at them? Talk to the little girl in the pictures. How does the conversation go? Write down your feelings and thoughts and then take the activity one step further: Choose a few of the photos and create an altar to your younger self. Add any objects, toys, mementos, or other items that appeal to you. Place it in a private place or in the place where you do your program assignments, where you can visit your younger self often. You decide what's best for you.

Further Exploration and Discovery

Go through the questions in "Your Checklist for Reflection" on page 50 for each of this week's writing exercises.

There's a big difference between dwelling in the past and exploring past hurts for the sake of freeing yourself from pain. Dwelling in the past has a "poor me" or "why me?" undertone. It sounds like "I'll never get over this. It shouldn't have happened, and I can't do anything about it now." *Exploring* past hurts, on the other hand, has an air of curiosity and compassion. You feel open-hearted. You can feel the loss *for* that younger one. There's a better likelihood that you will grieve the hurt and loss and that this healing will lead to greater freedom. Once you become an adult, *you are the only one who can help that young person who still resides in you.*

If you haven't already done so, try reading your letter to your young one aloud. This piece of writing, in particular, can be powerful as you hear your written words spoken out loud. What do you feel as you hear these words spoken to your younger self? Does anything surprise you? Did writing the letter to the young one inside help you feel more connected to her? Does she need more attention from you? The connection with her is one you'll want to foster as time goes on.

When you pay attention to a place inside you that's been neglected, old thoughts and feelings are likely to surface. This is natural. We want you to take in these words of wisdom and *believe* that it's never too late to heal.

Take note of which messages in "My Child, You Matter, and You Matter to Me!" resonated with you and which ones didn't, and pay attention to your reactions. It's quite possible that some mixed feelings or confusion have arisen. When words don't match behaviors, it can feel very confusing to a young girl. The lack of congruence can influence a lifetime of experiences and relationships. Sometimes (although not always) the young one inside can end up feeling like she didn't matter. Imagine just how difficult this would make her emotional and psychological development!

It's important to convey that even well-intentioned parents can behave in ways that inadvertently hurt their children. We're not suggesting spending time and energy on blaming parents for what they did or didn't do. Most do the best they can given the resources they possess. It's also important to state that, sadly, some parents do cause extensive damage to their children. If their own needs were not met adequately when they were young, they might not be able to meet the needs of their own children. And if their needs were met, meeting their children's needs comes more naturally.

Take another look at your family map and "sit" with it for a while. If you're aware of any wounds your parents experienced when they were young, can you see why they might not have been able to pass on some of the "you matter to me" messages to you? Even if a parent never heals, it's okay if you do. It's not too late for you to heal. And you can do it for yourself without their involvement.

Be Even More Curious: Optional Exercises

If you have time and the inclination to do more for the younger you this week, read on.

1. Take your young self to a toy store and buy her the toy that she wants. Indeed, let your young one have her way here. Don't rush. She might need a while to reconnect with what she wants. If it feels like the right thing to do, wrap her choice up as a gift and let her have more fun later when she opens it. Try spending a few hours together, perhaps taking her for an ice cream cone or some other kind of treat.

2. Draw two large overlapping circles (a Venn diagram) on a piece of paper or in your journal. In one circle, place the verbal messages you received from your parents and in the other the non-verbal messages. Write only the matching verbal and non-verbal messages in the center of the Venn diagram, where the circles overlap. These messages might have been positive or negative.

3. Are there positive messages that were never conveyed to you that you wanted or needed, or that would have made a difference in your life? Decorate the lid of a jar with colored paper, sparkles, or any other decoration. This jar will be your mailbox. On separate sheets of paper list the messages you wish you had received and place them in the jar. Think of them as love notes to yourself. Open the jar and read them from time to time. You might want to keep this jar close to the altar of your younger self. You can also make

a collage using words and images from magazines that represent your helpful messages – both the ones you did receive and the ones you hoped for but never experienced.

4. Imagine if the young one could write back to you. How might she reply to the letter you wrote her?

What to Hold Inside This Week

You are proceeding nicely and will continue to do so without doing more than the primary exercises each week. Please don't underestimate what has already transpired during the past three weeks. Be gentle with yourself.

Pay attention to whether or not you feel connected to your younger self. Move toward softness as you connect with her. Take some quiet time to love and appreciate her. Write to her. Reach out to her. Get to know her. She needs you and needs to understand that you, her adult, are protecting her. If you require help with this, close your eyes and picture a baby you love sitting in the center of your heart. Put your hands over your heart to hold her there. See if that helps you connect. If you're not yet able to have warm feelings for her – for whatever good reason – try to be okay with that. Be easy on yourself. Just notice what is there and see where it eventually leads.

Be aware as best you can of how your adult self is still trying to work through unresolved childhood needs. Some women discover during this week's exercises that they've never experienced unconditional love. For example, Samantha realized that she hadn't received any of the positive messages in the "My Child, You Matter, and You Matter to Me!" list.

This revelation overwhelmed her and brought up a tremendous loss that took some time to grieve over. It also helped her understand that she had been unconsciously expecting her intimate partner to fill this void. Her partner, of course, couldn't do this for her; but Samantha herself could, by grieving her loss. Gradually she felt more self-compassion. She consequently exerted less pressure on her partner to try to make things right for her.

On the other hand, Birgit had received the spirit of several messages on the list, both verbally and non-verbally. While feeling grateful for this, she also noticed that she had some heightened energy with: *You don't have to perform or jump through hoops for my love. I love you for who you are and not for what you do.* Her parents were putting subtle but constant pressure on her (and her husband) to have a child. They wanted to be grandparents. Perhaps they wanted this more than they wanted Birgit to follow her path. Writing about this gave Birgit more clarity about where she felt entangled in their expectations.

While you progress through this learning process, remember self-compassion – meaning loving yourself without judgment. Use your journal to keep track of new insights.

As you watch for times and places where you might be trying to meet needs that should have been met when you were young, bring your observing eye to your *reactions* and your *responses*. Notice how quickly a *reaction* comes, and how much information your body gives you when you *respond* instead. Learn to become aware of the differences. Feeling the distinction between these two can guide you to the subtle (and maybe not-so-subtle) places calling out to be healed.

Stay with *I don't know* (intentionally and on purpose), and pay attention to how it feels not to share your process with others.

Self-Care

When you tune in to self-care this week, consider what your younger self needs and desires. See if you can treat her to a little tender loving care. What would nourish her? How about preparing her favorite food for her to eat or doing something she loved to do? Does she need permission to indulge? Can you give her that permission? Did she get the message that me-time is selfish? If old messages or feelings emerge as you explore self-care options, use your journal to write about them.

One idea is to give your younger self permission to take a long, luxurious soak in a bubble bath, or visit a spa and be treated to a massage. Pampering yourself with a leisurely soak or hanging out in a spa setting can support your emotional work while it promotes healing. For this week's self-care, pampering is primary. When was the last time you finger-painted – and did you realize you can get finger paints especially for the bathtub ☺?

The self-care I did for myself this week was…

You Are Not Alone

Here are two more stories to help you to feel connected to a larger community. Read about Amy Lynn and Louise only if it feels supportive to you, depending on where you are on your journey. If reading about them distracts you or interferes with your process, check out the stories later. You decide what feels right for you. Above all, take care of yourself.

Amy Lynn's Story

In my twenties: I want a baby; I just don't want one now.

Thirty to thirty-five: I want a baby; I just don't want one now. I think.

Thirty-five to thirty-eight: I want a baby; I just don't want to have one with a husband I don't love.

Thirty-nine: I don't want a baby. I just need to face it.

I felt my way, 100 percent, through all of it. I had a very visceral, negative reaction to everything representing a child. I called the abortion clinic the day after I found out I was pregnant. If I could have thought my way through it then I would have a child now, but I could never convince myself, no matter how hard I tried, that I wanted a baby. I knew I didn't want to be alone, but I also knew that the solution to loneliness wasn't having a baby.

My birth mother was twenty-one years old and got pregnant while having an affair with a married man (for whom she worked) who had four kids of his own. Upon hearing about her pregnancy, he wanted nothing to do with her or me. After she had given birth, I became a ward of the state until I was adopted at two weeks old. I'm pretty sure my birth mother was scared and felt alone and abandoned. I have these feelings a lot, and I think it's probably what she felt most of the time I was in her womb. I think she probably loved that man, and he rejected her. I don't know her, though. I've never met her.

My adoptive mother was strict and direct. She was nice when you did something she wanted you to do (usually regarding God or chores), and extremely cold and emotionally unavailable when you did something that displeased her. She did not like physical contact. And I remember tolerating her foot-rubs, even though they were too hard and kind of hurt, because she was, at least, touching me. She loved God more than she loved anything. She used fear of going to hell and guilt to discipline us. She was fickle and would change the rules all the time, usually after she had "prayed about it." She was hard to live with. Since I could never win her love or support and did not understand the rules to get this, I wanted to get away from her, so it didn't matter if she was mean or disappointed in me or not. I would never use fear or guilt to raise a child. I would never make a child feel scared of burning in hell. I would never tell a child that if they prayed hard enough their dad would come home. She was psychologically abusive and I can see that now; but she's also got her issues, so maybe it's a type of mental illness.

My dad was the only person who could comfort me after the age of four or five. He was a very calm person. He was raised as a Buddhist in Malaysia but was born in China. My earliest memory is of his being kind and bringing me a toy. I also remember lying on his chest sobbing, finally feeling safe after something had scared me. My mother never physically comforted me that I can recall. He moved away (was separated) from us for months at a time, from when I was an infant through growing up, because he and my mother had issues. They should not have been married or adopted children together. I missed him a lot. He was the fun parent, but he left the raising of us completely to my mother. He was a doctor and was always rushing to someone else's needs. He never was on time or came home when he said he would. But he was also non-judgmental, and very understanding of everything kids do and feel. He gave us too much freedom because my mother gave us none. He did not get involved in our lives in a bad way or in a good way. He was forgetful and did not find traditional things important, so we felt alone a lot. But if you truly needed him, he would be there. He said that when I was a kid I told him, "Dad, I'm never, ever having a baby." I didn't know I told him that. I don't remember saying it. But I love him for helping me affirm my decision. It helps me to know that I've felt this way for a long time. It made me feel like someone finally understood me.

It surprised me how mad it made me that everyone expects you to change your interests and focus on them when they get pregnant. I never realized how entitled and narcissistic that is. Our society accepts it as natural and normal because everyone is supposed to want kids. I realized I'm in a minority class by choosing not to have kids. And as such, I now know how it feels to be discriminated against.

When one of my close friends would get pregnant, everything changed regarding their priorities and they became all about the pregnancy and the baby. It bugged me, and they didn't want to talk about anything but stretch marks, sonograms, and strollers. Things I classify as super boring became super interesting in their heads once they were pregnant. I found out that after a few years the good friends do come back once the newness of the baby thing wears off. They want to have and be good friends again and not just have everything be about the baby. They no longer want only these weird friendships they made over the last few years with other Stroller-Strides-type moms.

I have a really big family. Both my parents had two additional kids from second marriages, so there are eight of us. I love my siblings more than anything in the world. We are all very, very close. I always felt that I would miss having a big family like the one I grew up in. Then I realized I will always have them and their children (my nieces and nephews), and they will always be my big family. I didn't need to start one of my own; I could just keep the one I had. I also realized that of all the roles in a big family, the role of mother is not for me. That's more for someone like my older sister. I like the role of class clown.

Amy Lynn was thirty-nine when she made her decision. Her husband wanted them to have children. After she accidently became pregnant and had an abortion without telling him, she was finally able to tell him that she didn't want to have children. It had been extremely difficult up until then to tell him so. They are now divorced. Her decision not to have children was the straw that broke the back of her marriage; but it can also be said that the clarity of her decision finally helped her end a marriage that did not suit her. Amy Lynn found her courage to fully face her truth not to have children, make the changes that truth asked of her, and divorce her husband.

She endured a difficult childhood with a physically present but overly religious mother who used religious beliefs to an extreme measure, controlling and scaring her young daughter, and later alienating her. Amy Lynn wonders today if her mother was mentally unstable. It is certainly a possibility. It's also quite possible that her mother was and is psychologically wounded and has tried to use rigid religious beliefs to compensate for a weak internal psychological structure. Amy Lynn's mostly absent father was a saving grace. He could see his daughter for who she was and gave her concrete signs of love and care. Even though he wasn't around much while she was growing up, Amy Lynn experienced what genuine care feels like. He continues to be a valuable, supportive person in her life.

We were very sorry to hear that Amy Lynn had received some unprofessional marriage counseling early on when she and her husband were trying to work through their different positions. The therapist told her she should have a child – that it would be good for her and good for her marriage. Fortunately Amy Lynn didn't take this advice.

It took Amy Lynn time – in her case many years and four abortions – to accept her desire not to have children and to give herself permission to act accordingly. Terminating her pregnancies was the right option for her. Difficulty in giving oneself permission to know and follow one's truth is a recurring theme for many women.

While Amy Lynn worries at times about financial and emotional security, and sometimes feels lonely, she values and enjoys her time with friends, family, and her dog. She is also grateful for her freedom. When asked if her relationship with children has changed now that she has decided not to be a mother, she said, "I feel relieved around them somewhat. I don't have to worry if they're bugging me, or if this is what my kid would do, or how I'll be able to go on an airplane with a screaming kid, because I know I'll never have to do it. So I guess my relationship with kids has improved. They no longer represent my possible life."

What Amy Lynn wished she had known earlier in her life was "that I'd never feel a biological clock or that need to have a baby; I waited for one to start ticking for a long time. I thought that happened to everyone, eventually; but as it turns out, it doesn't, and no one told me that." She has this advice for other women facing their choice: "Listen to your gut. Listen to what your body tells you when you're around children. Don't let other people influence you with the fear of being alone or the fear of an empty life, because fear is not a reason to have a baby. "

Louise's Story

I was in my early twenties when I thought seriously about the decision to become a mother. I knew when I was a child that I wanted to be a mom; it was just something I knew I was going to do. As I entered my twenties and left my home state to move to California, I knew it would take me several years to establish myself. I did not think it would take me as long as it did to have children. I kept waiting for that "perfect" relationship. With a couple of previous partners I was ready, but they were not. I kept waiting for them to be ready. Then time kept slipping by.

Certainly watching my parents pass away after having been married for fifty years had an influence on my desire and timing around having children. I had hoped more than anything that I could be with someone – a partner – to start that process with. But since I had already sacrificed about seven years waiting for that person to be ready, I decided I was going to do it on my own even if the relationship dissolved, which it did when I was pregnant, more or less. I also made a conscious decision to find a man (friend) who was willing to be the father, willing to be "Daddy," because I was extremely close to my father and wanted my child to have a dad in his life. I knew I was going to raise this *child on my own, but wanted this person in my child's life even on a limited basis. Backing up a bit, I had thought I would get married (to a man; didn't come out as a lesbian until my late twenties) and have kids and probably be a stay-at-home mom. When I discovered myself, so to speak, I still knew I would have children; it would just entail a different sort of path. My parents died in 1999. I finished my master's program in nursing in 2000 and shortly after graduation started the plans of trying to get pregnant.*

I had confided in my parents before they passed on. I specifically remember my mom asked me how in the world I could have children without a spouse or man in my life. I told her I hadn't figured that part out yet, but that I knew I wanted to try to find a male friend who was willing to not only donate his sperm but who was interested in being a father figure of some sort. I also confided in a couple of siblings. One brother, in particular, was not supportive, claiming I did not have the resources and it was a bad decision. But most of my siblings were supportive. My role model was my sister. She was a single mother and a strong woman, and I knew that I could do it as well as she if I had to.

My mother was fearful for me: fearful that I would not be able to do it on my own; fearful for any potential mistreatment that I might experience in society as a whole for being not only gay, but a gay mom. She was feeling very protective and nervous at the same time. Unfortunately she was not able to be here for her grandchildren, having passed on two years before my son was born.

Did I regard her differently? Well, she had her children naturally with my father, and while I know she decided to have children, I also believe she just kept having them (nine of us!) because it was the Catholic thing to do and all of her friends were in the same situation. Big families were the norm back then. Had she procreated in our generation, she might not have had as many, as I know it was very hard on her in many ways.

I came to my choice clearly during and after my parents' passing. I knew it was time, not only because I was getting older but because I was able to truly experience, for the first time in my life, the meaning of family, the bonds and ties that we have with our family members. These bonds are not repeatable in any other relationship, I don't think.

As for my relationship with my mother while growing up, there were many joyful moments, but it was mostly strained, especially during my teen years. She favored her boys, and consequently had painful relationships with all of her daughters. Several of my sisters told me that she felt closest to me among her daughters. It took a lot of work on my part – and hers – to mend things and grow close. That repair started in my early to mid-twenties and continued until she died when I was thirty-seven years old. When I came out in my late twenties, she was very upset and turned her back on me, stating that I was making a bad choice. So it was as if we had to start over again; more repair work had to be done. I have two brothers who are also gay, and she was much more accepting of them, telling me they did not have a choice, but that I did.

I had an extremely close relationship with my father growing up. He was my ally. I felt he understood my pain, though he didn't feel like he could do anything about the discrepancies between how females and males were treated in our family. He also spent time with me as much as he could and time spent with my mom was rarer. My father was similar to my mother in his fears about how I was going to handle it on my own. However, he knew I loved children in the same way that he did and felt I would be a wonderful mother. He always told me to make decisions that would make me feel happy, no matter what.

When I was pregnant with my second child, I chose not to find out the sex. I thought I was having a girl, but everyone in my world convinced me I was having a boy, so I began to believe that. I was honestly terrified of having a girl because I did not want to treat my daughter the way I had been treated. Since I already had a son, I was so scared I would favor him over a daughter and repeat the pattern in my family. I later came to learn that my mom was treated unfairly in her family growing up with a brother, *and so she was simply repeating what she had experienced. I wasn't sure if I could break the cycle.*

When I delivered my baby, and the doctor announced it was a girl, I sobbed tears of joy. I knew in that second it WAS going to be different with her and me. And it is. I am not repeating the cycle. Apart from my own mother's pain, which she, unfortunately, carried over to her children, she was a loving mother and cared for her children incredibly well. Despite the difficulties, I did feel loved by her. She always cooked us meals with such care, bought us the nicest clothes, tried to spend one-on-one time with me, took me out to lunch, etc.

The most enjoyable aspect of my life is my children. I cannot imagine my life without them. I knew it would be wonderful to be a mother, but I had no idea how much happiness and fulfillment it would bring me, and I love my career as well as my fitness and athletic endeavors! Being a mother has given me more than I could receive in any other capacity; the gifts are endless, and I have an even greater appreciation and love for children than I started out with!

My biggest struggle is trying to find a constant balance. Being a single mom who was laid off from a stable, well-paying job a year and a half ago has brought many challenges. I am trying to support my family while building my practice, and that has taken an inordinate amount of time and energy away from my children. So I am constantly

> *trying to have enough time for them, trying to work a lot, trying to take care of myself as well, trying to maintain a social life with my close friends.*
>
> *When I decided that I wanted to have, preferably, an actual man (versus the sperm bank) help me have a child and be involved on some level, I realized what a huge favor I was asking of the person I chose to pursue my dream with. I felt so indebted and grateful to him, and I still do!*

Louise was the eighth of nine children. She grew up in a family in which her mother treated the boys very differently from the girls. She was close to her father and worked to have a better relationship with her mother up until her mother's death. Her parents died within five months of each other, and Louise identified their deaths as the impetus for her to begin conceiving her first child. Until then she had wanted to be a mother but kept waiting for her relationship to be ready so she could do it with a partner. Her parents' deaths were a great mobilizer. Now Louise is the mother of a boy and a girl. She is doing it on her own, although her children have a father figure in their lives. She is essentially a single mom, with no regrets.

Louise admitted feeling extremely alone in the process of conceiving and having her children, especially emotionally. She became empowered to move forward, fulfilling this vital role of mother, especially with her second pregnancy. The in-vitro fertilization was arduous but ultimately successful. Louise remains aware that she might have to deal with prejudices being a single mom who is also gay. Her mother's doubt that she could make it on her own as a parent made her sad, but also reinforced her convictions. Louise wanted to prove her mother and other naysayers wrong. Bolstered with the inner knowledge that she would make a great mom, Louise became present and giving in a way she feels parents need to be.

Louise believes it's important not to know everything that will happen, and to accept some mystery. This helps maintain her faith in single motherhood and the gifts it brings. She advises any friend struggling with this issue: "Believe in yourself and your dreams, and don't listen to or surround yourself with any negative energy or attitudes."

Week 4

Getting Your Bearings and Calibrating Your Compass

"A perfectly good final choice can have everything to do with 'it feels right' or 'it feels wrong' as long as you have listened, through a rational process of self-inquiry, to all the voices that contribute to that feeling."
–Phyllis O. Ziman Tobin[4]

How are you doing so far? Thinking about the particular path of your journey, can you point to one time in the past week when you were especially satisfied with yourself about something? Were you able to discern between your *reactions* and your *responses*? Have you noticed yourself reacting or responding to things differently than you did in the past? If so, do you have any insights yet as to what might be going on for you?

These questions are intended to help you track your feelings. Tracking your feelings is an essential way to stay connected to yourself. Your developing the ability to track feelings allows valuable new information to surface from within.

Last week you took a peek at your younger self. You began to explore her needs, particularly the ones that were overlooked or never met. You also took the time to notice what messages – verbal and behavioral – you did or didn't receive. Was the message "you matter" conveyed to you? And if so, how? Children – like all human beings – thrive when they know their presence makes a difference in the world, and especially when they get the message that they are important to their loved ones. *Children need to receive the message that they matter.* If you didn't receive this message when you were young, it's not too late to reclaim its truth now.

Is it getting easier to be with the ambiguity of *I don't know?* Is The Mantra helping you? Whenever you recognize that you've veered off the path of the journey, try returning to *I don't know* as easily as you slid away from it by visualizing an infinity sign and coming back to the intersecting middle:

I don't know is where you can return over and over, not where you must rigidly remain. Hanging out in *I don't know* should feel fluid, and will get easier with practice.

Week 4 Guided Visualization

(Adapted from and inspired by "Yes-No Situation" by John O. Stevens in *Awareness: Exploring, Experimenting, Experiencing.* Boulder, Colorado: Real People Press, 1971.)

Of all the guided visualizations in our program, this is the one that makes many women wonder, "What does all this have to do with deciding whether or not I want children?" Rest assured, the exercise has everything to do with empowering you to *know what you want*, which is crucial to how you approach decision-making.

Trust that your attentive mind will go where it needs to go. When your eyes are closed, you engage the part of your brain that isn't as easily accessed when your eyes are open. Have someone read the visualization to you or record it for you so you can listen while your eyes are closed, as its power also lies in the element of surprise. If that's not possible, make a recording yourself so you can listen with eyes closed to deepen the experience of where the visualization takes you. If you read the visualization to yourself, read it silently and slowly to give yourself time to savor the experience. Close your eyes now and then to open to the power of your imagination.

Remember that the experience you have is what matters most, and there's no wrong way to do it. Have your journal and writing tool nearby so you can record your impressions and images immediately.

To prepare, choose a quiet place where people and noise won't disturb or distract you, and a time when there's nothing else for you to do and no one who needs your attention; this time is solely for your benefit. Either sit comfortably in a chair or, if you prefer, lie down on the floor.

Remember a Time When...

Now that you're ready, become conscious of your breathing. Let your eyes close gently as you take a deep breath and exhale. Inhale and hold your breath for five counts. Then exhale until most of the air has left your lungs. Inhale again and slowly exhale, letting out an audible sigh through your mouth while you count silently from ten to one. Continue breathing slowly and deeply. As you breathe, you relax. Allow your natural breath to bring a deep sense of peace and well-being. Feel your body relax and let your mind free-associate. B-r-e-a-t-h-e.

Imagine never knowing inadequacy. Imagine a world without the word *mistake*. Imagine that living, learning, and growing means moving in the direction of what you want and what is true for you. Imagine you are the only judge of that direction and you have your creative way of getting there. Imagine this for a moment and b-r-e-a-t-h-e. No matter what has happened in the past, see if you can let yourself be delighted completely with exactly who and how you are now. After all, there is no other way to be. Take a moment to think about one thing that you appreciate about yourself.

Recall a specific situation in which you said yes but wanted to say no – a time when you went against yourself or your wishes. It's possible there are many situations from which to choose. Pick one. Trust the first thing that comes to mind. It can be minor or seemingly unimportant, or it can be something significant. It could have happened years ago or just yesterday. If you're not able to come up with a specific situation, think of a time when you felt as if you didn't know how to stand up for yourself. Check in with your breath. Picture your situation and continue when you have it clear in your mind.

Take a minute or two to visualize the situation as if it were happening right now. Let it play out slowly in your mind. Where are you? Who is with you? How do you feel being there? Who is speaking? What are they saying? What do you feel right now? Are you tightening up anywhere? Has your breathing changed? Bring the situation alive as if it is occurring right now.

Shift your attention back to the moment when you said yes. Pay attention to the tone of your voice as you say the word *yes* and to how you feel. What does it do for you to say yes? What do you gain? How might you benefit by saying yes? What do you avoid? How do you feel about saying yes in this situation?

Go back to the moment just before you said yes. Now say no and anything else you would like to add to your no. What else would you communicate if you had permission to be completely uncensored? Take this opportunity to express fully everything you'd like to about saying no. It doesn't have to be rational or socially acceptable.

Notice your tone as you say the word *no*. How do you feel? Do you feel good? Do you feel afraid, guilty, or relieved? Does it feel strange or out of character to say no?

How does the other person respond to you after you say no? How do you feel about their response? What is your reply if you have one? Are you aware of anything else you have not expressed? Are you holding anything back?

This visualization is not about judging yourself, but about paying attention to your body and noticing the feelings that come along with saying no. Go ahead and say good-bye to this particular situation and slowly come back to the present. B-r-e-a-t-h-e.

Keep your eyes closed while you slowly return to your present environment, allowing a few moments to be with your emotional and physical sensations. Breathe.

When you're ready, slowly open your eyes and begin to write in your journal. Record your immediate thoughts, feelings, insights, and anything else you want to about your experience.

Immediate Writing after the Guided Visualization

If no images came to mind, or your thoughts did not provide you with something tangible, speak to that in your writing. When you finish writing, continue reading.

The guided visualization began with the words:

Imagine never knowing inadequacy. Imagine a world without the word *mistake*. Imagine that living, learning, and growing means moving in the direction of what you want and what is true for you. Imagine you are the only judge of that direction and you have your creative way of getting there. Imagine this for a moment and b-r-e-a-t-h-e. No matter what has happened in the past, see if you can let yourself be delighted completely with exactly who and how you are now. After all, there is no other way to be.

What happened when you listened to the first part of the guided visualization? Did you take it all in? Did it feel good to hear? What feelings came up for you? What did you experience in your body? Did you feel tears surface? Did you feel your body temperature change? Did your throat or belly tighten up at all? Did your forehead wrinkle? If you feel like adding more to your writing, do so now.

Next you were asked to recall a time when you said yes but wanted to say no. Were you able to retrieve this memory easily or did the event take time to identify? If it was difficult to come up with a situation, was it because so many examples came to mind or was it because you can usually say no when you want to?

Some people can say yes more easily than others. If you are more likely to say yes than no, does the yes come from your true desire? Or does it have a tinge of obligation, guilt, fear, or doubt? If you typically say no more easily, explore whether there are times you say no when you'd rather say yes. If so, are you denying your pleasure? Are you avoiding being open to new opportunities? Might you be setting overly rigid boundaries?

Like all the guided visualizations, this one works on you behind the scenes. Even if it seems nothing has come up for you now, trust that you will feel the effects down the road.

When your writing feels complete, check in with your emotional state. Are your feelings manageable? If you feel overwhelmed, follow these instructions:

Take a deep breath, then exhale as slowly as possible, letting all the air escape your lungs. Allow your body to take in a breath on its own. Continue this several times until you notice a sense of calm. Then tap your feet on the floor. Follow that by tapping the tops of your thighs with your hands. Then tap your arms with your hands. Clench your fists and then release them. These actions help reconnect you to the present and ground you. Doing this is especially important when the emotions you experience feel overwhelming or just too much for you to manage. If you need to take further action to feel reconnected or grounded in the present, stand up and stamp your feet. Then reach your hands up in the air and stretch.

Look around the room and notice objects that bring a gentle smile to your face. Is your focus where you want it to be? Are your emotions manageable? Before you continue, make sure your attention is where you need it to be.

What Happens in Week 4

Each week something new gets touched inside, and this assists in unearthing what needs to surface. This week you'll learn more about being able to say yes and no when you want to. We break it down into discrete, easily digestible bits that allow you to explore with sensitivity your tendencies, patterns, and impediments.

As you engage with this week's activities, we invite you to give some thought to the cultural messages you've absorbed about saying yes and no. What beliefs have you inherited from your family or friends about what's okay or not okay to say? Do you feel you have permission to state your opinion even if the majority doesn't share it?

By the end of this week, you'll have a new relationship with the words *yes* and *no*. You'll recalibrate your inner compass and you'll gain valuable clarity about how your new relationship to these words will influence how you make decisions.

Feeling Yes

Giving yourself permission to want something, to feel the fullness of your desire regardless of the outcome, is a crucial step that allows you to arrive at a conscious yes or no decision. It's your birthright to feel and know what you want. Your internal physical and emotional sensations give you this information.

Have you been taught that there's shame in wanting something? Has someone else's sense of entitlement impacted you in a negative way? We're not just talking about material possessions; we're talking about knowing what your internal desires are when you feel *yes* toward anything – abstract or material. Feeling and knowing what you want provides the essential background *you need* to make informed decisions.

Alas, the word *want* is often associated with greed, envy, or commercialism, and it can undoubtedly be a source of suffering. It can be true that the less you want, the less prone you are to disappointment. But the negative consequences of not knowing what you want can be extremely high. And just because you want something doesn't mean that there are just two outcomes. You don't have to act on that feeling *or* experience disappointment when your desires aren't met.

Adjusting to the idea that wanting something is merely personal information can take some time, but it's worth the effort. The rewards are immeasurable. Practice by browsing a magazine or catalog, cruising the Internet, going window-shopping, or just closing your eyes and imagining. As you do, notice what draws you in or quickens your heartbeat. These desires can be material items or outcomes to particular situations. While exploring your relationship to wanting, notice what thoughts, memories, and feelings are evoked. That's all you have to do.

Feelings of anger, sadness, self-judgment, and loss can come up at first. If anger arises, it could be the emotional remnant of an internal conflict. That internal conflict might be in part related to self-judgment – that it's not okay to want. For example, when you were younger you might have learned that sharing a felt desire with someone only brought you negative or critical feedback. If negative feelings or memories occur as you participate in this week's exercises, try to redirect your attention to the wanting, or to how your body reacts to those feelings.

You are simply after information about you and your inner desires. Acting on this information isn't as important right now as getting better at identifying sensations in your body and connecting them to particular desires. It's okay to open up to this information. It's okay to go after what you want. Maybe something is blocking your way. If so, the first step to developing a stronger connection to your desires and to yourself is to become conscious of it.

Saying No

Denying yourself the experience of wanting, or feeling your yes and having a difficult time saying no, are both being untrue to yourself. Girls, in particular, are often raised with the message that they need to say yes even if it puts others' needs before their own. Society has conditioned women to deny their satisfaction for another's. In fact, this has been perpetuated for so long that many women are not even aware of it. Does this sound familiar? With each generation, younger women are changing this mindset by finding their voices and discovering they have permission to say no. Notice where you are on the continuum of feeling it's okay to say no. Do you feel you have more permission than, say, your mother or her mother did?

Women have many ways of rationalizing not saying no. One of the most common involves the belief "If I *can* do it, I *should* do it." In other words, ability trumps desire. But though you may have the time, skill, talent, or experience to *do* any number of things, that doesn't mean you have to say yes to them. Just because you *know* how to work on bicycles doesn't mean you *want* to spend half your Saturday fixing your neighbor's bike. Just because you *can* meet a friend for half an hour for coffee doesn't mean you *have* to squeeze it into a packed day. Just because you *know* you'd make a good parent doesn't mean you will or *should* ultimately be one or want to become one. There is an important distinction between ability and desire.

Sometimes you have to say no even though your decision is unpopular. Feeling uncomfortable is sometimes unavoidable. And a little bit of temporary discomfort is not so bad, especially when you can reward yourself with the enduring sense of empowerment and your healthier, more authentic relationships with others – and with yourself – that come from clearly communicating your truth. Learning to say no appropriately does get easier with practice.

The Consequences of Not Being Able to Say No

Not being able to say no when you want to can have unfortunate consequences. You can end up feeling anger or resentment toward the person or situation to which you said yes, or generalized feelings of powerlessness, annoyance, or irritability. This creates a serious internal dilemma, one that clouds your day if not your life. If it is a habitual problem and you just can't say no to others, it complicates your interactions with them and contributes to less authentic relationships. It can also cause erosion of your self-esteem.

Should you decide to become a parent, no is something you'll have to be able to say to your child – gently, firmly, and over and over again. If you're fearful that your child will take over your life because you don't know how to say no easily, there are resources available to help support you in learning to set clear limits. Whether or not you ultimately decide to become a parent, being able to say no will liberate you from basing important decisions on fear, and it will benefit your life in countless other ways.

Handling Disappointment

Another common difficulty in feeling and expressing a clear yes or no has to do with your relationship to disappointment. Have you experienced disappointments that just feel too painful to face? Disappointment is a natural – and important – occurrence of living. When you're a child you develop a healthy relationship to it if you are lucky enough to have an adult around who helps you fully own your feelings and work through disappointments as they occur.

Unresolved feelings of deep disappointment can have a life all their own well into adulthood, especially if you aren't consciously aware of them. They impact decision-making. You might anticipate being disappointed, so you hold back from what you want, which can develop into a pattern of denying yourself what you want. It can become so automatic that you're not even aware you're doing it. If you hold yourself back in fear of disappointment, you can lose out on the good that might also come your way. Even if you protected yourself from potential pain, the cost is missing out on potential pleasure that might be right around the corner. Or you might imagine that by saying no to someone, they will feel as badly as you felt when someone said no to you. You can't know another's exact experience. You do that person a disservice by thinking you can, and what's more, you only succeed in bypassing your truth when you try to anticipate someone else's.

Here's an example of how this played out for Sue: She experienced freedom once she separated out earlier disappointments from her current life. Having grown up in a family in which alcoholism prevailed, she got used to ignoring her disappointments. While participating in the program, her journal became the depository of many painful memories, which she then explored more fully and was able to grieve about over time. She became a nurturer of her earlier self, and she became more resilient in the face of her adult disappointments.

Your job is to feel and perhaps grieve your disappointments when they occur. You might even find it beneficial to grieve a backlog of old disappointments as Sue did. Remember that it's not your job to make sure others don't experience disappointment. You can trust that others will find their way when they become disappointed – just as you will find yours. And even if others don't find their way, it isn't your responsibility to find their way for them.

Making Decisions as a Two-Step Process

Knowing what you want is necessary before you can make a conscious decision! The knowing and the decision-making are, in fact, related but discrete entities. The two-step decision-making process looks something like this: Your friends ask you to go to dinner after work. You habitually say yes because it's what you always do without question. What if you paused long enough to ask yourself, *What do I want to do after work tonight?* Maybe it's to go out with friends, or maybe it's to go home and have a quiet night with your book and your cat. What if you responded with your decision to the invitation only after you first knew your desire?

Decision-making is relatively easy when your desire and your decision match. If you divide every decision you make into the two steps, you feel more connected, more empowered, and more accepting of yourself. There will be times, however, when you find that your desire and your decision are not congruent. You can arrive at a decision of yes with a desire of no for a few reasons: you feel it's the right thing to do at the time; or you know you'll feel better about it in the long run. Here's a common scenario: Your boss asks you to stay late to finish a project. You know you don't want to because you'd rather go home. You can feel your desire of no loud and clear. However, you make a decision of yes because you also want this project finished and you want to feel part of the team. Given x, y, and z reasons, it feels like the right thing to do. When you break it down this way, you aren't untrue to yourself.

When your desire is no but – for whatever reason – you decide to say yes, you're less likely to feel annoyed, fearful, or resentful about your decision if you've taken the time to acknowledge your desire first. A conscious decision to override your desire of no with a decision of yes feels very different from going straight to yes without pausing first to discover and know the clarity of your underlying desire.

There can also be times when there is a legitimate reason to arrive at a decision of no with a desire of yes. At the end of your journey through this program you might gain the clarity that you want to be a mother. You weigh your desire against the reality – your longtime partner does not want to have another child (perhaps they have children from a previous marriage). So you *make the decision* to stay with this partner and find other creative ways to meet your desire. Your decision of no is different from your desire of yes, but you are clear on why both exist.

A discrepancy between a desire and a decision can also suggest something else entirely. After you've made your decision, even though you understand the decision is the right one, you might feel bullied, regretful, or mad at yourself, as if you had no choice. Or you might feel bullied into saying yes while inside you're still silently screaming no. But your feelings of being *externally* coerced could be unfounded and the discomfort you're experiencing is coming from an *inner* struggle, an echo of something that occurred in your past. We go into this in more depth a bit later in the program.

This is what has happened for Holly. She continually felt that her manager at work was placing unreasonable demands on her by asking her to put in more time and effort on the project she shared with three others. On the face of it, what she reported seemed accurate. However, upon careful exploration, she realized that she *often* felt that others asked her to give more than she was willing to give; even though she would say yes, she felt used. Her yeses were accompanied by some hesitation *and* a sense of obligation. Holly unearthed an inner conflict dating back to soon after her father died when she was thirteen. Just at the point in her life when she would have naturally been exerting more of her desires and testing herself out in the world, her mother began asking her for more and more emotional support, essentially hindering and even closing down Holly's adolescent development. With time and some very courageous work, Holly brought peace to this part of herself. She felt freer and more hopeful. With this piece of work behind her, she could now say no when she wanted to and say yes without feeling resentful. She realized she had carried this internal conflict into her situation at work and her personal relationships.

The two-step method described here can help you get in touch with your feelings and determine if, in fact, you are aligned with or fighting against yourself. If you struggle a lot with knowing and following through with inner desires, you, like Holly, might need outside help to unravel the knots inside. This is something a professional can help you do.

It is through the consciousness of this two-step decision-making method that you change how you decide yes or no. Try it for yourself. Pausing to explore what you want gives you a solid base from which to make informed decisions. Beginning this week, try to consciously break down every decision that comes your way – small or large – into the two steps and see how it goes. Most women find this approach very liberating. Good luck!

Be Curious: Assignments for Week 4

1. In this week's first assignment, we encourage you to free-associate. It's important to let what comes to your mind flow onto the paper without hesitation or censure. Don't think too much – and have some fun! The writing does not need to make sense or be rational. You can compile a list or write out sentences. Do whatever you want. Really!

    Be Curious: Let's play a little with the words *yes* and *no*. Write "YES" on the top of a blank page. Sit for a few minutes and let "YES" fill your mind and body. Feel the word and say it out loud, then notice what feelings and thoughts come to mind. Write a stream-of-consciousness about the meaning it has for you. Remember that it doesn't need to make sense. Take some time to absorb the full experience of "YES." You might even want to set a timer so you take plenty of time, say ten minutes. Trust yourself. There is no wrong way to do the exercise.

    Now write "NO" on the top of another blank page. Let it fill your mind and body, feel it, say it out loud, and notice what feelings and thoughts you have. Write a stream-of-consciousness about "NO." Take some time, perhaps ten minutes, to absorb the full experience of it.

Some women find more freedom in yes, and some in no, which is very personal. We want you to explore your relationship with the words and how you hold each of them in your mind and body.

2. Be Curious: Now let's play a bit more with the physicality of yes and no, and calibrate your inner compass. Say the word *yes* out loud. How does it feel in your body? Notice the feelings in your face and your mouth when you say yes. You might want to watch your face in a mirror. Is there tension in your facial muscles? Is your mouth soft, puckered, tense? Say yes over and over again, experimenting with different tones and inflections such as urgency, anger, silliness, and tranquility. Try saying yes in the voice of a victim, experimenting with passivity, timidity, and resignation. Then say it loudly with an aggressive, sarcastic, or forceful tone or energy. Say it with as much happiness in your voice as you can muster. And finally, do anything else you can that comes to mind. Drop your inhibitions as best you can. You can also do this with someone else, going back and forth with different tones, playing off each other. Have fun with it! When you feel that you've exhausted all the possible ways of experiencing yes, do the same for no. Notice all of your emotional and physical sensations as you play with the words *yes* and *no*, and upon completion write about your full experience before moving ahead.

3. Be Curious: At the risk of feeling disappointed by not getting what you want, make a list of everything you want (at least on this particular day). From little to big, mundane to exotic, worldly to personal, ethereal to material, physical to emotional, write down whatever you can allow yourself to want. The intention of

this exercise is actually to feel the sensations that arise in your body as you consider all your desires. Notice what happens when you feel wanting or desire. You are gathering information about yourself. After you've made your list, write about your sensations and anything else that came up for you.

4. Be Curious: Review your family map this week. As far as you're aware, who struggled with saying yes or no? Who seemed able to stay true to their inner truth? Do you recognize a good role model, someone who was able to make decisions with self-respect, conviction, and ease?

Further Exploration and Discovery

Review the writing for each of the four exercises above while considering the exploratory questions in "Your Checklist for Reflection" on page 50. Then use the following questions to help you explore even more:

Do you feel that your relationship to yes and no already feels slightly different? Upon completion of this assignment, many women realize they have attached positive and negative meanings to these words. What if neither is good or bad, positive or negative, empowering or deflating? What if yes or no is not about the words at all? What if *empowerment* is fully understanding exactly *why* you are saying yes or no, and owning the truth of what brought you to say it? Real empowerment means internally processing with clarity. Real empowerment takes that *knowing* and uses it to meet your minute-to-minute experience with confidence. Women find that after doing this assignment their relationships to the words as positive or negative fall away. The words themselves don't dictate empowerment. Empowerment comes from knowing *who you are.* You are the definer of you. Hopefully a new and improved relationship to yes and no is well on its way.

Was it fun playing with the words *yes* and *no* out loud with different tones? If it wasn't fun, was it at least enlightening? Even if there was some embarrassment, you gathered new information. For example, did you discover that one tone was more difficult than another for you? Did you use the same tone as a particular intention even when you meant to imply something else? If it wasn't fun and you would like it to be fun, try doing it with a six-year-old!

As you read aloud your list of desires, see if you can consider your feelings purely from the viewpoint of an objective observer. How difficult was it to make a list of your desires? If it was challenging, ask yourself, *Do I deprive myself of what I want because it can lead to disappointment?* or *Do I deprive myself of what I want because _____?* (fill in the blank: *it's selfish/greedy/hedonistic, something bad will happen,* etc.). Whether it was easy or challenging, be curious and non-judgmental with yourself. After you've done your discovery and exploration, put the writing aside and check out this week's optional exercises.

Be Even More Curious: Optional Exercises

These suggestions aren't necessary to gain results from the program, but if you have time and wish to understand more about yourself, they'll help.

1. Think about where, when, and how you might deny yourself a particular item or experience. Do you say no too quickly, especially when you want to say yes? Write about one of these situations.

2. If you struggle with saying no, write a letter from the forgiving part of you to the part of you that struggles to say no. It might look like this:

   Dear _____, who doesn't know how to say no when she wants to, I forgive you. I realize you've done the best you could. You needed help early on to learn about setting limits and feeling entitled to say no, and it wasn't available. I can see that now. You are a good person. You have permission now to say no. You have permission now to write about all the things that got in your way. It's not your fault that you've struggled with saying no, and it's not too late to turn things around. [Continue the letter on your own.]

3. Play the "Let's Just Want" exploration game with a young person who is at least four years old and with whom you have a good relationship. Let them know it's a game of finding out all the things they want, and that you want to understand what it is that they want. You can go shopping, to the park, or look through catalogs or magazines. Ask the young person what they want or like over and over again: "...what else do you want?...what else do you want?" This is not to tease the child, and it isn't about commercialism; it's about letting them know you are interested in

them, allowing the experience of desire and wanting, and sharing it without judgment or shame. It isn't about securing the wanted items; it's about paying attention to the young person so they can feel seen in the delight of their desire.

Young people want to show adults who they are and what they love and have the adult be delighted in them. The object of their desire can change in a heartbeat. Adults and parents can get confused about children wanting things they don't need. Young people want to feel "seen" – acknowledged – and understood, and when their desires are recognized it helps them feel that they are being seen, which helps them feel connected to others and consequently to themselves. Feeling connected is ultimately more important to them than acquiring the actual things. When you give children your undivided attention, they love showing you who they are.

You can also play this game with an adult friend. The two of you can go on a wanting spree and delight in each other's desires free of judgment, criticism, and practicality.

After you play, write about what occurred and see if you learned something about yourself; memories might surface. Do you recall adults being delighted in you? Were you seen as a young person, or do you remember what it was like not to be seen? Did you have to push down or hide what you wanted? Did negative sensations or feelings occur when you wanted something? Write it all down. See what comes.

What to Hold Inside This Week

Take some time to slow down and feel. See if you can carve out some emotional check-in time each day. It doesn't have to be long – even fifteen minutes of sitting quietly and checking in brings benefits.

As you go through your week, notice your immediate responses to people – colleagues, friends, or family members – asking you for favors or making requests (or demands) of you. If you can, before responding, practice pausing, looking inside, and asking yourself, *What is my desire here and what do I want to do about it?*; and then, *Even though I have the ability to meet this request, I don't need to. Do I want to?* Try tracking all requests and your responses this week.

Notice if you can feel your desires clearly. Notice when you deny yourself something you want. Break down as many decisions as you can into two steps. First ask, *What do I want? What is my desire?* Then ask, *What will be my decision?*

Continue to explore how it feels in your body when you want something. Are you able to feel desire and enjoy it even if the desired object or experience doesn't materialize? The sensation of wanting can be fun and instructive in and of itself. Even when it comes to the simple moment of choosing between coffee and juice, pause long enough to explore what you really want. Practicing with things of no great consequence helps build the muscle for more important situations.

This week, when you feel joy and abundance, notice how entitled you feel to experience these emotions.

Remember your tools: the journal-writing and The Mantra. Taking time to write and to recite The Mantra each day can help you immensely.

Above all appreciate yourself, and say out loud, "I matter," as you continue this journey of self-discovery.

Self-Care

What happens when you wander without an agenda? If you're lucky, your senses bump into the world around you with a freshness that exhilarates, restores, and renews. This week you've been exploring the differences between yes and no. What if your self-care activity or ritual embodied a way to feel, to sense what you're drawn to (yes) or uninterested in (no)?

Can you spend some time at a gallery, or an art or science museum? Let yourself wander. Rather than trying to see everything, or spending time processing with your left brain, see what draws you in. Follow what interests you without questioning why. Notice what doesn't. Play with this idea. There is no right or wrong way – only your way. Have some fun.

If this suggestion doesn't grab you, spend some time doing something that really opens up your awareness. If you're inclined, do some journaling about what comes up. Whatever you do, make sure it isn't something that you feel you *should* do!

The self-care I did for myself this week was...

You Are Not Alone

Meet Tess and Ghea. Their stories are different, but both women are eloquent in their sharing. As we've said before, if it feels better to wait to hear about other women's processes, do just that. If you find comfort or companionship reading these while you're on your journey, go right ahead.

Tess's Story

High school graduation wasn't too far away, and I remember thinking about having eight children with my then boyfriend. Even then it seemed like an inferior plan. When I look back, I think I only considered having children when my future was uncertain or scary.

When we got married, we agreed that we didn't want children, but we would leave the door open in case we changed our minds. Once in a while one of us would entertain the idea, and the other would say, "Wait ten minutes and tell me if you still think this is a good idea." It became a bit of a joke. We would talk about it for a little while and talk ourselves right out of it. Then when I had finished grad school, I felt a distance between my husband and me and a lot of uncertainty about what was next for me. For a little while (more than ten minutes – perhaps a week) I seriously entertained the idea of having a baby. It was an act of desperation. I knew that, but for that week I was romanticizing about having a baby. I mentioned it a couple of times. He gave me the ten-minute line.

Then one night we were lying in bed, and I told him how much I had been thinking about it, all the things that weighed on me. I concluded by telling him that I thought it was an attempt at avoiding the next step in my life. I had finished grad school, and I didn't know what to do next. That was a dumb reason to have a baby. I just needed to get tough and start finding out what I really wanted to do next. I was just scared. It was one of those clear moments for me. So he turned to me and said that he thought he should get a vasectomy. It wasn't a discussion. It was a declaration. It felt like a defense mechanism because he didn't trust my judgment. I was so pissed. Although I was now sure I didn't want children and a vasectomy would make my life easier, I resented his presentation of the idea. After taking care of the birth control so responsibly for all those years together, the idea that he could no longer trust me to keep him from being a parent was a slap in the face. What I didn't know then was that his best friend had just caught his wife sabotaging their birth control and trying to get pregnant when they had agreed not to. I had a momentary lapse of sanity, and he thought he needed to protect himself from me. I should have known what was coming.

My second husband is the love of my life. We found each other via similar paths of heartache. I am happy that neither of us has ties to former spouses or higher priorities due to children.

I thought about the lifestyle of a parent, and it just didn't appeal to me. So I waited to see if I would feel any different as I got older. I watched my friends' lives change. Some were so happy and suited for parenthood. I could see why they chose it. It just wasn't for me. I enjoy working and having a career. My work is interesting, challenging, and satisfying. I knew that I could not do both (work and parent). I remember thinking that being a parent was way too important to leave to chance or emotion. It was a very serious commitment. If I wasn't totally committed to parenthood, I had no business being one. I sometimes think about what will happen as I get older, but I have no guarantee that I will get old. My confidence in my decision keeps growing. I have had no regret.

I think I went through a period of intolerance toward children that were not part of my family (snotty noses and fingers, annoying behavior). That evolved into sympathy toward children with crappy parents. Now I have sympathy for both.

My mom was a stay-at-home mom and a great listener. She rarely gave advice. She just listened while I talked out whatever was on my mind. While I now confide in her less, we are still very close. We talk often, and I see her often. She and I seem very different. She is a natural listener and extremely patient. These are skills that I have to work very hard at. She had all the important mommy skills: nurturing, caring, and giving. I have good math and leadership skills. I don't think I would say I want to be as she was, but she was perfect at being my mom. Looking back, she was so naïve and dependent when I was young. It seemed to work for her. She was happy, but that isn't my style. I thought my sister and mom were great mothers. They were dedicated to their roles. I didn't think I could put the same effort into being a mom that they did. I didn't have the passion for it.

In spite of many siblings, my dad found ways to make our relationship special. My dad is a recovering alcoholic. He was drinking when I was growing up, but I have a handful of memories before his drinking got bad, like sitting next to him in his big chair watching baseball while he explained the game to me. The pile of memories while he was sick have faded away. Decades of contentment have replaced them. We are quite close now. Earlier, my dad didn't understand why I wanted to go to college, but he seemed to go along with the idea. (Why didn't I just get married and start a family like women are supposed to? Blah, blah, blah. He never said those words, but I imagined that was what he was thinking.) When I told him I wanted to go to grad school and get a PhD, he realized that I was on my path.

Tess is in her early forties and comes from a large family of seven children. She was raised Catholic but currently has no religious affiliation. She thrives at work with a challenging and fulfilling career. She loves her husband and the life they share together. They have time to pursue their personal interests and spend quality time with each other. Tess enjoys the luxury of working on being a better partner, sibling, aunt, and daughter. She has tremendous gratitude for her good fortune.

Since Tess and her first husband both stated early on that they did not want children, this probably wasn't the reason the marriage ended. More likely there were other more complicated issues at stake. Most likely she learned more about herself and her needs and desires during her first marriage and this helped her find a better-suited partner the second time around.

Soon after Tess made her decision, she noticed that her friendships with female friends changed as their lives took different turns than hers. She said, "As my friends started having children, our relationships drifted apart. I understood. They needed to focus on these little creatures. That was the whole point of having them. I was going to grad school while they were going to Chuck E. Cheese; two different choices, not better or worse, just different." To women who feel conflicted about their decision she offers this advice: "Focus on your partnership first. Then really listen to yourself. Do you have a passion for this role? What do you imagine your daily life to be like?"

Ghea's Story

I had a bunch of role models, all of them different from my mother. One was a woman who left her career to raise her children, another decided not to have a baby, and still others continued with their careers and also had babies. What I understood early is that motherhood is not something related to what and how, but it is related to following one's wish. That makes all the difference. The ones who chose it were perhaps busy but satisfied; the others who didn't choose but answered to other people's requests (or what they thought was their duty) were quickly unhappy.

First it was a career issue for me; then I understood that my husband was my child. After he and I split up, I was by myself for eleven years. Then I met my current companion with these two little girls who had lost their mother to cancer. I decided I wanted to help them grow up. My ex-husband acted as a child, so with him it was quite easy to understand that there was no room for other children. On the other hand, after deciding to become a stepmother, there followed a deep understanding that I wanted a family of my own.

My mother was really happy when she knew she was pregnant with me. She had some risk of losing me, so she had to spend a couple of months in bed. Then she decided to go to a private clinic to give birth to me. She was, and is, so anxious; she was afraid then that someone might switch babies in the hospital. That was also her fear when my older sister was born.

My mother and I loved each other, but we had very different approaches to life. During my teenage years I was in an open conflict with her. It took a lot of personal work on my side to grow into an adult, peaceful relationship with her. Now I deeply accept her just the way she is.

As a stepmother, I act very differently from the way my mother did. I'm able to show how much I love "my" girls. I speak with them about everything, and I answer all of the questions they ask. I spend time with them; we like doing things together and they can say to me that they don't like something I have done.

My father was my role model. I liked to talk with him and share opinions and experiences, as he did with me. We had many common interests and overall similar inquiries into spiritual, philosophical, and political areas. We did not have the same ideas, but we loved to discuss them with each other anyway.

Ghea, now in her early fifties, spent approximately nine years thinking seriously about her choice of whether or not to become a mother. She lives in a country that is changing but still holds traditional views, where it is expected that women marry and have children. She began her decision-making process at age twenty and was twenty-nine and married when she decided no, that her husband was enough of a child. She described her feeling then as one of relief. She was forty-seven when she made the reverse decision, to become a stepmother, by saying yes to life with her partner and his two young daughters. Their mother had recently died of cancer, and Ghea became their principal mother figure. This decision filled her with happiness.

It's interesting that Ghea's graduate degree thesis was on the mother-daughter relationship. During that period of her life she was very involved in social activities aimed at raising women's consciousness about sex, pregnancy, birth, and contraception. She personally was informed and felt that she could make her decision wisely without professional help. She is independent, yet did share her decisions with her female friends. Today she finds fulfillment in her job and her relationships with the two girls. She has this advice for other women who are trying to decide: "Keep room for yourself and your wishes."

After Ghea reached her decisions – first not to be a mother, and later to become a stepmother – she didn't notice any changes with her female friendships. She said, "I always had many friends and they made different choices, and I can understand and relate to all of them." Her relationships with her sisters did change after she decided to become a stepmother: Two sisters, one older and one younger (both with children), said they felt closer to her because finally they all shared a common role.

Unfortunately, Ghea's father had died and never knew that she became a stepmother. She noticed her peer relationships with men changed slightly after she became a stepmother. She felt men recognized her abilities as a mother, and this gave her more credibility with them. As for any changes she noticed with children, she said, "I always loved children, and when I decided not to have babies I was a lovely aunt (extended also to my friends' babies). Then, when I became a stepmother, my 'competencies' with children expanded even more."

After eight years Ghea and her companion, the father of her two stepdaughters, ended their relationship. He plans to marry another, and Ghea sees her biggest struggle as adjusting to what this impending marriage will do to her relationships with her stepdaughters. They will all have to find a new balance. She is positive about getting through this transition, keeping her commitment to the girls, and remaining realistic in her expectations. The girls are eight years older than when the relationships began, and they will also have a say in any decisions that are made.

Week 5

The Dialogue

ɞ There's an important distinction between dwelling on the past and
revisiting the past in order to heal. ʗ

Settle in, take a breath, and open your mind. Focus on a positive
memory from the past week. Bask in it for a few moments while
owning the courage and commitment that sustain you.

Last week you explored your relationship to expressing yes and no.
You learned how feelings of powerlessness and resentment can arise
when you go against your innermost desire. You also now have a better
understanding about the two-step method of decision-making. It was
a week of focusing more closely on yourself and what you want rather
than attending to others.

How did it feel to pause before saying yes and no to requests from
others? What feelings came up? How did it feel to notice sensations of
desire or wanting? Did you feel entitled to have them? Was it comfortable?

It's not unusual at this point in the process to start having
uncomfortable feelings you can't quite identify. Don't worry; nothing's
wrong. In fact, something could be very right. What's happening is this:

your internal world is loosening up, and what once felt fine, or at least okay, might now be somewhat unsettled. It's a positive sign that your psyche is opening up to clues about *surrendering*, the same clues that lead to clarity.

Just allow the emotional rumblings that have been cumulatively stirred up over the past few weeks to continue to percolate in your subconscious mind and in your body. As this process deepens, you can trust that it has a life of its own, and it is fine to let it just hum along in the background while you keep moving forward. If it helps, try saying this with some volume: "I'm safe and it's to my benefit to let things hum along."

Week 5 Guided Visualization

(Adapted from and inspired by "Parent Dialogue" by John O. Stevens in *Awareness: Exploring, Experimenting, Experiencing*. Boulder, Colorado: Real People Press, 1971.)

These exercises bring into awareness information from your unconscious, which helps you on your journey of discovery. There are two components to this week's guided visualization. Both involve thinking about your parents. The labels *mother* and *father* are used. If those don't fit your situation, use whatever labels work. Only you can know what's best for you.

"Choosing" is the first part. Trust that your attentive mind will go where it needs to go. When your eyes are closed, you engage the part of your brain that isn't as easily accessed when your eyes are open. Have someone read the visualization to you or record it for you so you can listen while your eyes are closed, as its power also lies in the element of surprise. If that's not possible, make a recording yourself so you can listen with eyes closed to deepen the experience of where the visualization takes you. If you read the visualization to yourself, read it silently and slowly to give yourself time to savor the experience. Close your eyes now and then to open to the power of your imagination.

Remember that the experience you have is what matters most, and there's no wrong way to do it. Have your journal and writing tool nearby so you can record your impressions and images immediately.

To prepare, choose a quiet place where people and noise won't disturb or distract you, and a time when there's nothing else for you to do and no one who needs your attention; this time is solely for your benefit. Either sit comfortably in a chair or, if you prefer, lie down on the floor.

Choosing

Now that you're ready, become conscious of your breathing. Let your eyes close gently as you take a deep breath and exhale. Inhale and hold your breath for five counts. Then exhale until most of the air has left your lungs. Inhale again and slowly exhale, letting out an audible sigh through your mouth while you count silently from ten to one. Continue breathing slowly and deeply. As you breathe, you relax. Allow your natural breath to bring a deep sense of peace and well-being. Feel your body relax and let your mind free-associate. B-r-e-a-t-h-e.

Picture your mother sitting in front of you. You may see her as she is today or as she was when you were young. Whatever comes to mind is fine. B-r-e-a-t-h-e. Make eye contact with her. Observe how you feel being in her presence. How does her energy feel? How does your energy feel? How old do you feel? Notice what feels good and what doesn't feel good. B-r-e-a-t-h-e. Sit with all your feelings whether they are calm, neutral, or otherwise. This is about being aware of your feelings and not judging them. While mindful of your breath, say good-bye to your mother for now. Sense the space in front of you without her there.

With eyes still closed, slowly take two complete, deep breaths with awareness. Picture your father sitting opposite you, as he is today or as he was when you were young. Whatever comes to mind is fine. B-r-e-a-t-h-e. Make eye contact with him. Notice how you feel being in his presence. What is his energy like? What is your energy like? How old do you feel? Notice what feels good and what doesn't feel so great. B-r-e-a-t-h-e. Sit with all your feelings, whether they are calm, neutral, or something else entirely. This is about noticing rather than judging or trying to figure anything out. Take a few breaths and say good-bye to your father for now. Feel the space without him there.

With eyes still closed, consider your reactions to the two different scenarios. What felt the same? What felt different? Which one evoked or even provoked the most emotion or energy, positive or negative? With whom do you have more unresolved issues? This is the parent to choose for the next part of the visualization. You can always repeat it with the other parent or with any parental or authority figure with whom you feel you have unresolved conflict or wounds.

Before continuing, write down any insights, thoughts, or feelings you've just experienced. Keep writing until you feel finished. Sometimes the writing at this point either reveals or confirms the better parent for the next part.

The Dialogue

This part is a guided dialogue between you and one of your parents or another important adult figure, living or deceased, in your life. The point is to have the opportunity to do some important and necessary work with an adult who played a significant role in your growing up. Their influence could have been positive or negative. Either way, invite healing to take place.

Now that you're ready for this segment, become conscious of your breathing. Let your eyes close gently as you take a deep breath and exhale. Inhale and hold your breath for five counts. Then exhale until most of the air has left your lungs. Inhale again and slowly exhale, letting out an audible sigh through your mouth while you count silently from ten to one. Continue breathing slowly and deeply. As you breathe, you relax. Allow your natural breath to bring a deep sense of peace and well-being. Feel your body relax and let your mind free-associate. B-r-e-a-t-h-e.

Imagine your entire body is wrapped in a blanket of soft white light. The light fills you completely with healing energy and love. Staying aware of your breath, move your attention to your heart, becoming aware of the space between your physical heart and your back. Picturing this area behind your heart, take a breath into that space. Breathe naturally into that space for a few conscious breaths. Then breathe naturally throughout your entire body.

Focus your attention on the parent or parental figure you chose. Picture them sitting facing you. Take some time to see this parent sitting in front of you. Make eye contact. How are they sitting? What are they wearing? What kind of facial expression do they have? Notice these and other details.

This time is uninterrupted for you. You have your parent's undivided attention right now. Even if you don't believe this would be possible, for whatever reason, see if you can imagine it happening anyway.

Imagine your parent wants to know what you have to say. Begin communicating in your own words, being completely honest about everything you'd like to share. Express things that you've never said out loud but wanted to. Maybe there are things that have been said that deserve to be said again. You may want to speak about resentments you've held back or anger you were afraid to show; perhaps love that never got expressed in the way you would've wanted. There might be successes you haven't shared. Are there struggles you'd like to tell them about or secrets that are ready to come out now? You might have questions that you want to ask but haven't until now.

Now is your chance to share everything that feels important to you. Be aware of how you feel as you do this. Notice if your body tenses, and if it does, where. Breathe into any tension that arises and allow your breath to help release it. Are you able to experience a connection with your parent as you express your thoughts and feelings? Are you able to stay in contact with yourself at the same time?

If your parent were to reply to all that you've just said, what would you want them to say? How would it feel to actually hear what you want to hear? Keep breathing.

What do you want to say back to your parent? How do you feel as you say it?

How do you experience the relationship? Is this the relationship you want with this person?

Take a few moments to consider what it is that you need or want from this parent. Tell them what you want or need from them. Take time to say exactly what you want them to do for you or say to you. Be aware of how you feel as you do this. Stay with your feelings as you ask for what you want or need.

Even if you know in your heart that this won't ever happen, or your parent is not able to meet your request, try in your imagination to have them do or say what it is you need to hear from them anyway. In this *imagined* dialogue, see if you can have your need met.

What are the emotional sensations you feel now? B-r-e-a-t-h-e.

Keeping your eyes closed, slowly, and at your own pace, say good-bye to your parent for now and return to your present environment, allowing a few moments to be with your emotional and physical sensations. B-r-e-a-t-h-e.

When you're ready, slowly open your eyes and begin to write in your journal. Record your immediate thoughts, feelings, insights, and anything else you want to about your experience.

Immediate Writing after the Guided Visualization

Your initial thoughts and feelings are more valuable when they're expressed immediately. Write until nothing else needs or wants to be said, and then sit quietly for a few minutes to make sure there's nothing more to come. The first few moments following a guided visualization are sacred, and it can be very difficult to regain access to the same thoughts. Don't rush yourself, and continue reading only *after* you feel finished with your immediate writing. Trust that there is meaning in your writing even if you're yet to see it.

Relationships with parents are complex no matter how much healing has taken place or how much work you've done previously. If during or after the visualization you found yourself feeling numb or drawing a complete blank, or perhaps feeling unsettled, overwhelmed, or resistant, do your best to write something about those states. Don't make assumptions about their meaning. Take advantage of any reaction you had and write about it. When feelings are evoked – for whatever reason – invite them to come forward and welcome them as much as possible to see what insights might follow. If you have trouble finding the words to express your feelings at this time, trust that everything will become easier with time.

When your writing feels complete, check in with your emotional state. Are your feelings manageable? If you feel overwhelmed, follow these instructions:

Take a deep breath, then exhale as slowly as possible, letting all the air escape your lungs. Allow your body to take in a breath on its own. Continue this several times until you notice a sense of calm. Then tap your feet on the floor. Follow that by tapping the tops of your thighs with your hands. Then tap your arms with your hands. Clench your fists and then release them. These actions help reconnect you to the present and ground you. Doing this is especially important when the emotions you experience feel overwhelming or just too much for you to manage. If you need to take further action to feel reconnected or grounded in the present, stand up and stamp your feet. Then reach your hands up in the air and stretch.

Look around the room and notice objects that bring a gentle smile to your face. Is your focus where you want it to be? Are your emotions manageable? Before you continue, make sure your attention is where you need it to be.

What Happens in Week 5

This week's exploration takes your relationships with your parents to a deeper level. We guide you carefully through any unresolved issues, as well as issues that you thought were resolved but aren't. We revisit a couple of themes from Week 3, and we explore how the desire to be free from pain can motivate you to heal old wounds. The activities and strategies offered teach you how to care for and heal your younger self.

You might feel your work on your relationships with your parents is complete. If you've already delved into some work on your family of origin, you are fortunate. Do continue with the exercises, as they take your previous healing work to the next level. You might even find some increased empathy and appreciation for your parent(s).

Women often have an overwhelming urge to skip or skimp on this week's exercises. You might feel a lurking sense of dread, or you might even feel some fear at the prospect of unlocking the door to a past filled with neglect and abuse. We want to give you both hope and the tools you need so you can tend to the leftover embers of whatever still needs healing within you. No one can do this work but you, and you can do it with understanding, self-compassion, and love. Trust that as you begin to work through this week's assignments, any feelings of hurt, guilt, blame, or defensiveness will begin to melt. Even an initial recognition that you experienced hurts or wounds early in your life that you're still carrying around can enhance your understanding tremendously.

When we use the words *parent* and *parents* this week, we do so inclusively. Think of the person who filled that role. We are aware of the wide variety of possibilities, so make the word work for you.

Revisiting Unresolved Issues

It's easy to underestimate how the past spills over into the present. Unresolved problems – even small ones – can wreak havoc on your current life and get in the way of knowing whether or not you want to become a parent. If that isn't reason enough to want to heal what's unresolved, the prospect of finally being free from the pain and suffering of carrying around old wounds can be a powerful motivator.

Let's take a closer look at your relationships with your parents while you were growing up. What messages did you receive from them about yourself? Were the messages explicit or unspoken? From these messages, what did you internalize? How do you feel about your relationships with your parents today? Have they changed over time? Are they better now because you've worked on them?

At times we're asked, "Can a relationship with a parent change if I'm the only one changing it?" The answer is absolutely! While the actual particulars of the past cannot be changed, your relationship to them can. When you change, you'll notice that those around you start changing – or, at the very least, you experience others' expected behavior differently. As an adult you have the opportunity and privilege to explore the time when you were young, tender, and very dependent. What was impossible to face back then *can* be faced now. You have internal and external resources available to you now that you didn't have back then, and it's in your best interest to tend to these hurt places inside so they don't block your path to clarity.

There's an important distinction between *dwelling on the past* and *revisiting the past in order to heal*. Dwelling on the past is a continuous loop of feeling sorry for yourself. Dwelling on the past makes you a current victim and requires that *someone else* make it right for you.

Dwelling on the past assumes a hopeless stance that *things can never be different*. When you *revisit* the past to heal, you move into the driver's seat. You witness, you grieve, and you have compassion for yourself and others. You don't blame yourself or anyone else. You can forgive yourself for how hard you've been on yourself and you can forgive yourself for what you had no control over. Unlike dwelling on the past, revisiting the past to heal is a dynamic process that has a beginning, middle, and end.

Understanding Needs Frozen in Time

Let's look more specifically at a particular kind of unresolved issue, one that's often at the core of early trauma. Human beings young and old need to feel close, connected, safe, and loved. If such needs went unmet when your childhood development required them to be met, they cannot be filled later in life the way they could have been then. It's an opportunity lost forever. These needs become frozen in time, and they color how you process nearly every later human interaction. This happens because below the surface you're still trying to get that early need met. Conversely, if your early needs were reasonably well met, you are probably relaxed and patient about getting current needs met.

Frozen-in-time needs can bring significant challenges into current relationships. They can cloud judgment about what it is you truly need in the present because you can easily confuse what's legitimately painful now with the hurt of the past. Unmet needs can feel like holes in your heart; while it's a common belief that one's adult partner can fill these holes, it doesn't work that way. While you may keep trying to find a partner who can meet needs that were unmet in your youth, what's necessary is a conscious acknowledgment of your situation. As you open up to acknowledge your unmet needs, you naturally begin to grieve what never happened. This healing experience of grieving is what dissolves the hurt and creates new potential for meeting current needs effectively.

Are you aware of any old unmet needs? If so, are you now trying to get them met by your partner, boss, friends, or parents? Do you repeatedly try to gain recognition at work only to find that when it comes it doesn't fill that hole inside? Do you crave reassurance from your partner, and when it's demonstrated find that it's never enough? Do you want your parents to see you accurately, and find yourself feeling sad or angry when they don't see you as you are? Are you always feeling let down by others?

Consider these questions for a time and see what awareness comes to you. To show how devastating frozen-in-time unmet needs can be, and how they can be healed, we share a bit of what happened for Samantha. Grieving and healing her unmet frozen-in-time needs freed her from a lifelong eating disorder and dramatically improved her intimate relationship.

If you remember, Samantha grew up without hearing or experiencing messages that she mattered. She hadn't known unconditional love. Her mother's undiagnosed (therefore untreated) bipolar disorder meant that chaos often ruled in her household. Samantha's primary emotional and psychological needs to feel wanted, loved, and seen for the wonderful little being she was were never met. She took refuge in food. In her teens and twenties, she became bulimic, a very serious eating disorder. By the time she was in her thirties she had discovered a recovery program that helped her see how she had used food to control feelings that were uncomfortable for her. She also did one-on-one psychotherapy for a brief time.

By the time Samantha participated in this program, she had already learned that she had unmet needs and that they continued to exert influence on her current life. While working the program, she was able at last to tend to this place within herself. Her younger self was relieved of her burdens and her adult self successfully negotiated more realistic expectations from her intimate partner. Her relationship to food progressed into one of healthy sustenance rather than a reaction to her unmet needs.

We've heard numerous women share this belief: "A child will fulfill my needs and love me like no one has ever loved me." On a certain level this can be true. But this *expectation* puts an unfair burden on your child. Your child's role – and right – is to feel loved and nurtured and to be dependent on you as you were once dependent on others. A child won't fill a hole. The only way to heal the pain created by unmet needs is to grieve the loss; as you grieve, frozen-in-time needs thaw and gradually melt away. Self-appreciation, self-compassion, and love eventually prevail. Healthier and happier relationships follow.

Generational Inheritance

The accumulation of hurts you carry around might not be entirely yours. Some of the intensity or depth of those hurts could belong to a parent or grandparent. While parents do the best they can with the resources they have, it's quite common for people to pass down unfinished emotional business unintentionally from generation to generation. Children can be burdened with problems a parent doesn't want to face or know how to face.

Perhaps the only way to be sure that an issue in your family has been put fully to rest and not just pushed underground to be recycled by a future generation, is to explore it. While you're working this program by doing the exercises, take the time to think afresh about things you might not have questioned before. Examine the everyday behaviors you witnessed or experienced growing up that were familiar and seemed so normal; it might never have dawned on you to question them before. Try to break through that haze and ask yourself why things were the way they were. Look further afield for generational patterns.

Pull out your family map. Are there unresolved issues in your family? Might your parents be holding on to something that they haven't faced. Could it even have been passed on to them by your grandparents? Do you feel emotionally indebted in some way to your parents; were they perhaps also beholden to one or both of their parents? Are there spoken or unspoken rules in your family by which you still live? Are there expectations, aspirations, or judgments that came from your parents that still constrict or oppress you? What aspects of your relationships with your parents *don't* you question? Are these relationships as you would like them to be? Families are complex entities and sometimes it's hard to see these things. Make a list of abilities, attributes, or issues you might have inherited from your family. Note any questions that come up as you look for patterns.

As you explore your family's patterns, you can expect some pain to surface around any unresolved issues, whether they are newly discovered or ones you thought you'd already worked through. We hope the pain is tolerable and that you find the steadfastness – and yes, the courage – to tend to and heal any layers of hurt inadvertently passed on to you by your family.

Here are two examples of *generational inheritance* at work to show you how it can play out. One of the participants in our program, while observing her family map, discovered something about her father she'd never been conscious of before. She knew that he'd been orphaned at an early age and adopted by his aunt and uncle. The woman in this illustration had two sisters and two brothers. Her brothers were married, whereas she and her sisters were all single. As she put together her family map, it struck her that her grandparents' deaths and her father being orphaned by age seven had somehow given her and her sisters the unconscious message that they couldn't abandon him again by creating intimate adult relationships. Irrational perhaps, but this kind of unconscious transmission happens all the time. This awareness freed her from the grip of the unconscious message.

Do you remember Birgit who, along with her husband and two dogs, was leaning toward not having children? Her parents wanted to be grandparents. As she worked through this program, Birgit developed a deeper understanding of her parents' need for grandchildren. Both of her paternal grandparents died during WWII in a concentration camp in Poland. Her father survived only because he had been sent to live abroad with a distant relative. Taking this history into account, Birgit developed a heart connection to her parents that allowed their conversations to be more healing and less adversarial.

Be Curious: Assignments for Week 5

This week's activities give you the chance to illuminate any issues that are still tender and take your healing to the next level. It's important to remember that there is no wrong way to do the assignments. Whatever way you approach them and how they unfold for you is perfect!

1. Letter to My Parent

This writing exercise might be something you've done before. You might even find yourself thinking, *Oh no, not this again.* Fear not! Every single time you write a heartfelt and honest letter to a parent, you're a different person in a new time and place in your life, and you'll write about different things. No matter how many times you've made an effort to do an assignment like this, it's highly effective.

The parent you chose during the guided visualization is the one to write to, and the goal of this particular assignment is to push yourself a bit further, perhaps to that place that still feels uncomfortable. It's about finding what might still be unresolved, or solidifying something that is only partially resolved. This exercise is effective even if your parent was rarely part of your life or you never had any contact at all. Some women write their letter to the mother who put them up for adoption. Others write to a father they never met or a parent who's deceased.

Some women have difficulty with this exercise because their present-day relationship with their parent feels good enough and they don't want to rock the boat or show any disrespect. Regardless of how things between you may have improved, trust that there's value in exploring the full spectrum of your relationship with your parent over time. Your letter can chronicle a relationship that has been transformed from not so great to pretty good, or the other way around. Either way, you'll experience personal growth. Your letter can simply convey how proud you are of your parent's efforts to improve things between you, or it can express specific appreciations.

As you write, let yourself go out on a limb. Try not to censor your writing. Being inappropriate or irrational is perfectly acceptable. Say what's never been said adequately enough, whether it's *I love you, You never did this or that and I'm not over it yet,* or *I don't care if you've apologized and turned your life around; I'm still angry.*

Your letter needn't be rational, conventional, or even reasonable. It doesn't have to make sense chronologically and it doesn't have to be written in a way your parent would need to hear it. You can visualize your parent to be any age, and you can allow them to change in age as you write. Keep in mind that you might have internalized messages and behaviors that your parent never intended for you. Allowing yourself to write without an agenda helps bring this material to the surface so the healing process can begin.

Writing this letter is solely for you and your healing. Your parent need never see it. Some women end up with a letter they later decide to give to their parent, but this is not the goal. If you feel you have absolutely nothing to say, write about the struggle you're having finding something to say.

Be Curious:

*Dear*_____,
There are so many things I want to tell you. Some of this you've heard before and some you've never heard...

2. Your Parent Responds

This second exercise is less conventional and often feels more challenging than the first, but it's a wonderful healing tool. Imagine yourself as the parent to whom you just addressed your letter. Embody that parent, but in their most evolved and enlightened state – a fantasy parent, if you will. In the voice of that idealized parent, answer your previous letter in the *most loving and compassionate way possible.*

Write as a loving parent who has gone to bed and become enlightened while they were sleeping. Write as your loving parent who now sees everything differently and wants to apologize, express their abiding love for you, and repair any damage done. Allow your mind and body to bask in the deliciousness of love and redemption that is created as you write this letter.

Don't overthink it; just write and see what comes. Let yourself say everything you need to, no matter how big or little it seems. You can write more than one version of this letter in order to develop and deepen it.

The difficulty some women run into with this exercise is this: "But my parent would never say that." That may be true, but it isn't the point. The point is to write *what you need and want to hear*. Pretending goes a long way here. We've witnessed some deep healing in those who really milked writing this letter. Here are some samples of statements they needed to hear, in no particular order:

"I am so sorry I let you down. I have no excuse, and I will do better going forward."

"I should have gotten help back then. You deserved better."

"I am so glad I was at your basketball game. I was truly in awe of your performance even though I never showed it. I admire you and your strength."

"You put up with so much from me. I apologize for being an alcoholic, and I don't ask for your forgiveness. I just hope that through my actions now we will be able to have the relationship you always wanted to have with me. I love you so much."

You're not alone if you have trouble doing this particular exercise. Some women have so much anger at their parent or are so disappointed in their parent's inability to see them that they don't feel receptive to that parent's imagined vulnerability and softness. Do the best you can. Coming back to it at a later date is also an option. While some women find writing this letter very liberating right away, others have had to wait weeks to feel ready to take it on.

Be Curious: This is how your fantasy parent's letter to you begins:

> *Dear [your name or your nickname],*
> *Thank you for telling me all of this. You're accurate about everything you said. I love you and...*

3. Children's Emotional Development

Here the aim is to help you identify and express what emotion your inner child needs help with. Increasing awareness of that emotion helps you take better care of yourself. Don't overthink it, and be gentle with her and yourself. It's a chance to at least understand your inner child more, and possibly even re-parent her in the here and now.

Given what you know now, what emotion would you say is hard for the young version of yourself to have, hold, or express? Where does she get stuck? Is there a temper-tantrum buried deep inside? Is there a good cry just bursting to get out? Are old confusing messages causing a gridlock of fear and worry? Children who feel safe can express their emotions quite easily and naturally. They often just need help understanding what they are experiencing. That can come through labeling feelings accurately and normalizing them when they are overwhelming. When children feel that they have been understood and their needs are respected, they bounce back quickly and keep going along. They don't get stuck. See if you can tend to your inner child's emotions.

Be Curious: Starting from what you know today about yourself and your younger self, with what emotion do you imagine you need help? Write it down on a piece of paper in large letters and place it somewhere visible. While going about your everyday life, collect a few images for a collage that speaks to the emotion you've written down. If you have the time to create the collage this week, terrific; but you can work on it over the next two or three weeks. When you have at least fifteen images, play with them using scissors, paste, and whatever other materials seem right to create your collage. Place the finished creation near your altar to reflect this emotion back to you. If the emotion arises in you, let yourself express it to the best of your ability. Tell yourself and your little one that these feelings are natural and transitory, especially when seen and acknowledged.

Further Exploration and Discovery

Read your writing assignments aloud, starting with your letter to your parent and their response. Hearing these two letters aloud connects you more deeply to your emotions. As you read and note your feelings, consider the following:

What is it that I still want from my parent? Do I still feel disappointment, and if so, about what? Do I notice any generational inheritance at play?

When I reread what I wrote more slowly, what does my heart feel? What about my throat and my belly?

Do you feel that everything that needed to be said has been said? There's an opportunity here to break through internal barriers that you might have put in place many years ago for your protection. They could still be blocking you in some way. Take this opportunity to add to your letters until you feel certain they are complete.

Review "Your Checklist for Reflection" on page 50 for more guidance exploring this week's activities.

Be Even More Curious: Optional Exercises

1. Repeat this week's guided visualization and/or writing exercise with another parent or parental figure. This could be a godparent; co-parent; mentor; biological, step, or foster parent; or another adult who had a big influence (positive or negative) on you. You can do them with as many people as you wish to provide endless opportunities for healing. If you do the letter writing, make sure you do both parts; the complementary letters make a powerful healing tool.

2. Write a fantasy letter from one of your grandparents to one of your parents. What might your parent like to have heard that would've made a difference in how they raised you? This is a good time to look at your family map to spark ideas.

What to Hold Inside This Week

It's natural to feel quite a bit of tenderness this week. It can show up quietly, with a vengeance, or anywhere in between. The most important thing to remember is that any pain you feel only wants your attention. Feelings are fluid, and they are merely asking that you notice and accept them. As emotions well up, they can be more than can easily or quickly be worked through. Go at your own pace. Tend to what you can now and make notes in your journal about things that need follow-up later on. Further down the road you can give more attention to these issues.

Remember to be kind and gentle with yourself always, but especially this week. You're undergoing a deep, emotional operation. Give yourself – the patient – some extra slack, and rest when you need to. You might even want the help and support of a psychotherapist. Consulting a professional is not a sign of weakness; on the contrary, it's an act of courage.

You are precious and loveable. To know this and feel this is your birthright. During this week, feelings of shame, sadness, and anger often surface. If this is true for you, spend time journaling about what you notice and what you feel. Feeling shame only means that you unearthed one of the toxic by-products that tag along with unhelpful internalized messages. *You have nothing to be ashamed of.* It's not your fault that you're still experiencing this very painful emotion. There is merely healing work to do, and you have the tools for this work right here in this program.

Notice how it feels not to share the details of your journey with others, especially as more feelings surface. In the middle of this introspective process is most definitely *not* a good time to open a dialogue with your parents or other family members. Just record your discoveries and pause to be introspective and honest *with yourself.*

It's a good week to review your family map. Is there anything you'd like to add to it? You might begin to notice that details of your map have greater or lesser importance as you continue your healing work.

Keep your journal handy to record the thoughts and feelings that arise throughout the week, and remember to use The Mantra to help calm any restlessness.

Self-Care

Consider giving your feet (often so neglected) a well-deserved gift. Feet support us. They keep us firmly planted on the earth. They are the conduit of our rootedness. Fill a large container with hot water, add some salt (Epsom or table) and a few drops of an essential oil or oils of your choice, and sit comfortably with both feet submerged for at least ten minutes. If you can, treat yourself to this indulgence more than once this week. Maybe try different essential oils each time you soak your feet, noticing if they inspire different memories. A good foot soak is very grounding and especially enjoyable right before bedtime. Ahhh…

The self-care I did for myself this week was…

You Are Not Alone

Read Makayla and Cheryl's stories whenever it feels right for you – now or later.

Makayla's Story

These all played a factor: having a partner, family, religious/spiritual upbringing, and age. I never envisioned being a single mom so I couldn't give the issue of motherhood serious consideration until I found myself in a committed, long-term relationship. Growing up in a Jewish household, rich with community and tradition and where there was much emphasis on the concept of "generation to generation," certainly played a factor. I don't think I realized how much of a factor it played until I went through the Motherhood group. It tied into family as well. Growing up, there was the assumption that my siblings and I would have kids. It was like the idea of college; the question was not if, but where. As I approached my fortieth birthday and actually saw friends go through declines in their fertility, I was keenly aware that if I wanted a child I didn't have ten years. I didn't want to be a fifty-year-old first-time mother of a newborn; I felt like I needed to figure it out soon.

My mom was and still is a very important figure in my life. She clearly loved being a mom, loved her kids and her family, put time into building a strong community, and seemed to live a fairly balanced life. She also had a life outside of us, which I appreciated. She is someone who is amazing at relationship-building.

I remained close to my mom after I reached adulthood (not quite sure when that was, maybe around twenty-five after I completed school?). I would tell her what was going on in my life; she knew my close friends and they were considered extended family. The only exception to our open communication was on the topic of dating. I had a "three-date" rule: not until the third date with someone did I tell her about him. She would get so excited about my dating; she couldn't help herself. So as a matter of privacy and not to get her hopes up (and mine too, I'm sure), I followed the three-date rule pretty closely.

I would very much like to be like my mother in many ways. She truly lives life to the fullest and has this ease about her. As I mentioned earlier, she creates and sustains a beautiful community. She is emotionally available and a great support for her family and friends. She loves being a mom and wife and she adores family. I think I am like her in the sense that I am also energized by people and love organizing social activities with the purpose of creating community. I get emotional like her. I think the main difference with us is that she never developed a formal career. She took pride in other aspects of her life and never saw herself pursuing intellectual ambitions. I take great pride in my career, and my graduate schooling was very important in my development. My career gives me a sense of satisfaction and confidence that I don't think my mom had the opportunity, or possibly the desire, to experience.

I also felt supported by my dad. He was the rational one, less emotional than mom, but I knew at my core if I needed anything, he would be there. I had a hard time talking to him about "girl things" when I was approaching adolescence, but that went away as I reached early adulthood. He would be the first to describe himself as the steady, rational, "what you see is what you get" kind of guy.

I overthought things before I went to one of the support groups Ann led. I'm a lawyer. I analyze. I can give a list of pros and cons and argue either position well. That's my educational training. So on this particular topic, I kept thinking through the issues, writing laundry lists of pros and cons. Once I let go of the lists and just felt my feelings, it became very clear. All the rest, the externals, I could figure out. It was the feelings that I paid attention to, and the feelings were very profound for me.

I think I knew deep down that I wanted to choose yes before I even started the group, but then I got caught up in overthinking it, wanting to support my partner who had real reservations about becoming a parent, and my own struggles about how to "do it all." Sometimes the exercises we did in the group or the writing assignments didn't make sense to me or didn't seem to relate to making a decision, but I trusted the approach. I trusted that whatever was coming up was relevant in some way.

Whenever I considered not having a child, I felt incredible regret and sadness, but there was also some relief that my life would continue looking the way it does now, which is full and rich. Of course, I know that this is an illusion of being in control and thinking life won't throw any curve balls my way. There was grief when considering either choice. If I decided yes, there were feelings of grief around not having the same life I do now: not having as much time for things or people I cherish, and losing the luxury of not being responsible for anybody *but myself. If I decided no, I felt incredible sadness and grief around not experiencing this incredible thing called motherhood. That feeling ultimately seemed much deeper than the grief I felt around a decision of yes. And it was helpful to recognize that there were feelings of loss with either decision; that simply because I felt grief did not mean I made the wrong decision.*

Even though we decided yes, I had a hard time actually visualizing getting pregnant and having a child. I began to feel anxious, and felt that because of my age it wasn't going to happen. It was hard not to feel pessimistic since close friends of mine who were the same age as I were going through fertility treatments unsuccessfully. After the group ended, I saw Ann, the group therapist, individually to try to manage the anxiety and figure out ways to stay positive. That was really helpful. I was able to envision what I really wanted to happen and began to live with the attitude "of course this will happen."

I don't think it's a coincidence that several weeks after that individual session with Ann I got pregnant! I think it was a whole host of reasons: the work my husband and I both did in the twelve-week program; the dietary changes we made; and, as I said before, my truly living with the idea "of course this will happen."

Makayla was forty years old when she and her husband separately went through the program. Fortunately for them, they independently came to the same decision: They wanted to have a child and start a family. They had been married four years and were together two years before marriage. Before participating in the group, Makalya felt stuck. She didn't quite know how to deal with her ambivalence and she didn't know how to talk honestly about it with her husband. The group allowed her to feel supported by other women, and she didn't feel alone. She also felt empowered to make the decision by herself, for herself.

Makayla has this advice for others facing this issue: "This is an incredibly personal decision and it's important to take the time to go through a process and be intentional about it… whatever decision you ultimately make is perfect."

Cheryl's Story

I did not feel my husband was as invested in the decision-making process as I was, at least in the beginning. I always felt that the burden of the decision-making was on me since he said that he would go along with whatever I decided. However, I didn't feel that those were his true feelings on the matter. I also didn't feel very informed or empowered, as I didn't know many people who were as ambivalent about the decision as I was. I had friends who made conscious decisions not to have children, but I didn't know of anyone like me who was truly ambivalent.

My husband, in fact, did not want to have a child. He went through the Fatherhood group (while I went through the Motherhood group), and this clarified his true feelings on the matter. It was very important to me that I had a partner who truly wanted to have a child if I were to consider this. I cried when I heard that my husband's decision was a no. I felt sad about the loss of what could have been; how our lives would be different. Later I felt relieved and happy that we came to a decision together. It no longer felt like I was making the decision alone.

I know my mom didn't think much about whether or not she wanted children. It was just something that was expected after getting married. I know only that I was born in a hospital in Chinatown and that my parents lived with my father's parents after I was born. My mom did tell me it was difficult living with her in-laws and that they did not treat her very well.

My relationship with my mother is the same after the decision, but I view her with more respect and pride for what she's done with her life. She did the best she could with her set of circumstances. I used to think that she took the easy way out by being a stay-at-home mother and not pursuing a career. However, now I realize how hard a life it was caring for me and my brother alone, as my dad wasn't *around much. I found out that my mother did have career aspirations to become a teacher, but gave that up when she came to the U.S. and married my father. I feel sorry that she didn't get the opportunity to live out her dreams like my brother and I.*

My mother worries that no one will care for me when I get older. This upsets me because I feel that this is not a legitimate (though understandable) reason to have a child. Children don't always care for their parents when they are older. I explained to my mother that it is not a guarantee that my child would even take care of me in the future. She doesn't seem to understand this.

I did not expect to feel sadness after coming to my decision. I expected more relief and happiness as opposed to sadness. I can't tell whether my sadness is the grief of not experiencing the life that I could have had or sadness because I really want to be a mother and am not going to be. After talking it over with the Motherhood group therapist, I do think it is the former.

Cheryl is a dedicated family physician. She used this program and her work with Ann to help clarify that no was the right choice for her. In her questionnaire, Cheryl said she was very surprised to realize in hindsight that she and her husband had never talked about children before they married. They had been married eight years and Cheryl was thirty-six when they made their decision to lead a child-free life. She said, "My relationship to my husband didn't change, but we do seem more relaxed about things when talking about children, such as when we talk about my new nephew. There is a sense of relief that we have both come to a decision that is right for us."

Cheryl found a role model in one of her married, child-free co-workers. This woman's fulfilling life inspired Cheryl and helped her see what a life without children can look like. This co-worker has a full social life; she loves art and travel and can spend time pursuing both passions. She and her husband travel to Europe regularly and seem to flourish in the freedom they enjoy. Cheryl contrasts this with how stressed-out and unhappy another friend with a child always seems to be. When asked how she feels around women with children, Cheryl said, "I already felt awkward around women with children, and I still do to some extent. The only difference now is that this doesn't affect me negatively as much as it used to. I have just come to accept that we have different lives, and that's okay." She wonders if she will always have difficulty interacting with families with children or if their circle of friends will change going forward.

Cheryl wishes she'd known that the Motherhood-Is it for me? program was available years ago. She also wishes she'd known that other women also silently suffer with indecision. In addition to the professional help she sought, Cheryl shared with her co-workers and close friends that she was actively trying to decide. While she kept her deeper feelings to herself, she let friends know that she wanted their support.

Cheryl feels that she and her mother were quite close when she was growing up. She feels that today, through no fault of their own, they don't have common ground – their lives are so different – but she has empathy and understanding for her mother. Her father was less present when she was young, almost always either working or playing mahjong with his friends. Cheryl said they are closer today, and she has a better understanding of him now that she is an adult. Cheryl's only sibling, her brother, recently had a child. Her parents have refocused on their first grandchild.

Cheryl has this advice for women who feel they are in a similar place: "You are not alone. There are probably more women struggling with this issue than you are aware. Don't let the externals hinder you from discovering the real truth within you."

Week 6

Your Mother – How Well Do You Know Her?

"In helping women make their choices I have learned how the task of choosing can be transformed from something overwhelming into a systematic process that encourages not only constructive decision making but personal growth too."
–Phyllis O. Ziman Tobin[5]

Congratulations! You finished five weeks of the program. How is it going for you so far? We know there can be times – especially in the middle of the process where you are now – when you feel like you're sinking to the bottom of a pit of hopelessness, so remember to balance things out by acknowledging what's going well. Be assured that as time goes on it does get easier and all your hard work will yield results. Whatever your individual situation, it's not too late to experience substantial healing.

Last week, as you explored your parental relationships, you tried to unearth what was unresolved that might still need some attention. Have you gained insight into a family pattern or recognized any unmet childhood needs in yourself? Perhaps you've already begun to acknowledge missed opportunities and grieve their losses.

It's important to facilitate this grieving and healing process by exploring your thoughts, feelings, and insights in writing. Letter-writing is powerful and never loses its value, so do this practice again at some point. If you're aware of a tender spot that still needs some attention, acknowledge it by writing in your journal so you can tend to its eventual healing.

Week 6 Guided Visualization

(Adapted from and influenced by *Motherhood Optional: A Psychological Journey* by Phyllis O. Ziman Tobin. Jason Aronson, 1998.)

This week's guided visualization has two parts, each presenting a series of questions for your consideration. You'll be instructed to write after each part. You need two chairs for this exercise. Place the chairs facing each other, about three feet apart. Begin by sitting in one of them.

Trust that your attentive mind will go where it needs to go. When your eyes are closed, you engage the part of your brain that isn't as easily accessed when your eyes are open. Have someone read the visualization to you or record it for you so you can listen while your eyes are closed, as its power also lies in the element of surprise. If that's not possible, make a recording yourself so you can listen with eyes closed to deepen the experience of where the visualization takes you. If you read the visualization to yourself, read it silently and slowly to give yourself time to savor the experience. Close your eyes now and then to open to the power of your imagination.

Remember that the experience you have is what matters most, and there's no wrong way to do it. Have your journal and writing tool nearby so you can record your impressions and images immediately.

To prepare, choose a quiet place where people and noise won't disturb or distract you, and a time when there's nothing else for you to do and no one who needs your attention; this time is solely for your benefit. Either sit comfortably in a chair or, if you prefer, lie down on the floor.

Part I – Mother

Now that you're ready, become conscious of your breathing. Let your eyes close gently as you take a deep breath and exhale. Inhale and hold your breath for five counts. Then exhale until most of the air has left your lungs. Inhale again and slowly exhale, letting out an audible sigh through your mouth while you count silently from ten to one. Continue breathing slowly and deeply. As you breathe, you relax. Allow your natural breath to bring a deep sense of peace and well-being. Feel your body relax and let your mind free-associate. B-r-e-a-t-h-e.

As you settle comfortably in your chair, feel your feet on the floor. Tap them a few times. Feel the weight of your body sink into the chair. Starting at the top of your head, let your face, neck, and shoulders relax, then your torso, belly, and legs. Clench your fists and then relax them. Bring your attention back to your natural breathing. Try to feel the physical space between your heart and your back. Breathe into that area behind your heart. Feel your shoulder blades drop (or fall) and slide down your back. Resume your natural breathing.

Invite your mother to sit quietly in the chair facing you. She wants to be there. As you ask your mother the following questions, notice your own emotional and physical reactions as you hear the answers. Notice how you feel even if she doesn't answer. There are no right answers. There are no wrong answers. There is only whatever information comes to you. Right now just breathe, make eye contact with your mother, and listen to the answers.

"Mom, did you like or enjoy being a mother?" Notice how it feels to ask. What does she reply? If you don't get an answer, notice how you feel.

"How dependent were you on your role as a mother for your sense of self?" Breathe and notice if a response comes.

"Did the demands of motherhood compromise your sense of self? If so, what was that like for you?" B-r-e-a-t-h-e.

"Mom, what else besides me was meaningful to you?" B-r-e-a-t-h-e. Does she answer? Notice what it feels like if an answer does not come. B-r-e-a-t-h-e.

"If you had not become a mother, what would you have done with your life? Where would you have focused your attention?"

"Two more questions, Mom. What was your greatest joy in being a mother to me?" Pause and let the answer come.

"And, knowing what you know now, what is the one thing you regret most about how you raised me?" Breathe and be with whatever feelings are present.

Say thank you and good-bye to your mother and watch her exit the room. You are now in your private space once more, facing an empty chair. What does it feel like to be there without her presence? B-r-e-a-t-h-e. Slowly open your eyes and write about your experience, feelings, and thoughts. When you have written all that you want to, continue.

Part II – Mother and Daughter

Close your eyes again and bring your attention back to your breath. Take two or three conscious breaths with your attention moving from the top of your head all the way down to your toes, reconnecting you to your relaxed body.

Imagine you are directing the next questions only to yourself. Again, there are no right or wrong answers, and there should be no judgments or shame. There is only the information that comes to you.

"Do I want to be like my mother as a person? As a woman? As a partner? As a mother?"

'If I choose to become a mother, would she want me to be a different mother than she was? Can I be a different kind of parent than she was? Would she expect me to be like her? Would she want that for me?" Take in a breath and notice what feelings are present inside you.

"Would she approve of me if I did become a parent like her? Would she disapprove of me if I did not?"

"Do I feel I ought to be like her?" B-r-e-a-t-h-e. Where does your mind go with this?

"Does she think I should be a parent? Does she think I should not be a parent?" Be with the information that comes to you. It might come as words, images, feelings, thoughts, or something else. Notice what comes and b-r-e-a-t-h-e.

"How dependent would I be on my role as a mother for my sense of self or sense of identity?"

"What is meaningful to me in my life?"

"Does my mother know what is meaningful to me?"

Keep your eyes closed while you slowly return to your present environment, allowing a few moments to be with your emotional and physical sensations. Breathe.

When you're ready, slowly open your eyes and begin to write in your journal. Record your immediate thoughts, feelings, insights, and anything else you want to about your experience.

Immediate Writing after the Guided Visualization

Write even if it felt like nothing much happened for you. If you didn't have the answer to any of the questions, what was that like for you? What questions made you think about things you haven't considered before? As you reflect on all the pieces of information that come to you this week, remember that each by itself might not have an obvious meaning, but nothing should be swept under the rug or dismissed as unimportant. Record everything – the lumps of coal as well as the jewels.

When your writing feels complete, check in with your emotional state. Are your feelings manageable? If you feel overwhelmed, follow these instructions:

Take a deep breath, then exhale as slowly as possible, letting all the air escape your lungs. Allow your body to take in a breath on its own. Continue this several times until you notice a sense of calm. Then tap your feet on the floor. Follow that by tapping the tops of your thighs with your hands. Then tap your arms with your hands. Clench your fists and then release them. These actions help reconnect you to the present and ground you. Doing this is especially important when the emotions you experience feel overwhelming or just too much for you to manage. If you need to take further action to feel reconnected or grounded in the present, stand up and stamp your feet. Then reach your hands up in the air and stretch.

Look around the room and notice objects that bring a gentle smile to your face. Is your focus where you want it to be? Are your emotions manageable? Before you continue, make sure your attention is where you need it to be.

What Happens in Week 6

All human beings want to love, be loved, and connect with one another. Nowhere is this desire more deeply rooted than in your relationship with your mother. Alas, the mother-daughter relationship can sometimes be fraught with complexity and even pain. The more you understand about your relationship with your mother, the more you can come to clarity and unblock impediments to happiness in your adult life. In delving more deeply into the nature of motherhood and examining the relationship you had with your mother, you'll be turning over many stones. We give you the tools your curiosity needs to access critical information.

If something keeps coming up for you as you do this week's exercises, even if it seems trivial or mundane, it's worth further consideration. We want you to regard recurring themes as indicators that there is something to look at within you. Regard these indicators as invitations to free yourself from any unconscious or unhelpful messages you might have internalized. These messages – or the fear of passing them on to a future generation – might play a role in your not knowing if you want to become a mother yourself.

You might need to modify the term *mother* to make this week's material and exercises work for you. Perhaps you have a stepmother, biological mother, or adoptive mother. You might need to explore more than one maternal relationship, starting with your birth mother. Most women find that one person – the one who filled the primary role of mother – stands out for them. Start with her.

As you explore your relationship with your mother this week, you'll likely bump into three versions of her: the mother you knew growing up, the mother you know as an adult woman, and the mother figure you unconsciously internalized when you were young. This third mother is the one you need to get acquainted with. Her influence might be much stronger than you are currently aware of.

Even though it takes time and effort (perhaps more than you can accomplish in a single week), it's not too late to start untangling any unhealthy connections between you and your mother. These questions can help you begin to explore who your mother really was and is, and identify perceptions that might be inaccurate:

Did you feel nurtured by your mother?

Did she convey that you mattered to her?

Did she seem ambivalent about you or the role of motherhood?

Did she convey that she loved being a mom, or that the role was overwhelming?

Did motherhood stand in the way of her doing what she wanted to do for herself?

Were there externals or other pressures that inhibited the way she wanted to mother?

How did your mother change once her children weren't dependent on her?

How would you describe your mother as she is today?

Generational Inheritance Revisited

Like everyone else, your mother inherited and internalized her own set of experiences, issues, and messages during childhood. If she wasn't able later to examine and heal her own early struggles, it's likely that she unintentionally passed them on to you. That means that some of the confusion, anger, or sadness you carry around could belong more to your mother (and possibly to your mother's mother) than to you. While this can be a painful truth, it can also be liberating to discover that the depth of pain you carry isn't necessarily all yours. It's *still* something you have to deal with, however. While we as daughters can inherit some of our mothers' painful baggage, it falls to us to tend to our personal healing – for ourselves as well as any possible future generation.

Internalized Messages

Every single interaction between a mother and her daughter carries some non-verbal message such as "You are precious to me," "You'll never be as smart as your sister," or "If you're a good girl, you'll be rewarded." These messages accumulate to create an internal schema that shapes and informs your understanding of yourself and how you perceive and relate to the world around you. Internalized messages can reflect perfectly healthy beliefs, or they can be distorted or inaccurate perceptions that lodge themselves in your psyche and create impediments to happiness in your life.

If, for example, you grew up in a family in which little love was demonstrated, you might have internalized a message with a strategy: *If I love fiercely and always think about the other, then I'll be loved in return, and I will survive.* Out of this strategy you might have come to unconsciously believe that having your own child would be too burdensome. Or you might have developed the underlying belief that having a child would be a guaranteed way to finally get the love you always wanted. Either way, your belief ends up limiting your ability to make a conscious choice.

Sue uncovered a good example of an internalized message gone awry while working through the activities of Week 6. Her earliest memories were of a stressed-out and overwhelmed mother. Sue's mother lacked the physical and emotional support she so badly needed (often true in alcoholic family systems), and, feeling powerless to make changes, just put one foot in front of the other, often displaying a grumpy, critical demeanor to her children. Sue internalized the belief that it was *her* fault that her mother was so exhausted and unhappy. What also sometimes happens, and would have been worse, is that Sue could easily have internalized the belief that she was unwanted or that her mother was indifferent to her. Sue's overwhelmed mother likely had no idea that her own state could implant in Sue the internal message "I don't matter very much" or "If I just stay invisible, I won't get hurt." Another overwhelmed mother might feel completely frustrated with herself because she can't be the mother she hoped to be. The daughter of such a mother might internalize the message "Mom hates being a mother and she hates me."

If you find yourself brushing this topic off quickly with sentiments like "My relationship with my mother is great – no negative internalized messages here," we strongly urge you to take a closer look. In exploring internalized messages, some women uncover a quality or attribute of their mother that seems positive on the surface but has actually been masking an unhealthy dynamic. While exploring her relationship with her mother, Holly reported, "My mother was always very loving to me, and I loved her back intensely. We are still very close." Through a process of untangling, Holly came to realize that as a child she felt a tremendous responsibility to fulfill the role of the perfect daughter and to keep telling her mom just how wonderful she was. Someone with a purportedly close relationship with her mother (as Holly felt she had) can feel deep down that she doesn't have a right to have children because her mother still needs her attention. An internalized message such as this can be at the root of ambivalence toward motherhood, especially if it lives in your unconscious.

Attachment Wounds

D. W. Winnicott, a pediatrician and psychoanalyst from the United Kingdom, made valuable contributions to our understanding of what constitutes a healthy, strong bond between a mother and her infant baby. His observations added to the literature of *object-relations theory* in psychology and dispelled the myth that a mother must do everything right, or essentially be perfect. He developed the concept of a *good-enough mother*. The good-enough mother, rather than being perfect, is authentic and mostly consistent in her intentions to care for her child. She has good and bad days, but her intention to love and care for her child is perceptible. She has reasonable internal and external supports for maintaining continuity of care. This allows her baby to be more relaxed. In this relaxed state, her baby can *feel from the inside out* rather than experience internal stress in reaction to an external world in which her needs are not acknowledged or met. The mother's continuity of care provides the backbone for the infant's sound physical, emotional, psychological, and cognitive development. It also provides the foundation for the child's ability to develop an authentic self, one who can more easily access innate resiliency and creativity.[6]

A disruption in the mother-daughter attachment such as a difficult emotional connection, a long absence, a major illness, post-partum depression, or a divorce can result in an *attachment wound* for the daughter. When a girl experiences something so difficult, her quick intelligence jumps in to decide how best to survive. Sometimes a survival decision, rather than being one specific reaction to a given situation, turns into a mental pathway that colors her understanding of herself and the world. Such pathways then inform new experiences and go on to limit her abilities and future possibilities.

Let's look at a couple of examples of what an attachment wound looks and feels like:

Holly internalized the message that she had to be the perfect daughter so that her mother could feel that she was a wonderful mom. On the surface, this doesn't sound like a big deal. Linking Holly's experience of years of depression, difficulty forming lasting intimate relationships, and nagging sense of missing something in her life, she began to realize that perhaps her mother wasn't the nurturer Holly had remembered her to be. She now suspects that her mother had something in her make-up that made it impossible for her to see her daughter rightfully as a separate being with her own needs, desires, and personality. Holly concluded that her mother, not with malice but through her own needs, used Holly to prop herself up, and that this caused an attachment wound for Holly, through no fault of her own. Now that Holly has more insight, she feels much better about herself. She is working with a psychotherapist to help her fully understand the consequences, grieve her losses, and heal. She is astounded by how pervasively this attachment wound rippled through and influenced her life.

Samantha, too, was profoundly impacted by a difficult emotional connection to her mother. Her mother was emotionally more available than Holly's, but because of her untreated bipolar disorder, her availability was inconsistent. This registered with her young daughter as confusing, even chaotic. Samantha retreated emotionally, taking comfort from food. She felt alone and isolated. Her older brother wasn't around much, and the age difference didn't lend itself to the feeling that she had in him an ally. She did, however, have her Aunt Bea, who was her saving grace. Samantha credits her Aunt Bea with sustaining Samantha's sanity, and by grieving what she didn't originally receive in her mother-daughter connection she then could believe she was (of course!) worthy of being loved. This belief grew into self-confidence, which nourished her capacity to be more vulnerable with her partner, Elise.

Personal Boundaries

Boundaries – healthy and unhealthy ones – were referred to several times during Week 1, though not by name. While creating your family map, you represented individuals with discrete circles and squares and indicated marriages and children with connecting lines. The circles and squares didn't overlap because we're separate human beings with separate thoughts, feelings, and experiences, even as we're dependent on each other for love, closeness, and connection.

In Week 3 you learned about the clear messages a child needs to hear. When a girl hears these messages and sees the matching behavior along with them, she feels safe and can develop physically, emotionally, and psychologically. This helps her establish a sense of herself as separate yet able to connect with loved ones. In Week 4, when you explored your true response (yes or no) regardless of how you thought it might impact other people in your life, you were working toward clear, healthy boundaries.

Healthy boundaries develop *when the environment and the interpersonal relationships you grow up in are respectful of you as a separate being with your own needs, desires, and aspirations.* This does not mean that you would have always gotten your way. Setting appropriate limits for a child is an important building block in establishing healthy boundaries.

An environment – or family system – that fosters healthy boundaries respects the individuals who share that space. There is respect for privacy, personal possessions, and personal space. There is acknowledgment of your value – not for what you do, but for who you are. You are encouraged to express your desires, even if they aren't always fulfilled. Your emotions are met with care and interest, and they are labeled or named when it is important to do so, to help you understand your inner world. You are supported when you are overwhelmed so that you can feel inner stability.

Perhaps you are one of the fortunate ones who grew up in such a setting. As a result, you likely have reasonably functional boundaries and can say no and yes when you want to. You probably rarely feel bullied or victimized.

Sadly, many of us were not raised in an environment that helped us cultivate intact boundaries. Maybe one of your parents was so emotionally wounded that they lacked personal boundaries and treated you as an extension of themselves rather than as a separate person. For example, let's say your unspoken role was to meet your parent's needs, and when you didn't fulfill this function you received the message that you somehow weren't worthwhile. You would never have had the chance to experience yourself as a valuable and separate human being.

Let's look again at Sue's early life. Her father was alcohol dependent; her mother struggled to bring order to the ensuing chaos; and, until her parents divorced, the household suffered greatly. As Sue was growing up, this was her *normal*. As she later learned in her Adult Children of Alcoholics group, the personal fallout of this type of family environment can be devastating. Attention isn't paid to the needs of the children.

When Sue participated in the Motherhood program with us, she shared with the other women in her group that it wasn't until she was in her thirties that she began to realize where *she* actually was in her relationships. She had always tried to anticipate others' needs, as she had tried to do with her father. If his needs were correctly anticipated, he might not become volatile. This constant focus on another person prevented her from developing a healthy, intact sense of self, so she could not develop proper boundaries. What usually follows in such situations is lack of clarity about what one wants or desires. Or even worse, it becomes irrelevant. The good news for Sue is that she found support resources and over time developed more intact boundaries for herself. As a result, her relationships with many friends improved, while some friendships ended – the unbalanced and unhealthy ones that she needed to end for her self-development.

The degree to which you maintain healthy boundaries has everything to do with your decision about having children. You have to know who you are and what you feel, independent of anyone else, to be able to work out what you want and why you want it. But the reality is that maintaining healthy personal, psychological, physical, emotional, and spiritual boundaries is necessary for you to thrive whether you become a parent or not. Close friendships and intimate relationships suffer when your boundaries are fuzzy; rational expectations become skewed, and not knowing how to get your needs met successfully can be both daunting and painful. And, certainly, healthy boundaries are an important consideration if you do decide you want to become a mother. Without them you'll struggle unduly with your emotions whenever your child struggles with theirs.

How do you get healthy boundaries if you've never had them? Start by continuing your exploration with the exercises of this program. The more you consciously explore your inner world, the more you understand where *you* end and *another* begins. You can educate yourself by reading some of the literature that is readily available. Many accessible books have been written about cultivating healthy boundaries. And, like Sue, you can find a dedicated community like an Adult Children of Alcoholics group where you can practice developing healthy boundaries with like-minded individuals. For more focused practice, consider individual or group psychotherapy, in which you have the opportunity to scrutinize interpersonal exchanges in greater depth.

Boundaries are subjective and personal. You ultimately decide where your boundaries lie and how fluid or rigid they are. See what you discover this week as you deepen your understanding of what constitutes healthy boundaries, especially those you have with your mother.

Where on the continuum from unhealthy to healthy would you place your mother-daughter boundaries? What can you learn about the physical, emotional, and psychological space between you and your mother? Do you feel you have permission from your mother (and yourself) to think and feel freely as a separate person? Do you actually have to be geographically far away from your mother to feel separate? Where and how does your mother-daughter relationship feel effortless? Does your mother-daughter relationship feel rigid or intrusive? As you learn about your inner world, these questions are relevant even if your mother is not physically available to you. Now is a good time to gently take stock and find out.

A Woman's Rite of Passage

Following the discussion of personal boundaries, we shift to the important task of understanding how you are different and separate (emotionally and psychologically) from your mother and how being separate benefits your decision-making skills.

The formative relationship with one's mother should ideally begin with a healthy dependency. As a young woman matures, an important rite of passage occurs as she takes the time and effort to separate psychologically from her mother as best she can. She moves from dependency to healthy independence. This is never truer than when a woman makes her *own* decision about becoming a mother or not.

As you work through this week's suggestions, consider with care who your mother actually was and is and allow your developing awareness to illuminate how you differ from her. Note similarities and differences, making an effort to separate her influences from your intrinsic self. It's a good week to notice whether you have made assumptions about who your mother is, especially if you have put her in a box based on how she treated you. Take some time this week to reflect on your earlier writings, including the exercise from Week 2 on defining motherhood. See if you notice any recent shifts in your awareness.

You'll benefit this week by staying curious. It's not at all disloyal to tease out who you are from who your mother was and is. Rather, it's respectful to both of you. You have so much to gain from this exploration; you can come away seeing your mother as a separate, imperfect, but very human being – a woman who might have had her own hurts that remain unresolved. And you'll find yourself freer to move forward in your life.

Changing Your Story

Some of you will realize you had a good-enough mother. Others will have a long list of what was wrong with their mother's way of parenting. It can be painful to look objectively at your mother's limitations and see how imperfect she was and is, especially if you idealized her when you were young. Remember that you *had* and *have* no control over who your mother was or how she behaved. No matter how wounded your mother might have been, it was not your doing or your fault that things unfolded as they did.

If you feel you didn't get what you needed from your mother, there's an important lesson to be learned. While your mother can't address the needed repair work now – even if she wants to help you and has the necessary skills – healing or repairing *is* within *your* power. To begin, allow yourself to recognize what you might have missed out on and genuinely feel its loss. Let yourself grieve for the mother who wasn't who you wanted her to be; this will actually help you accept and value the woman she actually was and is. When you can tend to your own pain, without judgment of your mother or yourself, you are well on your way to being healed. You move away from feeling helpless and powerless to effect change in your life, and shift yourself toward a very different life story. Face the truth of what was. Make your peace with it. It will open up your path to clarity.

Be Curious: Assignments for Week 6

When we say there is absolutely no wrong way to do the writing assignments, we mean it! Your writing does not need to make sense, be rational or linear, or even consist of complete sentences. It only needs to be meaningful to *you*. As you write, let your mind free-associate. Stream-of-consciousness writing allows your unconscious mind to step forward.

The first writing assignment brings to you again the questions from this week's guided visualization. Read them carefully before you write your responses. Your answers here take over where the guided visualization left off. They help you access fresh information and develop a more complete understanding of this most complex relationship. As you work the exercise, more questions will likely come to mind.

1. Read these questions first silently, then aloud. Respond in writing with whatever comes to mind. If you don't know an answer, write about how it feels not to know. We have Phyllis O. Ziman Tobin to thank for many of these questions. They can be found in her book *Motherhood Optional: A Psychological Journey.*

Be Curious: In thinking about your mother, let yourself wonder...
   a.   Did she enjoy being a mother?
   b.   How dependent was she on her role as mother for her sense of herself?
   c.   How much did the demands of motherhood compromise her sense of herself?
   d.   What else besides you or her children was meaningful to her?
   e.   If she weren't a mother, what would she have focused her attention on?
   f.   What do you think was her greatest joy in being a mother to you?
   g.   What, if anything, might she regret most about how she raised you?

And now, why not wonder...
   h.   *Do I want to be like my mother as a person? As a woman? As a partner? As a mother?*
   i.   *Would she expect me to be like her? Would she want that for me? Would she want me to be a different kind of mother than she was?*
   j.   *Would she approve of me if I became a parent like her? Would she disapprove of me if I didn't?*
   k.   *Do I feel I ought to be like her? Can I be a different kind of mother than she was?*

l.   *Does she have views about whether or not I become a mother?*

m. *How dependent would I be on my role as a mother for my sense of self or sense of identity?*

n.   *What is meaningful to me in my life? Does my mother know this about me?*

2. It's helpful to take a step back and take stock of how others perceived your mother while you were growing up. Doing this can validate your experience, or stir up some uneasiness or confusion. Discover what happens for you.

Be Curious:

a.   *How did the community and other family members see my mother?*

b.   *In what way was this view of her similar to my perception?*

c.   *In what way was this view of her different from my perception?*

Further Exploration and Discovery

Reread your responses to the two writing assignments above and consider the exploratory questions in "Your Checklist for Reflection" on page 50.

Did the exercises stir up unexpected questions and feelings about your mother? Did old hurts resurface? Even if you feel that things are good enough between you and your mother, or if an old hurt with her has already been worked through, taking another look can be fruitful. It might surprise you to learn that useful information comes up even more noticeably or unexpectedly for women who feel that up till now they've had a *good* relationship with their mother.

While the initial goal of the exercises is to explore your reality and not to include your mother in the equation, you might feel the desire to involve her if she is available to you. We recommend you don't do this while your own process is still incubating. Better to wait until you're further down the road. We do, however, advise you to make notes in your journal about what you want to discuss with her at a later time.

Note any new questions that arise. If your mother is no longer living, or your relationship is so strained that it's not possible to make these inquiries, there is still plenty you can do on your own. Be creative. Perhaps one of your mother's siblings or a grandmother is around. You deserve not only to survive but to thrive, and the relationship with your mother deserves to be as good as it can be, regardless of your circumstances.

Be Even More Curious: Optional Exercises

If you have the time and desire to take your exploration further this week, try one or more of these additional suggestions:

1. Repeat the guided visualization, replacing your mother with your father or another parent (especially useful if you had more than one mother figure). Follow up with writing out the answers to the questions as you did in the first "Be Curious" assignment.

2. Create two separate collages, drawings, or paintings, one that represents the essence of you and another that represents your mother. Work with one at a time and give yourself the chance to really feel the differences. Place the end products where you can

"visit" them to feel how they are different and/or the same. Feel the sameness and the differences as you later admire your work.

3. If you have a flair for the dramatic, why not try what psychologists call *chair work*? Place two chairs opposite each other. Sit in one chair, and using the guided visualization questions from Part I for this week as a guide, ask your mother or mother figure a question. Then move to her chair and answer you, her daughter. Then move back and either respond or ask another question. Play this out until you feel finished, and write about what happened in your journal.

4. What were the verbal and non-verbal messages you received from your mother about becoming pregnant, having babies, and becoming a parent?

What to Hold Inside This Week

Our experience tells us that this week's work can be daunting. You're brave and you can do this. Stay close to the truth of that, as well as very close to your heart, all week. Be gentle with any feelings of loss that surface. Try to spend a little extra me-time each day, sitting quietly to write in your journal. If during the week more emotions show up than you expect, welcome them with open arms as best you can. You have perseverance. You can meet what comes with open eyes, an open mind, and an open heart. You can be your own best nurturer; practice right now. Give yourself a real bear hug – yes, you read that correctly: wrap your arms around yourself as tightly (but comfortably) as you can. Say clearly and with conviction, "I *am* one magnificent woman!" Breathe mindfully and repeat the sequence two more times.

Continue to be curious about your interactions with others, your thoughts, your feelings, and any old or new behaviors. Since you began this inward journey, have you noticed that you feel or act differently around the people to whom you are closest? This is to be expected; you're stirring things up in your heart and mind at a very deep level.

If you're feeling particularly vulnerable this week, you might want to revisit the first and second guided visualizations presented in Week 1. Reach for comfort. Reach inside yourself to connect with your internalized good-enough mother, and ask *her* to nurture and fuel you with self-love and caring. Try to hold on to your birthright. You deserve to feel love and be loved no matter what has happened or is happening now with your real mother. Take plenty of rest and make time to sit quietly or meditate and record reflections and insights in your journal. If you need to add some items to the section of your journal designated for future follow-up, do so.

Self-Care

Do something this week that really nourishes and recharges you. What nurtures you? Does your younger self want to weigh in with a different view? While we have two nurturing suggestions – treating yourself to a massage, and taking a long, leisurely walk in nature – there are countless ways to nourish and renew. Pick whatever most appeals to you, carve out the time, and make it happen. Yes!

The self-care I did for myself this week was...

You Are Not Alone

This week Nicole and Nina share their personal stories that are strongly influenced by their mothers. Both women stress how they needed to *feel* their way to their decision. Read on when it feels true for you to hear their stories.

Nicole's Story

I think my mother's diagnosis of cancer made me think about it more. My father had passed away the year prior to her diagnosis. It made me think more about family, loss, what was really important to me, and that maybe I was cheating myself out of a lot of love and closeness because of not wanting to risk that much. Now I am facing possible fertility concerns. I pushed my body probably right up to the point where the door is closing on being able to get pregnant (at least on my own). I had a fertility blood workup done right when I started trying and that all looked good, but that doesn't guarantee you anything. As I type this I am waiting to see for the seventh time if I'm pregnant. I'm not interested in pursuing invasive treatments, but have been trying acupuncture. If I have waited too long, I will have to accept that and that will be hard.

I think it was always in the back of mind when I was young, and I think I just thought it would work out somehow. Then in my thirties, I started to wonder if maybe it wasn't going to happen. I didn't have much luck or, more accurately, taste when it came to men. They were cute, charming, but flaky, and almost always unwilling to commit. Then I would overcorrect and find someone who adored me who I had absolutely no connection with and then go back to cute, charming, and flaky. I finally met a good man who was cute and charming and who I connected with when I was thirty-nine.

Looking back, I probably wasn't really ready to commit to a relationship before him. I respected him and loved him and thought now things would fall into place, but by that time I was questioning whether having children was such a good idea. I was set in my ways: mostly sleeping in and going out to dinner and movies a lot. Looking back, deep down I think I knew I wanted one, but I stopped believing in the idea of a family, or maybe I never believed in it because of how I grew up. I knew that I could trust myself to accomplish goals that I set for myself and create a life I would be happy with on my own. However, trusting in a relationship with another and having a child with them required a level of confidence in my future that I didn't have.

The other problem was that my partner at first said he was open to the idea and six months in said he wasn't. Now I was faced with losing someone who took so long to find, to pursue the unknowns of parenting. I was so confused about it all. I would ask myself, "If you wanted one so badly why didn't you try harder to settle down earlier?" I thought maybe that meant I might be fine without a child, and I was just rocking the boat in my first really good relationship. The saddest part was that the closer I got to him and the more I trusted the relationship, the more I wanted to have a child with him. He was a constant. If we fought, he was still there. If I had PMS, he was still there. If I had too much to drink and caused a stupid fight, he was still there. That was wonderful, but it made the decision so much harder. The struggle with that decision brought me to the Motherhood group.

At first I was trying to think my way through, which didn't work for me. When I started to feel my way through I made progress. Some women know for sure and that's great for them, but if you aren't sure, you aren't going to be able to figure it out by logically trying to decide. You're going to need help (like the group I had) and you're going to have to get deep down inside yourself for the answer. You will never be able to figure it out by weighing the pros and cons. I read every article and listened to every radio and TV show on

> *the subject, and though it helped me understand the why and why not for other people and the good and bad of both decisions, it didn't help me decide for me. For me, I needed the group. I needed to do the writings and talk about it a lot. I had to separate what I thought about motherhood from what I felt about it.*

Nicole lives and works in an urban area. At the time of her story, she was forty-two years old and had been in a committed relationship for over three years with a male partner who has a daughter from a previous marriage. On top of years of casual thinking about whether or not she would have a child, she spent three years agonizing over it – three years in which she felt alone and confused, even after talking at length with her partner, her friends, and her sister.

When it seemed to her that her relationship was at risk, she ultimately sought professional help and joined one of the twelve-week programs. Together with the other women in the group, Nicole began to uncover her deeper feelings. She said, "The group helped me get rid of some of the automatic thoughts and fears I had around having a child. It helped me get more in touch with just the feelings about it – both good and bad – and, in the end, there was a lot more good." When the group ended, Nicole knew she wanted to have a child if she could.

Her partner initially didn't want to have another child but changed his mind when he realized he would lose this valued relationship. As of this writing, they are trying to get pregnant. He says he will be okay with either scenario. Nicole, though not as casual about the outcome, feels that she and her partner are now closer to each other than ever before. In her own words, "When I knew we were going to try, I was happy and excited. Now I'm in limbo, but I will always be happy I tried." Nicole still has day-to-day struggles around the issue, but not the agony she went through before she decided. "If I get pregnant, this will be my path; if I don't, this will be my path."

The youngest of four, Nicole experienced early family life, especially a complicated relationship with her mother and a nearly non-existent relationship with her father, as negatively influencing her path of decision. She also can't recall having any real role models when she was young. As for growing up with her mother, she had this to say: "She would do wonderful things for you and she would be heartless at other times. I never doubted she loved me, but I know for sure by twelve years old I did not trust her, nor did I find comfort in her. It may have even been earlier, but I definitely remember feeling that way by twelve." Her mother's inconsistency toward her could contribute to the volatility and reactivity that occurs at times in Nicole's intimate relationships.

Now, as an adult, Nicole feels the relationship with her mother is still complicated, but less so. Much of her anger and reactivity has been relieved. Her mother's diagnosis of cancer had a softening impact, but the support group also helped Nicole heal some of her unresolved hurt by providing a safe place for her to focus specifically on key aspects of her mother-daughter relationship. Although Nicole's father is now dead, he doesn't seem to have ever held a significant position in her life. Their relationship was characterized more by an absence than a presence. This could bring up feelings of loss for Nicole down the line, even if the resulting feeling is one of potential loss – what never was – rather than the actual loss of something that once was.

Nicole aspires to be a different type of mother than her mother was to her. She would like to keep the good and change the bad. When Nicole became an adult, her mother shared with her the reasons she did what she did when her children were young; she claimed that her internal fragility pushed her to react to her children the way she did. The coldness that frightened Nicole when she was young is a big factor in the mistrust she developed toward her mother. Nicole would never want to be distant (angry at times, yes, but distant, no) toward her own child. Insight is good, but changing one's behavior takes time. Nicole seems aware of this and invested in making the changes that could help free her from perpetuating patterns. Through life experiences she is developing self-awareness and emotional maturity, good qualities for a parent.

It is worth noting that there have been three additional shifts in her life since she made her decision. The first is that she has engaged with her partner's daughter at a deeper level. She feels more of a commitment to his daughter – perhaps as practice (as she says) or maybe to show more of a commitment to her partner – but also Nicole can likely now envision the potential long-term relationship she'll have with his daughter in the years ahead. Second, she has noticed a change with female friends. Those who didn't want children have reacted to her movement away from them (even if only in perception), and this has caused some discomfort; conversely, friends with children have rallied around her. The third change is that Nicole has noticed that her family – mother and siblings – are all excited for her and are offering encouragement.

Nicole said she wishes she'd been able to listen to her heart at an earlier age and not been so afraid of asking for what she wanted and needed. She has accepted that no matter how good she is at avoiding hurt, stuff happens, and she will survive. She shared, "It sounds corny, but this saying does fit for me: 'Tis better to have loved and lost than never to have loved at all.'"

Nina's Story

My mother was very young when she had me. She hated my father and maybe I reminded her of my father. There was no love. Despite that, she did a lot of things for me. My parents divorced when I was two-and-a-half years old.

Both of them had terrible childhoods. Both of them were against having a child. My mother is different now, but when I was younger, she would say, "People with no children have only one concern and worry, but with children, they have a million concerns." My father was very proud of me for not having a child, since my half-sister has four children. As their grandfather, he has had to take on many unwelcome financial responsibilities.

I think if I were in a healthy and loving relationship I might have wanted a child.

Nina is an intelligent, sensitive, contemporary woman living very comfortably in modern society while her family background is steeped in traditional culture, especially where women are concerned. She moved to the United States as a young woman and has maintained emotional ties to her country of origin. Some extended family members and friends still live there.

Nina decided at age thirty-seven that she would not have children. She reached her decision on her own without seeking professional help or talking with friends or family. She felt capable of making up her own mind without consulting others.

Nina shared that her relationship with her mother was very painful and difficult all the while she was growing up, and that this has only eased in the past few years. The changes came about after a breakthrough in communication that allowed mother and daughter to relate to each other with greater appreciation and respect. They enjoy each other today in a way that wasn't possible before. As a young person, Nina felt that she hated her mother. These are strong feelings that possibly prevented Nina from fully exploring her feelings about her potential role as a mother. The fact that her earliest years were spent living in a country with a traditional culture with parents in a troubled marriage could also have contributed to her ultimate decision.

At the time she finally decided, she was nearing the end of her second marriage. Married first at age twenty-one to a man she felt would be unsuitable as a father, she didn't feel that choosing motherhood was safe with him. While at times she daydreamed of having a child, wondering if she would have a boy or a girl, she didn't feel secure enough to consider her options in that marriage. In her second marriage, she and her partner slowly became emotionally estranged from each other.

Nina has no regrets about her *no* decision. She feels fulfilled in her life, striking an important balance between professional work, creative work in an avant-garde theatre group, and her spiritual practice. She hopes that all women feel entitled to find their way to their own decision. She added with conviction, "Having a child is not for everybody!"

Week 7

Yes ~ No ~ Maybe

"I realized for the first time that childlessness can be about many things.
It is about biological limitations. It is about ambivalence.
Sometimes childlessness is just about wanting something else in life.
And sometimes childlessness is a combination of all these things."
–Mardy S. Ireland[7]

Not everyone can sustain the intention and commitment to do these exercises week after week… but you have! Pause long enough to feel your perseverance, because, in truth, you're moving forward despite any fear, pain, or uncertainty.

You might feel that since you've completed half the program, you should be halfway to your decision. If you notice this kind of self-expectation, allow yourself to breathe into the knowledge that this process is not a linear one. Continue to open up in order to receive more information in the weeks to come. There's still so much to discover. Even as you begin to have more and more clarity, gently move back into *I don't know* as best you can. You've nothing to lose by staying with *I don't know* a bit longer.

You spent the last two weeks focusing on parents. Last week was packed full, and you now have a good idea of what needs tending. Full healing might not have happened yet, but just having a picture of what is yet to be resolved can feel liberating. If you still feel a bit unsure about all of this, don't despair; it will become clearer as you continue to progress with the program.

Last week you examined your relationship with your mother. You considered who she was while you were growing up, and you paid attention to the degree of psychological and emotional separation from her that you've already achieved. It took courage to explore your personal boundaries. Are you happy with the current state of your physical and emotional boundaries?

Your relationship with your mother has a powerful impact on how you go about deciding whether or not you want to become a parent, and this is certainly true if you've been experiencing ambivalence. You internalized so much about her experience, whether you were aware of it or not. As new feelings are stirred up going forward, live with them as best you can. Give these new feelings room to express themselves. Let the unearthing continue, and keep going. Your clarity and resolve will come. It's safe to trust this.

You might feel by now that many unresolved issues have already surfaced, and yet here we are moving on to unearth more! You might also feel the urge to deal with what has already come to light rather than take in additional information. However, it's more important now to move forward, focus on the new material, and trust that what feels unresolved will be tended to or will fall into place, if not directly in the remaining weeks then afterward when you look at your next steps. Moving along your particular track will ultimately have a bigger positive impact than spending your time fixed on any one issue.

Week 7 Guided Visualization

For this visualization jewel, trust that your attentive mind will go where it needs to go. When your eyes are closed, you engage the part of your brain that isn't as easily accessed when your eyes are open. Have someone read the visualization to you or record it for you so you can listen while your eyes are closed, as its power also lies in the element of surprise. If that's not possible, make a recording yourself so you can listen with eyes closed to deepen the experience of where the visualization takes you. If you read the visualization to yourself, read it silently and slowly to give yourself time to savor the experience. Close your eyes now and then to open to the power of your imagination.

Remember that the experience you have is what matters most, and there's no wrong way to do it. Have your journal and writing tool nearby so you can record your impressions and images immediately.

To prepare, choose a quiet place where people and noise won't disturb or distract you, and a time when there's nothing else for you to do and no one who needs your attention; this time is solely for your benefit. Either sit comfortably in a chair or, if you prefer, lie down on the floor.

Yes? No? Maybe?

Now that you're ready, become conscious of your breathing. Let your eyes close gently as you take a deep breath and exhale. Inhale and hold your breath for five counts. Then exhale until most of the air has left your lungs. Inhale again and slowly exhale, letting out an audible sigh through your mouth while you count silently from ten to one. Continue breathing slowly and deeply. As you breathe, you relax. Allow your natural breath to bring a deep sense of peace and well-being. Feel your body relax and let your mind free-associate. B-r-e-a-t-h-e.

You're halfway through this program, but that doesn't necessarily mean you're halfway to knowing your desire or knowing what your decision will be. Trust in your own deep knowing that answers will come.

Envision that today you made the decision that you will *not* become a mother. You will not have a child or children. Yes, it's true: you decided to live a child-free life. And if you already have stepchildren or another child, you have decided you will not have any more children. What is your first uncensored thought? What are you feeling at this moment in time? Stay with whatever you are feeling or not feeling. If you're feeling numb, be with the numbness and continue to b-r-e-a-t-h-e. This has been a difficult decision to make; however, the decision process is over. You have decided.

Let go of any resistance you might have to embracing this decision. Give yourself complete permission to immerse yourself in your decision. Welcome all the feelings that come with this decision. Maybe you're feeling sadness, relief, joy, surprise, loss, fear, guilt, shame, confusion, worry, contentment, anxiety, anger, delight, or another feeling not mentioned. Whatever you're feeling, welcome any and all of them.

Breathe into these feelings, letting them be in your heart and body. Now that you've made the decision that you're not going to be a mom, who will you tell first? What will their reaction be? How do you feel about the reaction? Perhaps you won't tell anyone. Is there someone you don't want to tell? How do you feel about yourself as a woman now that you've made this decision? Is there another way in which you want to contribute to the next generation or participate in raising the next generation?

What course will your life take now? What is the first thing that will change? How do you feel about that? Who will be happy for you?

Who will be unhappy for you and think you are making a mistake? Does your decision change anything about your primary relationship if you have one? If you are single, how does this decision impact you? Does it change anything about other relationships with family members or friends?

Keep your eyes closed while you slowly, very slowly, return to your present environment along with this decision you've made, allowing a few moments to be with your emotional and physical sensations. B-r-e-a-t-h-e.

When you're ready, slowly open your eyes and begin to write in your journal. Record your immediate thoughts, feelings, insights, and anything else you want to about this guided scenario.

Immediate Writing after the Guided Visualization

The first minutes following a guided visualization are sacred. Immediate writing helps concretize what occurred for you and prevents valuable information from slipping away. If you didn't have the reaction you expected, write about how that felt. If you were disappointed with your reaction, don't leave it there; write about it. After you express everything that emerged, continue reading.

What was your initial reaction to the decision – and how are you feeling at this point? How did it feel that the decision was made for you? What does it feel like to be done with the decision-making process? This guided visualization can bring up strong feelings. Remind yourself that it's merely to help you get in contact with your innermost thoughts and feelings, *not* an indication of whether you actually should or should not have a child. Your reaction to this exercise is not a sign of whether or not you want to become a mother;

it's something to write about. Do not draw conclusions right now from what you experienced or are experiencing. Just log it and stay with it to the best of your ability.

When your writing feels complete, check in with your emotional state. Are your feelings manageable? If you feel overwhelmed, follow these instructions:

Take a deep breath, then exhale as slowly as possible, letting all the air escape your lungs. Allow your body to take in a breath on its own. Continue this several times until you notice a sense of calm. Then tap your feet on the floor. Follow that by tapping the tops of your thighs with your hands. Then tap your arms with your hands. Clench your fists and then release them. These actions help reconnect you to the present and ground you. Doing this is especially important when the emotions you experience feel overwhelming or just too much for you to manage. If you need to take further action to feel reconnected or grounded in the present, stand up and stamp your feet. Then reach your hands up in the air and stretch.

Look around the room and notice objects that bring a gentle smile to your face. Is your focus where you want it to be? Are your emotions manageable? Before you continue, make sure your attention is where you need it to be.

What Happens in Week 7

This week we invite you to accept the choice *not* to have a child and *not* to become a mother. Notice the two phrases: not having a child, and not becoming a mother. Do they feel the same or different to you? We ask you to embrace the *no* decision for a week. One important reason we ask you to "try on" and "wear" the *no* decision for seven days is so you can gain insight into your own situation and recognize how ambivalence might be playing a role in postponing or blocking your choice. You'll also have the opportunity to explore the toll your indecision might have taken on you, and you'll look at the impact of pressures or judgments from others or yourself. Through celebration, ritual, or ceremony, you'll formally acknowledge yourself for conscious decision-making. Prepare to be intrigued, and read on!

Making a Decision

Pretending with your whole heart and mind to have made a *no* decision provides you with information that can lead you closer to knowing your true desire. Some women find immediate relief that the agony is over and the decision has been made for them. Some experience the *no* decision with gentle ease because it's the direction toward which they've already been leaning. And others feel scared and/or unbearably sad to come to this final no. Whatever feelings come up for you, treat them gently and don't underestimate that this is a valuable way to access more information about yourself. The more you're able to open your mind and heart fully to this decision, the more easily that information can come forward.

Let's explore from your new vantage point how your life might change with this choice. What will you do first? Do you imagine being able to enjoy experiences that having a child would have precluded? Are you already regretting the loss of experiences you'll now never have? Or both? Will you decide to include children in your life or somehow contribute to the next generation in another way? Will you consider getting a pet? If you have a partner, how will your partner take the news?

Might this be a deal-breaker for your relationship? As you consider these questions, what feelings come up?

Even though you've been living with *I don't know* and you're still in the gathering-pertinent-information phase, there's absolutely no risk in taking on the *no* decision for one week. Whatever your deep-down individual truth is, it won't be swayed this week by pretending to have made a decision. Notice that holding the *no* position for one week is very different from going back and forth between yes and no every ten minutes. If you hear yourself saying *I can't do this*, gently bring yourself back to the *no* position that you're committing to for one week's time. You don't have to pretend to *like* the decision; you only have to pretend to have *made* the decision.

Understanding the Role of Ambivalence

Some women feel very maternal but don't necessarily have the desire to have children. Unable to resolve the tension between these two polarities, they remain in a prolonged state of ambivalence. Others avoid deciding until one day they realize they're too old to have a biological child. The decision not to have a child is made for these women by default. Sometimes a woman remains ambivalent to avoid facing her grief and other people's reactions to her decision. For a variety of reasons, more women than you realize have some ambivalence about wanting to be a mother.

Sustained, unhealthy ambivalence can stand in the way of your ability to move forward in your life in all kinds of ways. It ties up energy. It's immobilizing. It causes pain. Ambivalence curiously has the ability to move from person to person. Sometimes it keeps a *system* ambivalent; that's how powerful ambivalence can be. In a relationship (a system), one person can be ambivalent while the other is certain. If the positions later reverse, ambivalence can still be present in the relationship.

Ambivalence is not necessarily unhealthy, however. A healthy form of ambivalence does not render you immobilized; rather it is characterized by curiosity and the ability to sustain the uncertainty of not knowing without stress or judgment. You're in touch with how you feel, including negative feelings, and you aren't overly afraid of those feelings. You're not overwhelmed. Temporary feelings of ambivalence can be a sign to proceed with caution.

As the week unfolds, consider the role ambivalence has played in your struggle. It's important to take stock, but to do so without self-judgment.

Pressure or Judgment from Self or Others

Pressure to make a decision about motherhood can be self-imposed or come from external factors ranging from antsy parents and in-laws to the so-called biological clock. It can be real or imagined. It can be very difficult to untangle the knots caused by pressure, as self-imposed pressures can intermix with internalized messages from partners, parents, and others.

And then there's judgment. Deciding no can be a big deal in a society that still clings to messages such as "Having a child is a women's duty," "The only acceptable reason not to have children is infertility," and "Women have been having children since time began." Women have also, of course, *not* been having children – by choice. But the subject of having children or not arouses strong feelings even from people who seldom have opinions on anything, because it can intersect with their ideas about right and wrong. It can be hard to keep your sense of perspective and not succumb to societal pressure when you're essentially being assaulted with messages that bring with them the baggage of shame. You can feel compelled to pretend you want to be a mom even if you don't. And feeling *that* pressure can keep you stuck in the state of secretly hoping that your desire to be a mom will suddenly appear, believing *that* will relieve the pressure.

There are few topics as emotionally charged as this one, so for your protection, *remember to keep your process to yourself* for this week, too. It's important to have your complete inner experience without having to fend off comments from others, even if they're well-meaning. Contending with yourself is enough to focus on.

Be Curious: Assignments for Week 7

We stress again that your writing doesn't need to be in complete sentences or be rational. The writing assignments work best when your mind is free from constraints of right or wrong and shoulds or should nots. The writing unleashes the unconscious, and you access fresh information for yourself.

1. I've Made My Decision!

    In order to benefit from this week's assignment, for a full seven days pretend you've decided not to have children. This week's focus is on embracing a decision, and it doesn't matter much what your desire is or was. Don't bargain with your thoughts or feelings; make a decision to accept *this* decision (even though it was thrust on you). The more you convince your mind of this decision, the more feedback will come to you. Any reactions to this week's exercise are for your information only. Your reactions are not indicators of your desire or your final decision. Invite reactions. The reactivity inside you needs to surface so you can confront what you carry. Write about your experience a little bit each day rather than in one sitting, as your thoughts and feelings are likely to change day to day. Record in your journal every thought and every feeling that comes up. Notice what it's like this week to see women who are pregnant or young children playing. What observations and feelings do you have about friends, acquaintances, or even people you hardly know who live child-free lives?

Be Curious: *Today I decided not to be a mom and my feelings and thoughts about this are...*

2. Letter to the Child I Won't Meet

For some, this next exercise feels heart-wrenching. We don't intend to cause suffering, but it's important to excavate all the thoughts and feelings that can come up for you around the decision not to have a child. Do your best to stay with the discomfort and see what expresses itself for you. There are endless places you can go with this. What is needed to move on in the direction of not being a mom? Do you hope this child you won't have or be a mother to will end up with another family? Do you believe it's for the best? Do you feel sad about the missed opportunity? Write first and then explore what comes up about it later. You might want to wait several days or until the end of the week to write your letter. You may need to be with your experience of no for a bit longer.

Be Curious:

Dear Young One,
I've decided not to become a parent, and that means you and I will
never meet. There are things I want to share about you and about my
decision...

3. My Celebration, Ritual, or Ceremony

What if the society you lived in believed that discovering clarity was a far more important rite of passage than the content of any decision itself? What if we had rituals for arriving at conscious decisions? Can you imagine wanting to share and acknowledge the discovery of your truth with all your friends and family? Imagine making phone call after phone call to say, "Guess what? I finally know exactly what I want to do. I know that I don't want to become a parent. I'm relieved and excited because I was ambivalent about it for so long, and now I want to share my newfound sense of clarity and freedom with you." Then your friend or family member responds with something like "That's fantastic! Congratulations! Mazel Tov! I'm so happy for you. There's nothing better than knowing your own truth and living it. I'd like to celebrate with you. How shall we do that?" More phone calls get made and you begin to plan the event.

What will your celebration, ritual, or ceremony look like? You can invite one other person or many. You can light candles in an intimate setting or climb a mountain. Ask yourself, *Who in my life would I want to be present or nearby? What gifts will I need and want for my future child-free life?* Or perhaps you'd prefer to arrange something along the lines of "In lieu of gifts, please bring something written by you about a time *you* stayed true to yourself." The possibilities are endless, so jump in and be creative. Let your imagination be the limit.

Some women really get excited by this. It can feel so freeing. Others find it sheer torture. If the word *celebration* doesn't work for you, try creating a more solemn ritual to honor yourself for making a conscious decision that took time, energy, and thoughtfulness. If a more solemn ritual feels closer to where you are, you might find this exercise creates an opportunity to express what feels like overwhelming grief. Make time and space for attending to your grief. You and it deserve this attention. If the idea of celebration or ritual feels beyond your current ability and you don't feel up to it, don't worry about this perfectly common reaction; however, if there's a way to carry out the exercise in your mind or on paper so it brings you benefits, please try to do it. You'll be sure to gain some insights from the attempt.

Be Curious: *The details for my celebration, ritual, or ceremony (or some women rename this "My No-Baby Shower") are…*

4. Make a Collage!

If a full-on celebration or ceremony is just too far-fetched for you, create a lovely collage that embodies how you feel during this week. Use the magazine pictures and cutouts you've been collecting and add paint or drawings if you like. Have some fun with it!

5. Pressures and Judgments

Inquiring into your reaction of feeling pressured or judged can *tell* you a lot. If you don't like how being judged feels, and that tends to be the end of the story – without any exploration of *why* it doesn't feel good – then *be intrigued* about this discomfort and put it in perspective. That way, when others judge you or want to pressure you, the impact can be minimal. Your answers to the following prompts will lead you to greater clarity.

Be Curious:
When I'm feeling judged by others, this is what I believe about myself: (For example: *I'm stupid. I'm a loser. I'm a shameful person. I have no use for people. I'm alone. Bring it on! I don't care what you think; I'm good.*)

When I'm feeling pressured to fit into someone else's agenda or image, this is what I feel: (For example: *I can't think straight. I feel sad and lonely that I let it bother me. It makes me furious, but I freeze up and stay quiet.*)

Further Exploration and Discovery

You can spend the entire week on the recommended assignments. When you feel finished with them, take as long a break as you like and then go back and read what you wrote for each one while considering the exploratory questions of the "Your Checklist for Reflection" on page 50.

As you wrote about your decision, did new insights come? Things can start to shake up and separate out when you give yourself full permission to be in the *no* scenario. Even if you struggled to go into no, there is still something to be gained in trying. Can you notice what that is for you? Are you thinking about anything differently?

As always, we suggest you read your writings out loud, especially the letter you wrote to the child you'll never meet. Read so you can hear your own voice, and if tears come, welcome them as best you can. If tears turn into sobs, allow yourself to open to the part of you that's grieving. Witness and sit with your sadness. You might also feel relief that you can now let go of making a decision and fully say good-bye to what will never be. As you read the letter, consider to whom you're really writing. It could be the child you won't meet, but perhaps it's the little one within you who had to grow up too fast.

How did planning your celebration, ritual, or ceremony go? Was it something that came naturally to you or did you really struggle with it? This exercise is powerful, but it can be too much of a stretch for those who carry grief that feels too big to bear.

In fact, that is what happened for Samantha. She was forty-four at the time, and she'd been leaning toward a desire to have a child. Trying on *no* brought up tremendous sadness for her. She thought at first that the sadness would completely wash her away. With a little gentle coaxing, she designed a simple ritual that brought attentiveness and respect to her sorrow. She picked soft, soothing music. She placed a small bouquet of flowers next to a lit candle at the altar she had created for herself earlier in the program. She already had her childhood photos, a few mementos, and a good-luck totem there. She had nearby a box of tissues and her journal. She chose to read the letter she wrote to her young one. She struggled through it, alternating words with sobs. She didn't rush. She gave into the sadness that came. Eventually the sadness waves subsided. She wrote for a while in her journal and came to this nugget of self-truth: "I love myself and I deserve to live a full life." She noticed that this statement didn't depend on her having a child or not. Afterward Samantha felt an inner state of peace she hadn't felt before.

As you take a closer look at any pressure or judgment that revealed itself, was it familiar? Did anything new come up? It can be so difficult to untangle these things. Do the best you can by becoming more and more attentive and mindful of when you notice a pressure: *Is this mine or is it coming from another?* Internal pressures often start out as external ones. Releasing yourself from internal pressures is liberating, and the easiest way to do so is to become more aware of them when they crop up. Become your *own* best detective. Use your journal and see what insights develop over time.

Judgments can range from subtle to highly destructive. They are a bit harder to untangle. Like pressures, they can be self-inflicted or come from others. Inner judgments generally start out as external ones. As with pressures, it is important to gain the awareness necessary to untangle them. Since judgments can be deeply embedded in interpersonal relationships, it can feel like you're rocking the boat when you challenge another's judgments of you. The best first step with judgments is to gain more information. Pay attention when you feel any hurt or shame that arise when a judgment registers. What is this really? Where is it coming from? Is it familiar? Is it old? Is it new? Then you can decide what action you want to take, if any.

Birgit, for instance, didn't feel any *judgment* from her parents, but she did overtly feel the *pressure* they put on her and her husband to provide them with the grandchildren they hoped for. And she experienced judgments from extended family members. In fact she has a paternal aunt who used guilt to pressure Birgit any chance she got. It was so extreme that large family gatherings were uncomfortable for Birgit. She decided to write a firm and loving letter to this aunt asking her to respect her (and her husband's) right to choose the life and lifestyle that is right for them. She decided to send the letter after sharing it with her own parents first. Such an external action might be more blunt than your own situation warrants, but what's of key importance is that after identifying any judgments, you take care of yourself by putting them in their place as best you can.

Be Even More Curious: Optional Exercises

1. Continue to collect images and other cutouts that appeal to you. They'll be used for a project at the end of this program.

2. Notice the content, feeling, and tone of your dreams. They are keys to your unconscious.

3. This exercise is repeated from an earlier week. If you didn't do it then, check it out this week. As you think about your early childhood years, what messages did you receive (directly or unintentionally) that you might have internalized and that could still be influencing you today? For example:

I'm doing it wrong.
I'll never figure out how to do it right.
I don't matter at all.
I've never been good at making decisions.
My feelings don't count.
I'm not worth noticing.

There also might have been seemingly positive messages that were not helpful. For example:

"You're better than anyone."
"You're perfect."
"If it's a challenge, then don't do it. You'll just feel disappointed anyway."
"You don't need to push yourself. You're fine the way you are."

Take your time to think about this, make your list, and then write what feelings you have about these messages.

What to Hold Inside This Week

Wear your *no* decision for the entire week. Try to live it as if it truly *is* your decision. Let all the feelings that arise during the week surface while you try not to get in their way. Use an aid to remind yourself of your decision this week. Some women post a note on their computer to help them remember. Others wear a piece of string or yarn around their wrist. Try to live with the full, rich feeling of this choice; and if that means grieving, then grieve. If it means relief, then be relieved. We're not asking you to pretend to like it or not like it. We're only asking you to pretend that the decision has been made. Whatever feelings arise, be with them; write about them. There's no right or wrong way to be.

As this is all about your internal, uncensored process, we again remind you not to share any details (and in particular this week's decision) with others. This includes your partner, if you have one. This doesn't mean you can't share that you're in the midst of working through something that's complex and challenging. Share the bigger feelings around the work you're doing if you feel that brings welcome support. But do be cautious not to share the details so you won't have to deal with or manage someone else's feelings about your deciding not to be a mother.

This week is not about acting on anything; it's about living with and experiencing the decision of no inside of you. Be gentle with yourself. Contain inside yourself your decision and all the feelings that come up with it. Give yourself some me-time for this. Don't underestimate the power of this week's visualization even though the scenario was thrust on you. It is an extremely powerful and evocative week.

This week, as you live the *no* decision, make sure your journal is close at hand. As you move through your days, notice how the world around you looks from this vantage point of deciding not to have children. Make journal entries all week long to record your experiences and note your full range of emotions.

After seven days (and only seven days, as more time will not enhance its usefulness), go back to *I don't know*. Let go completely of the *no* decision. Pat yourself on the back for trying it on. Come back to the center, breathe the words *I don't know*, and read The Mantra a few times to help:

I don't know.

I don't know why I don't know.

It's not my fault that I don't know.

It's okay that I don't know.

I have had clarity before about many things.

My true desire matters and no one can know it better than I.

I am the definer of me.

The answers will come because they never left.

Only I can know what's true for me... It's all within me.

Self-Care

You've been exploring self-care and incorporating it into your life. Take a step back to gain perspective. How does the natural world support you? For example, the changing of seasons is a natural time to check in and notice transitions. Each season also has its particular energy, and our lives mirror this.

You may have your own idea for good self-care this week. If nothing springs to mind, see if one of these options appeals to you:

Winter – A time to draw inward and rest; a time of hibernation and incubation

You might be inspired to warm up to a fire. Spend some time cozied up near an active hearth, watching the blaze and enjoying the warmth. Curl up with a book. Enjoy a cup of hot cocoa. If you don't have a fireplace or woodstove available, seek one out at a friend's house or a nearby restaurant or café.

Spring – A time of renewal and regeneration

Plan your vegetable garden in a relaxed way. Go walking through places known for their springtime wildflowers. This is also the perfect time to start a culinary window herb garden. Sow seeds or plant your starter plants and watch things grow.

Summer – A time to kick back, be lazy, or play – in any order that suits you

Spend some time relaxing at a favorite beach and listening to the soothing sound of the waves. If you don't have access to a beach, a peaceful poolside is a good option. Run around, be silly, or make a big splash if you choose to.

Autumn – A time to let go

Light a candle. Write down three things (habits, negative thought patterns, anything else that comes to mind) on three small pieces of paper that you feel finished with or are ready to let go of. Burn each in sequence as you commit to letting go. You could say something like *I'm ready now to stop* _____. Breathe in deeply. See if you feel a difference now that you've said good-bye to _____. Be open to whatever comes next, and enjoy it.

The self-care I did for myself this week was...

You Are Not Alone

Two women share with you now their decision not to be a mother. For Danielle, it was always how she felt, while Sydney's decision came after a longer period of ambivalence and a miscarriage.

Danielle's Story

I have never, ever thought about becoming a parent. The desire was never there. At thirty-one, when I became pregnant, I recall feeling upset that it happened. After learning I was pregnant, my anxiety grew. I was anxious to terminate the pregnancy and my decision was firm. I was angry at myself for not being more careful. I was trying to finish school and not wanting that responsibility. I immediately talked with the person I got pregnant with, who was also a good friend, and we made the decision together. I did not struggle with the decision; I was relieved that I had a choice.

My choice has not affected my relationship with or attitude toward children. I teach young children and love what I do.

A year or so after my decision, I recall having some difficult times in my life. My religious upbringing moved me to question if God was punishing me for my decision. It was weighing on me. I sought advice from an older, spiritual, lifelong friend whom I trusted. She reminded me that God is not condemning. We are loved whatever choices we make. This conversation was a turning point in my life.

In early childhood, I recall my mother as caring and loving, but busy taking care of the family. I don't remember quality time with her such as reading a story with me. When I was approaching my teen years, she had an affair and separated from my father. During that time she was not there for me. It was a lonely and confusing time.

In early childhood, my father and I were buddies. He worked a lot, but often we would go fishing or enjoy rides in the country. It was my father who took me to pick my first kitten and to get my first bicycle. When the separation occurred, he faded from my life. He was in a state of depression. Our relationship was never the same.

In my early teens something happened that affected my perspective: The year was 1965 and the place was the Midwest. My older sister got pregnant at sixteen; she was sent to an "unwed mothers' home." Everything was kept quiet; no one talked to me about where my sister had gone or why. I was old enough to be told but I was left with my own thoughts. I can say that I was scared and confused. I assumed that my sister had done a bad thing.

Danielle, now in her fifties, never considered having a child. She feels she was "tested" with an unplanned pregnancy at thirty-one that she terminated. She was grateful this choice was legally available to her.

Danielle feels the impacts, positive and negative, that each of her parents played in her life. While completing the questionnaire, she discovered surprising discomfort when considering if she'd want to be a mother like her mother. What exactly was this discomfort? There exist complex layers within the mother-daughter relationship; this is true to some extent for all women. During a lifetime, these layers surface from time to time as events and circumstances allow. After working through some residual anger Danielle had toward her mother during her late teens and early twenties, could she still carry some residual hurt calling out to her now? Early hurts and unresolved conflicts often surface during midlife and the transition of menopause. Danielle's arising discomfort as she completed the questionnaire could have been a window into some part of herself that called her toward another opportunity to grow and heal.

Her father, quite a special figure in her young childhood, caused her further loss when Danielle was a teenager. Not only was she emotionally abandoned by her mother during her mother's affair, she then also lost her father as he slipped into a depression. Teen years can be hard enough, and while Danielle was trying to navigate the emotional and physical challenges of puberty, the adults in her immediate support network were not available to her – not intentionally, but the effect was the same. She and her siblings were left to their own devices. Could the separation of her parents have had a lasting impact in her life? If so, what might those influences be?

Danielle, the youngest of three children, admitted being impacted by her then sixteen-year-old sister's pregnancy. Did the pregnancy coincide with her mother's affair? Surely her sister's pregnancy and the way it was handled by the family hold importance for Danielle and other family members. Does she know what became of that child? Was the child put up for adoption? Does her sister know? Is there acknowledgement of this event today in the family?

Today Danielle has many children in her life through her vocation as a primary school teacher. She shared that if she had chosen to be a mother, she would encourage communication and self-love. No doubt this influences the way she interacts with and teaches her students. They're the beneficiaries of her awareness of what children need, based in part on her own early experiences.

Danielle acquired a vast network of male and female friends while cultivating, over decades, several very loyal friendships. In essence she created a family of friends for herself. She considers herself a spiritually oriented person and delights in the beautiful place she calls home.

She offers this advice to other women who are trying to make their choice about motherhood: "Seek personal support, and if desired, spiritual guidance also."

Sydney's Story

In my mind, a true mother is someone who wants to raise a child, not simply have one. And if that's the case, it shouldn't matter where the child came from since raising a child starts with nurturing, whether with a newborn or a twelve-year-old.

It started as an expectation – I'm supposed to have kids after I get married. Then it moved into a pressure – All my friends are having kids. Then into a burden – Oh crap, I'm getting old, my clock is ticking! Next it was a test – Let's give it a shot and see what happens. Then it was a temporary high – Shit, I'm pregnant! – which became a major reality check. I miscarried and didn't shed a tear, aside from the physical pain of it. Then it was the decision – Nope, kids aren't for us. And finally it was an emotional exhale of acceptance – We are complete without kids and really relieved and happy with our decision.

When I decided to try to get pregnant, the only person I confided in was a friend and co-worker who had two children. For some reason I felt she could help me most through it all. She was actually wonderful and supportive, and was the person who ended up taking me to the emergency room when I miscarried (it happened on *a work day). She stayed with me the whole time. The most important thing she did was ask me right after the doctor confirmed the miscarriage, "Do you feel sadness or relief?" When I immediately said, "Relief," she simply said, "There's your answer." She already knew I had been struggling with deciding, and even more so with the short-lived pregnancy.*

One other thing I did experience was accepting that I'm not as physically strong as I thought I was. After I went through the whole emergency room thing (And I swear I'm not trying to over-dramatize the miscarriage. It wasn't that bad; it happens to 20 percent of pregnant women, and mine was by no means tragic in any way. Unfortunately they made me go to the emergency room for fear of an ectopic pregnancy, which it did not turn out to be.) all I could think was, "That was just way too real." The stirrups, the sonogram machine, the ultrasound "probe" (that lasted over ten minutes), the whole physicality of it was just something I never want to experience again. I've never had a major surgery or broken a bone. I like to think I can handle pain well. I've had more dental work done than a teenager with an overbite and twenty-seven cavities! However, that type of realism and hospital-ness was just something I do not want to ever happen again, if I have a choice.

My husband was so supportive from the start. He encouraged me to make my decision even though he already knew how he felt. He said he never wanted me to resent him if he pushed either way. Later, after the miscarriage, I insisted he tell me his honest feelings since I wanted his reassurance and agreement that we were making the best decision together. As expected, he supported me fully. But more important, he admitted that he also did not want to try again. After he admitted that, it felt like the biggest weight had been lifted off my shoulders!

As for the overall decision-making approach, I definitely talked to my husband, sister-in-law, and sister about it. I spoke to my most trusted friends, whom I've known since third grade. I never really felt alone, per se, although I did feel a bit introspective and unsure that any of my close friends or family could really understand, since most of them are parents or were becoming parents. I found great honesty and candor from my best gay friend. He was the only one who truly validated my decision by telling me, "I've known both of you separately and now married, and I don't think a child is the best thing for either of you. You're both independent and like your lives just as they are." That meant the world to me that he was so honest, and I felt like my decision was okay.

My mother was very loving. She was very affectionate, always hugging and kissing me. For the most part, she was supportive of my major life choices; but she was raised in a very traditional household with conservative, Catholic parents. I know she waited until marriage to have sex, and when she found out that I hadn't, she was extremely saddened. We got past it, but I have to remember she was raised in a very different generation. My dad and I were very close; however, he was quite strict and conservative. We had curfews through college and we started working at age sixteen. By eighteen I was basically financially independent and was constantly encouraged to be a "gutsy little broad" to get what I wanted. Fortunately that did prompt me to try new things, go to new places, and travel abroad.

One important figure for me was/is my childhood piano teacher. We've been pen pals since I stopped taking lessons from her in college over sixteen years ago. She's like the wonderful aunt I never had. I actually have two aunts, but my parents have been estranged from their siblings ever since I was a child. She's amazingly understanding; she's supportive and, for lack of a better word, modern in her thinking. She is now seventy-six, although she could easily pass for fifty-nine. She has many grandchildren, but when I told her in person that kids aren't for us, she was wonderful about it. She didn't question it for a second; she just kept commenting on how rich our lives are – with each other, our careers, our fun lifestyle, and our dogs.

I also have another colleague who influenced my decision. She's in her sixties and married to a wonderful man also in his sixties and they have no children. They married later in life and they are always traveling; involved in auto clubs; have close relationships with their *siblings, nieces, and nephews; and live in an active adult community. I often said to her, "I want to be just like you when I grow up!" She's still sassy and fun and never seems beaten down, worn out, or bored. When I once asked her, "Do you ever regret not having kids?" she didn't hesitate and replied, "Yes, I do. But then I just move on from it and remember how great my life is. I wouldn't change a thing."*

I had thought it through with all the pros and cons, but I still didn't feel like I had reached a final decision until that day my friend asked me how I felt after the miscarriage. Then I definitely knew what I wanted. I actually appreciate that other women truly want to be mothers – it's just not for me. That said, my husband and I both agreed that if we happen to change our minds in a few years, we are completely open to and supportive of adoption through the state.

Sydney and her husband consciously considered several external factors when they were deciding. In no particular order they were: finances; their ages (mid to late thirties); her career (she has achieved her ultimate career goal); her small side business that is more of a hobby but provides valuable personal and creative time; lifestyle freedom; health concerns (history of family illnesses and hormone sensitivities); their satisfying sex life; outside pressures (mostly family, but also some self-pressure during their peers' child-bearing years); world overpopulation; Sydney's body image and self-awareness; their parents as potential grandparents; and finally, by the way, Sydney doesn't cook at all and feels that kids should have moms who can cook!

Sydney remembers her mother as very loving when Sydney was growing up. With the passage of time they developed more of an adult-adult relationship. Sydney can now see her mother more clearly as a real person, complete with strengths and weaknesses. Sydney readily identified qualities in her mother that she would emulate if she had decided to become a mother herself, and other characteristics that she would want to approach differently.

Her mother lives not too far away and they visit each other two or three times a year. As for their communication, Sydney shared, "I can talk to her about most things, but she's a bit self-absorbed in her advice-giving, such as 'I've been there, seen that, done that.' Ironically, it's not in a know-it-all way as much as a bragging way. I'm not sure why she feels the need to do this since we're grown children now, and it seems odd that she almost *competes* with her children. It's funny because parents should want things for their kids that they didn't have, yet my mom almost seems envious of our accomplishments and experiences at times.

"I didn't tell my mother about the miscarriage until a year later, but I was amazed at how supportive she was. She did her motherly duty of asking if I was sure, but then she just listened as I reassured her that it was the best decision for us. I asked her, 'Mom, what's the one thing every mom wants for her kids?' She replied, 'Just for them to be happy.' I responded, 'Well you can go ahead and check that box regarding me because I couldn't be happier with my life.' We both cried and hugged and it was a very important moment for me."

Week 8

Being Decisive

ଦ Choosing anything means leaving something behind. ଧ

Welcome to Week 8! Have you returned to the middle ground, the place between yes and no, with ease? If not, take some time to go there now. Draw in a few slow breaths while placing one hand gently on your heart and the other on your belly. Feel the palms of your hands rise on the in-breath and lower on the out-breath. Let your awareness follow each breath as it travels out to your hands and then back. Slow down… so you can admire yourself for taking on conscious decision-making.

How did living the *no* decision go for you last week? Were you able to embody it to your complete satisfaction? While some women get so much from this, it isn't easy for everyone. You did what you could. Let that be good enough and be assured that even if you were only able to do it half-heartedly, it still had an impact on you. You can always go back and repeat an exercise at a later point in time.

Week 8 Guided Visualization

First and foremost, there's no agenda for this guided visualization. Where your mind will go may be unknown, but you can trust your unconscious to bring forth images, ideas, and feelings. All that is offered up is related to the issue at hand, even if you might not think so.

Trust that your attentive mind will go where it needs to go. When your eyes are closed, you engage the part of your brain that isn't as easily accessed when your eyes are open. Have someone read the visualization to you or record it for you so you can listen while your eyes are closed, as its power also lies in the element of surprise. If that's not possible, make a recording yourself so you can listen with eyes closed to deepen the experience of where the visualization takes you. If you read the visualization to yourself, read it silently and slowly to give yourself time to savor the experience. Close your eyes now and then to open to the power of your imagination.

Remember that the experience you have is what matters most, and there's no wrong way to do it. Have your journal and writing tool nearby so you can record your impressions and images immediately.

To prepare, choose a quiet place where people and noise won't disturb or distract you, and a time when there's nothing else for you to do and no one who needs your attention; this time is solely for your benefit. Either sit comfortably in a chair or, if you prefer, lie down on the floor.

Being Decisive

Now that you're ready, become conscious of your breathing. Let your eyes close gently as you take a deep breath and exhale. Inhale and hold your breath for five counts. Then exhale until most of the air has left your lungs. Inhale again and slowly exhale, letting out an audible sigh through your mouth while you count silently from ten to one. Continue breathing slowly and deeply. As you breathe, you relax. Allow your natural breath to bring a deep sense of peace and well-being. Feel your body relax and let your mind free-associate. B-r-e-a-t-h-e.

You are on a journey of discovery; take a moment and be proud of your bravery.

Today you have made the following decision: You've decided you will become a mother, and you will have a child or children. Yes, it's true: *you are going to be a mom*. What is your first uncensored thought? What are you feeling at this moment? Stay with whatever you are or are not feeling. If you're feeling nothing, be with the nothingness. If there is a sensation of numbness, be with that. Continue to breathe into your feelings. This has been a difficult decision to make. However, the decision process is over. You've decided that you will become a mother. Let go of any resistance you have to embracing this decision. Give yourself 100 percent permission to try on this decision. Be welcoming to all the feelings that come with this decision. Whether you're feeling scared, joyous, resolute, elated, sad, surprised, a sense of loss, relieved, guilty, ashamed, confused, worried, content, anxious, angry, delighted, or another feeling not mentioned, welcome any and all of them.

Breathe into these feelings, letting them be in your heart and your body. Now that you've decided you're going to be a mom, who will you tell first? What will their reaction be? How do you feel about that? Is there someone you don't want to tell? How do you feel about yourself as a woman now that you've made this decision? How do you feel about assuming a role in raising a child who will be part of the next generation? What course will your life take now? What will be the first thing that changes? How do you feel about that? Who will be happy for you? Who will be unhappy with you or think you're making a mistake? Since you have decided yes, what does this change in your primary relationship if you have one? If you're single, how does this decision impact you? B-r-e-a-t-h-e. Does it change anything about your relationships with family members or friends?

Continue noticing how you feel. Keep your eyes closed while you slowly, very slowly, return to your present environment. Take your decision with you, allowing a few moments to be with your emotional and physical sensations. B-r-e-a-t-h-e.

When you're ready, slowly open your eyes and begin to write in your journal. Record your immediate thoughts, feelings, insights, and anything else you want to about this guided scenario.

Immediate Writing after the Guided Visualization

Writing immediately afterward helps concretize what occurred, so don't continue reading until you've written. Trust there's meaning in all your writing, even if you've yet to see it. Even if you feel like your experience fell flat, or you didn't have an emotional response or see images, write about how that feels.

When you finish writing down your initial responses, consider these following questions to help you flesh out your writing just a little bit more: What was it like to decide yes? Even if you saw it coming, were you also a little surprised? How does your life look now that you've decided to become a mother? Who will you tell? What does this mean for your relationship, if you're in one? What feelings do you have right this minute? Take time right now to add to your writing until there's nothing more to be expressed.

When your writing feels complete, check in with your emotional state. Are your feelings manageable? If you feel overwhelmed, follow these instructions:

Take a deep breath, then exhale as slowly as possible, letting all the air escape your lungs. Allow your body to take in a breath on its own. Continue this several times until you notice a sense of calm. Then tap your feet on the floor. Follow that by tapping the tops of your thighs with your hands. Then tap your arms with your hands. Clench your fists and then release them. These actions help reconnect you to the present and ground you. Doing this is especially important when the emotions you experience feel overwhelming or just too much for you to manage. If you need to take further action to feel reconnected or grounded in the present, stand up and stamp your feet. Then reach your hands up in the air and stretch.

Look around the room and notice objects that bring a gentle smile to your face. Is your focus where you want it to be? Are your emotions manageable? Before you continue, make sure your attention is where you need it to be.

What Happens in Week 8

This week you'll explore another choice – yes to motherhood – so you can see what comes up as you live that decision for a week. You'll look again at how to celebrate having made a decision. You'll continue to explore how ambivalence impacts your decision, and you'll discover that any choice, regardless of its outcome, invites loss even as it brings anticipation or excitement.

More on Making a Decision

We've often stressed the importance of discovering your desire first, but this week we ask you to suspend temporarily your exploration and milk your yes decision for all it's worth. You might be full of dread or anxiety about it, or you might be excited to try it on. Don't quit your job, file adoption papers, or even tell your partner that you're doing this exercise; the simulation is for the benefit of your internal, uncensored process only.

As you live your yes decision this week, remember that it's about wearing the choice of *being* a mom, not about the nuts and bolts of *becoming* a mom. If you have any anxiety or fear about getting pregnant, being pregnant, or giving birth, make sure these concerns are still tucked away in your externals jar.

One of the most important benefits of submerging yourself in yes is that you get to experience all the feelings that come with it. In particular, any fears or resistance you still harbor are likely to surface. You might wonder, *How am I going to mother a child when part of me doesn't want to?* or *How will I manage this when I don't have a partner or financial resources?* Feelings of anger could also arise.

When we imposed the yes decision, Sue felt anger flash loud and clear through her. She was surprised by this, as she thought she had already worked through a lot of this emotion, particularly the anger by-product from having her needs overrun in the alcoholic family system she grew up in. She had been leaning toward not having children, and yet this guided visualization was telling her she's going to have a child! This brought up another layer of deep hurt coated with anger – a hurt from years of having her needs and desires overridden. She'd been told repeatedly how to act and to be responsible for things beyond her years.

Once more she was being told what to do – to have a child – which went against her core feelings. Whether you feel anger, sadness, or something else, we want you to live the yes decision fully and see what comes up for you.

Choosing motherhood means different things to different women. What do *you* notice first? What are your worries? What excites you? Are there myths of motherhood that you want to debunk? Can your version of motherhood look the way you want it to? If you don't yet have answers to these questions, let them percolate this week.

Celebrating a Decision

So… you're going to be a mother! Can you imagine yourself welcoming this decision with the same degree of consciousness that you brought to last week's celebration, ritual, or ceremony? We're not talking about the kind of gathering that friends and family might hold in anticipation of the arrival of a baby, but rather a celebration marking the fact that you've undergone a long and arduous exploration and arrived at a conscious decision. It can be as simple as lighting a candle and taking some time to imagine how you want your new life to play out.

Or it can be as adventurous as what Samantha came up with; she planned a solo celebratory expedition. She hand-made the invitation and mailed it to herself. In anticipation of the event – a walk on the beach and flying a kite for her inner child, followed by a lovely picnic in her favorite area of a nearby park – she shopped for her favorite comfort foods. She also asked a favor of six long-time close friends. She asked them to write and mail a letter affirming what her friendship had meant to them over the years. On the chosen day, she packed her journal, the unopened letters, and her picnic, and drove to her favorite nature spot.

She enjoyed four glorious hours there, eating her nourishing lunch and savoring the treasured sentiments of her friends. Then she described in her journal how grateful she felt for everything.

You might find that the very process of planning your celebration, ritual, or ceremony brings up some further insights for your journal.

More on the Role of Ambivalence

When a woman thinks her indecision is a rational reaction to the *real* circumstances in her life, ambivalence can masquerade as a façade. She believes her ambivalence exists because of her external circumstances, when in fact she is struggling with several underlying issues. The circumstances of her life are much noisier in her head than the underlying issues, which she can't access. She blames herself for remaining stuck when it isn't her fault. She has trouble getting anywhere with the issue because she thinks she's ambivalent, when it's far more complex.

When we hear a woman say, "I can make a case for yes and a case for no and there are good reasons for both; I just go back and forth and get nowhere," we encourage her to examine fully the multiple threads of her indecision. When she does, a more accurate storyline usually emerges that might sound more like this: "I wish I'd started thinking about it earlier in my life. If I'd taken the time to think it through, I think I might have wanted children. Now I'm not so sure. It just didn't feel like a priority back then, and I never imagined I'd run out of time. Now I have to decide, and I feel stuck. I don't want to feel this pressure, and I feel sad and confused."

This particular woman's indecision involves a conflict between her internal yes to motherhood and her awareness that the timing is no longer optimal. She has some loss to work through: the loss of not figuring it out sooner; perhaps of not finding help earlier; and possibly also the loss of the actual opportunity to experience motherhood. She also feels the internal pressure, whether real or self-imposed, that's frequently a feature of ambivalence. As she opens herself to the grief and distress of this situation, additional unresolved losses could surface. Are you beginning to appreciate just how complex ambivalence can be?

Another element of ambivalence can be that somewhere, sometime, you were pulled away from *knowing what you desire*. You were pulled away from both the feeling of it and the actual entitlement to it. By "pulled away" we mean that not knowing was out of your control and not what you would have chosen for yourself had you been given the choice. The pain that results from being disconnected from your core self in this way can be enormous.

An example of this comes again from Sue. As a young child she had feelings, wants, and desires, but her attention was pulled away from them into her chaotic alcoholic family system. She felt she had to take on the role of trying to make things better. This meant sacrificing her internal knowing of herself to focus on outside issues: "Is Dad about to erupt?" and "How can I help Mom who is utterly overwhelmed?" Healing from the pain caused by being pulled away from her core self was a grieving process. In tending to her grief, Sue was able to reconnect with herself and develop more clarity.

Your ambivalence could also be part of a generational inheritance from your family of origin. Perhaps one of your parents had some ambivalence toward you and you unconsciously internalized the same emotional stance. Or maybe your family has an unresolved emotional issue of which ambivalence is a by-product, like Birgit, whose grandparents perished in a concentration camp. The trauma of a tragedy such as this can live deeply within a family psyche, even for generations. It is usually unspoken, yet has the power to create ambivalence that can stand in the way of making a life-changing choice, especially a decision about whether or not to have a child. The unconscious thought could be *If I have a child, something bad might happen to them.*

If ambivalence is something with which you've been struggling, what purpose or function might it serve for you? Is it possible you're hanging on to it because even if it feels like torture, at least it's familiar? Perhaps it feels too scary to move out of a false comfort zone of familiarity. If this resonates, have a look at what you gain from holding on to ambivalence.

Ambivalence is something that can be hard to grasp and equally difficult to talk about. There are likely complex and possibly competing issues at stake. It takes real courage to face the roots of your ambivalence, and it also takes courage to examine your options. Try to do it with kindness toward yourself and without shame or self-judgment.

Choice Invites Loss

In one of the first writing assignments we asked the question "As you face making this decision, what is your biggest fear?" Our intention at that time was that this question be purposefully vague; it was more important at that stage to see in what direction your mind was going to take you. Now that you've completed several weeks during which your thoughts and feelings have continued to evolve, you might have greater insight into your fears. What have you learned about them? One of the most common fears is that there will be feelings of loss or regret associated with a decision. Does that resonate with you? Who wants to face that?

The truth is that there's loss on either side of this decision. When you choose not to be a mother, you possibly say farewell to all the hopes, dreams, and fantasies associated with parenting a child. When you choose motherhood, you possibly say good-bye to the freedom and independence of the other unlived path, the one without children. Choosing *anything* means leaving *something* behind. What's more, with conscious choice there can be an initial heightened sense of loss just because you're more tuned in to your feelings.

Once a choice is made, however, something is also gained: the self-connection and empowerment that comes with conscious choice. When you proceed with your heart, mind, and eyes open, consciously accepting the associated losses, you also invite forward movement, an increase in your personal freedom, and the opportunity for growth and discovery.

Some grieving might need to happen this week. Facing your losses hurts. There isn't much more to do about this than to feel the physical pain in your heart, or elsewhere in your body, and allow the tears to come. Catharsis follows. Anticipated pain is often worse than the subsequent reality, and staying immobilized can be a defense against what feels like opening Pandora's Box. We're certain that you're capable of facing and processing any grief you experience, and we're sure it's in your best interest to do so. We designed this program to help your needed grieving happen as organically as possible. A lot occurs without you even realizing it, and grief has likely surfaced already while you've been engaging in the weekly activities.

Be Curious: Assignments for Week 8

1. I've Decided!

   You might not be happy about this decision. On the other hand, you might be completely delighted. Write whatever comes to mind – it doesn't have to make sense or be rational. Do your best to *live* the decision completely. Leave your desire aside for now. Respond to this writing prompt over the course of this week, perhaps every day:

   Be Curious: *Today I have decided to become a mother. My feelings and thoughts about this are…*

2. Dear Young One

   What do you want this child to know about you? How do you feel about their arrival? Is there anything you want to share about your decision-making? *How* this child comes to you doesn't matter for our purposes here. Your letter doesn't need to make rational sense either. Let your pen take you on an adventure while your mind and heart meander.

   Be Curious:

   Dear Young One,
   I've decided to become a mother, and this means you and I will meet in the near future. Here are some things I'd like to share with you…

3. My Own Ideal Birth

Some people are told a cherished conception or birth story over and over again. Others hear birth stories that fill them with embarrassment or humiliation. Many women have little or no information about their actual birth. This week you get to imagine the most loving and wonderful entrance for yourself. Compose the story of your birth the way you would have wanted it to be and the way you wish it had been communicated to you. Even if you already have a good birth story, how can you embellish it? Here you get to have fun and pretend. Pretending can stir up good feelings that have therapeutic effects on your body; your immune system likes them!

If for any reason you find this exercise to be painful, breathe into the feeling first. You might have to write about such feelings in your journal a bit before you can get to the writing or rewriting of your birth story.

Be Curious: *My birth story – the way I would have wanted it:*_____

4. Children's Emotions

Once you've sat with your immediate feelings about becoming a mother, take some time to consider the emotional reality of the work of parenting a child. It's particularly important to anticipate how you'll feel as you imagine your child's emotions, because those feelings will naturally trigger the parts of you that need healing. This is true for all parents. Which of your child's emotions do you think you'll fear the most? Which emotion do you feel you'll be most relaxed with? Where do you think you might need to pull in extra resources to cope with your child's emotions? Do you feel confident in your understanding of how children's emotions work?

Be Curious: *I'm most afraid that when my child expresses* _____, *I'll feel...*

Further Exploration and Discovery

When you finish this week's writing assignments, take a break before going back to read what you wrote. It's important to read your "Dear Young One" letter out loud. Then explore what you've written more deeply using the questions from the "Your Checklist for Reflection" on page 50.

Compare the experience of this week's writing to last week's, especially the letters you wrote to your young one. Which week's writing was easier for you? Was there any resistance to any part of these exercises? There is no need for judgment if there was. Just using compassion to notice and acknowledge your reluctance creates a natural opening for understanding what it's about.

Did you enjoy your ideal birth story, or did you feel lukewarm about it? Some women don't like this exercise because they realize that the only information they have about their birth is the date, place, and time. Holly's mother, on the other hand, had actually written a full account of her daughter's birth including the names of all the people involved in getting her to the hospital, the details of what happened all the way through to the birth, and a blow-by-blow description of what occurred after coming home from the hospital. It was a page long. Missing from the details, however, were any descriptions of feelings of joy. In fact, the report was void of any emotion whatsoever. Although Holly had far more information about her birth than most of us can imagine, she felt something was missing, and it was! She wanted to hear more about her mother's emotional experience.

While we cannot change the facts of the past, we can rewrite what we wish had happened and focus on the good feelings this new story brings. While focusing on the good feelings, you invite your central nervous system to rewrite (rewire) history in a way that you experience as nurturing. This contributes to your healing. It can also help open up the pathway to clarity. Rewriting your birth story can locate another piece of the puzzle you're completing for yourself. If you realize you have little actual information about your birth, you might feel inclined to find out more. Some women decide to ask their mother about their birth. If you decide this, pick your timing. Do you want to wait until the end of the program? Decide what feels right for you.

Be Even More Curious: Optional Exercises

1. Earlier in the week you envisioned a celebration to mark your having arrived at your yes decision. Take some time to write about what your celebration would look like, and don't hold yourself back.

2. Notice any dreams and write them in your journal. If a particular image from them speaks to you, draw or paint it. See where this takes you.

3. What verbal and non-verbal messages did you receive from your father (or another influential adult in your life) about becoming pregnant, having babies, or becoming a parent?

4. If an optional exercise from one of the previous weeks caught your eye but you decided not to do it then, see if it feels meaningful to do it this week.

What to Hold Inside This Week

You're going to bring up the next generation as a single mom, with a partner, or with your community. Breathe into it! Let it be so! Hold on to this decision as best you can without wavering, and view everything you can through this lens. Notice all the thoughts and feelings that come during the week and keep your journal close by.

Contain your experience to the best of your ability. Keep your yes decision to yourself so as not to open up to the feelings or thoughts of others. You'll have plenty of your own feelings, and they're the important ones right now. If you need extra help or encouragement, by all means ask for it. Let a supportive friend or partner know you're working hard on your path to clarity. Take extra time for yourself this week. Enjoy the journey when and where you can. Trust yourself.

We hope that all is going well for you as you work your way through this program. It can be natural at times to wonder if you're still on track. If at any time you feel disconnected from yourself, pick up your journal or your completed writing assignments and review what you've written to help you reconnect. Seeing how far you've come is sure to give you a boost.

Week 8 plays an important part in the overall program's success – *you get a chance to catch up with yourself after so much hard work!* The core assignments shouldn't take much time, so you'll have a natural breather and a chance to review your journal. Look for recurring themes or other discoveries. You can review the "Be Curious" sections of Weeks 1 through 7 to see if there's an activity you'd like to do again or an optional one that appeals to you. You can also just have a bit more rest and enjoy nurturing yourself.

Hold your yes decision for a full seven days (no more and no less). Holding it longer dilutes the exercise with no added benefit. Then go back to *I don't know.* Read or recite The Mantra a few times if needed. Let go of the yes decision and be proud of yourself for having embraced it as well as you did.

Self-Care

How has music served you at different times in your life? Get in touch with your inner musician. Play an instrument just for fun or select some mood music to listen to. Does a song ever pop into your head from the past? Search it out. Close the door to a room, plug in some headphones, and listen to your favorite music. Don't multitask; just listen, dance, or relax for at least fifteen minutes. Write in your journal if memories surface or if you feel something you haven't felt in a while. If music just isn't your thing, find another self-care activity this week that makes you happy.

The self-care I did for myself this week was…

You Are Not Alone

Both Susie and Molly decided yes to motherhood, Susie with her partner and Molly as a single mom. Read their stories when you choose to.

Susie's Story

My partner did not want to have a child. She said from the beginning that she did not want to have children. I had told her in the beginning that my belief was that I would love to have children but it wasn't an absolute requirement. I believed in fate and that if I ended up with someone who wanted children it would be great. But if I did not, it would be okay because it was more important first and foremost to find the person that you love. However, after two years, when my partner did not want to get married after I asked for her hand, I decided to pursue finding out what I wanted for my future. And that is when I started to think about having a child. My partner later said that she did not want to get married when I asked her because she knew I wanted to have kids. I believe it was because she was not feeling secure, safe, and happy at the time of my marriage proposal.

Since my work in the Motherhood program and our couples' therapy, my partner and I are getting married. We are also pursuing our second intrauterine insemination from a sperm donor. My partner has now said that she wants to be with me because that is what makes her happy and she will support our family if it has a child in it or not. When my partner makes a decision, she puts all her energy into it. She wants to make sure she has an equal role in the child's life. She has even said that she wants to stay home with the child so she can be a primary caregiver.

My process began with allowing myself to think of what I want for myself first and not think about what the other person wanted or needed. Through this approach I connected with my inner self. I also connected with the knowing that I would feel joy in raising a child and that I would be okay with whatever happened with my partner; that my partner would be okay. The most important factor became feeling okay with being "selfish" in asking for and pursuing what I want.

I did feel like a weight was lifted after my decision, and that while it may have seemed clear to others, I wanted to make sure I spent the time and dedicated energy to uncover all of my feelings and concerns about having a child.

While growing up, my mother ran the household. She set the rules and made sure we kept them. She was not always the most affectionate, but demonstrated her love by showing up to all my team's games and talking to all her friends about how proud she was of her children. My mom became more like a friend as I became an adult. I believe this happened because she had to grow up too quickly when she had me at eighteen years old. She has been able to live some of her young adulthood through mine. She would have supported any decision I would have made, though I believe she is happy that I've decided to pursue having a child and I would like to be a mother like she was and is. My mother is a very strong, loving, and generous person.

I grew up with a stepfather. He was the dad behind the scene while it appeared that my mom made most of the decisions. He is the quiet one, while my mom is the social one, and yet they have many things in common, things like camping and fishing.

Susie, a nurse, was forty-one when she made her decision. She felt some urgency. Her clock was ticking. She had been with her partner, soon to be spouse, for four years. Susie had role models – another lesbian couple – who had participated in a support group for lesbians trying to conceive. They shared with her the benefits received in the group. While attending couples' counseling with her partner, Susie also worked this program on her own. When she finished the program she felt she had full permission to make her decision and realize her desire – she wanted to have a child! She was clear about what she wanted and she felt excitement tinged with a bit of fear and guilt about forcing such a major issue on her partner and their relationship.

Susie's enjoyment in life today comes mostly through her relationship with her partner. She wishes she'd gone through a decision-making approach sooner. She also wishes she'd known she could ask for what *she* wanted and needed in a relationship. She has this advice for someone in a situation similar to hers: "Do *your* process first and then do couples' counseling as soon as possible. It is best to be true to yourself, not hide from what you want, and then ask for it in a loving way."

Molly's Story

I knew in my mid-thirties that I wanted children. But I wasn't behaving like someone who wanted children. I dated essentially unavailable and inappropriate men and at one point got into a serious relationship with someone who didn't want children. I would say that I was in denial for about ten years – wanting children but not being proactive about it.

Not being in a long-term, stable relationship, and struggling with financial stability, were always the two main factors that kept me from deciding to have a child. I never wanted to do it alone, and I didn't feel I had the resources. For many years my job was also a factor. I was a Waldorf teacher, work that required many long hours with little financial compensation. I also had fertility concerns. In 2003 I had surgery to remove a large uterine fibroid that would have presumably prevented pregnancy. Had I not wanted to try to get pregnant after that surgery, I would have chosen a solution much less radical. I think family pressures played into my decision too. If I was going to raise a family, I wanted to do it right, like my sister.

In my early forties I woke up and tried unsuccessfully to get pregnant with two different boyfriends, neither of whom seemed to have truly long-term potential. In fact I stayed in unhappy relationships with both of them out of desperation to have a *child. At age forty-five I made the decision to adopt on my own. It has mostly been about overcoming fear and learning to trust and believe in myself. The more I push aside the fear, the more opportunity and possibility seem to open up in front of my eyes. It feels almost miraculous.*

I have always regarded my work, teaching and tutoring children, as preparation for motherhood. I feel very maternal and adoring toward the children with whom I work. This attitude has only grown stronger since I decided to become a mom. Deciding to raise a child on my own has given me much more freedom and spaciousness in my choices regarding a partner, and as a result I am making much healthier choices.

I have grieved and grieved. I cried every day for three months when I finally accepted that I wasn't going to have a biological child, and I haven't been able to attend a baby shower since my early thirties. When my younger sister got pregnant with her first child I was thrilled – and devastated. When an old high school friend surfaced a few years ago and offered me his sperm, I went through a whole new layer of grief (it was undoubtedly too late). There is so much old sadness in me about not having a child. And now I have been matched with a little girl, at age fifty. I am astonished, thrilled, ecstatic, terrified... so many powerful emotions.

My mother died when I was thirty-two, when we were still discovering our adult relationship. She was still trying to understand me and I was still getting over my anger at the mistakes my parents made raising me. We had come to peace before she died, but I wouldn't say it was a mature adult relationship at that point. I very much want to be like my mother in the sense that she was silly, imaginative, and fun-loving. She gave me incredible opportunities. I hope to surpass her skills in understanding my daughter's unique difficulties, whatever they may be, and staying connected through difficult times.

Molly had to make practical decisions that involved changing careers so she could afford to be a single mother. She has attention deficit disorder, and this has made it, in her words, "very difficult to plan my life to see what is coming down the pike, so to speak." She has had to let go of expectations of how it was supposed to be. She found that she could do it her way, and she is doing it her way. Does she still have concerns? Sure. But they are not blocking her path. When one of Molly's close friends adopted a daughter from Nepal, Molly realized that she, too, could follow through on her wish to become a mother.

Molly feels that she was not strongly attached to her mother and that her mother's tendency toward mild depression meant that she was at times not available to her young daughter. Yet she was also "fun-loving and nurturing, even though she didn't understand my sensitivities and difficulties with sensory processing and attention." Molly's father was less predictable – a mix of adoring, charismatic, and fiery, with a tendency toward reactivity. He also didn't have a good sense of boundaries. He and his daughter were very close, and they argued with each other often. Molly is the middle one of three sisters. She felt both subtle and not-so-subtle judgment from her sisters, especially one of them, over the years. Since Molly has been matched with a child, she senses this sister is coming around and will be both committed and loving to her adopted niece.

If Molly could go back and change something about her choice, she would have made better relationship decisions and so had the option of getting pregnant and having children with a partner at an earlier age. The wisdom of age has taught her many things; one of the most important is that imperfection is good enough. She attracted many wonderful people to her life and created a nourishing support system. She has good friends she can count on. She has work she truly enjoys. Her biggest struggles include maintaining financial stability and balancing the different areas of her life.

Molly said that as she was going through her process of deciding, "I felt alone and supported, empowered and terrified, informed and stupid as hell, and I still do. But more and more empowered." What is her advice for others who are facing their choice? "Be brave! Follow your deepest heart's desire! Create the life you want and don't wait for someone to hand it to you on a platter."

Week 9

Gaining Perspective

cs We all have uncharted territories within. The most important reason to explore yours is that, once discovered, they give you direct access to your inner richness, vitality, and freedom. ♒

Y ou spent last week living with yes. How was that? Check in with yourself. Were you able to live fully the decision to become a mother without taking actual action steps? Perhaps you experienced firsthand how making a choice invites loss no matter what path you choose?

Do you feel like your journey is going well overall, or are you experiencing discomfort or even inner chaos from time to time? At this point in the program, women often tell us they feel like they know less than when they started. If so, take comfort; you're not alone. What can help is to take a comprehensive look at the writing you've done since Week 1. What stands out? What themes emerge repeatedly? What insights – glaring, subtle, or barely lurking inside your conscious grasp – have you gained? Don't try to overthink anything; just accept what your intuition tells you.

It's important to remember that most women don't find the Motherhood-Is it for me? program to be linear, so any temporary frustration or confusion is natural and not an indication that things aren't going well. So long as you've been following the weekly instructions, you can trust that you're on track. Clarity will come.

If you haven't yet fully let go of the yes decision, use The Mantra to do so now. Come back to embracing *I don't know* as best you can and open up to a new week of continued discovery.

Week 9 Guided Visualization

Even if you don't fully understand what comes up for you during the next part of this adventure, trust that your attentive mind will go where it needs to go. When your eyes are closed, you engage the part of your brain that isn't as easily accessed when your eyes are open. Have someone read the visualization to you or record it for you so you can listen while your eyes are closed, as its power also lies in the element of surprise. If that's not possible, make a recording yourself so you can listen with eyes closed to deepen the experience of where the visualization takes you. If you read the visualization to yourself, read it silently and slowly to give yourself time to savor the experience. Now and then, close your eyes so you can open to the power of your imagination.

Remember that the experience you have is what matters most, and there's no wrong way to do it. Have your journal and writing tool nearby so you can record your impressions and images immediately.

To prepare, choose a quiet place where people and noise won't disturb or distract you, and a time when there's nothing else for you to do and no one who needs your attention; this time is solely for your benefit. Either sit comfortably in a chair or, if you prefer, lie down on the floor.

A Surprise Detour

Now that you're ready, become conscious of your breathing. Let your eyes close gently as you take a deep breath and exhale. Inhale and hold your breath for five counts. Then exhale until most of the air has left your lungs. Inhale again and slowly exhale, letting out an audible sigh through your mouth while you count silently from ten to one. Continue breathing slowly and deeply. As you breathe, you relax. Allow your natural breath to bring a deep sense of peace and well-being. Feel your body relax and let your mind free-associate. B-r-e-a-t-h-e.

You've been presented with a unique and compelling opportunity! You received a gold-embossed invitation. It says that you've been selected to be a delegate on a special journey. It asks you to come immediately to a lush outdoor setting. When you arrive there, you meet two very friendly and competent scientists tending to a compact spacecraft.

To prepare you for your special journey, your vital signs are checked, and you are declared healthy and fit for travel. The door to the craft is opened by one of the scientists while the other points out the interior features to orient you and help you feel completely comfortable.

They tell you to relax, get in, get comfortable, fasten your seat belt, and, most important, truly relax with a capital *R*. Everything you need for this journey is either with you or within you. The scientists take care of the mechanical and technical details. They answer all your questions. You are ready. They close the door and off you go.

A few minutes after gaining orbit you feel a slight rumble, but otherwise all you notice is how still and peaceful it is as the spacecraft continues its journey. There's a digital readout that seems to display calendar dates. You notice it has become very active and is spinning random dates. It dawns on you that you are in a time machine. Just as you realize this, you feel a slight jolt as you land. The door to the time machine opens and you notice the date on the digital dial [If you're recording this visualization or reading it aloud for someone else, please add twenty years to this year and say that year in the next clause rather than "twenty years from today's date."]; it reads twenty years from today's date.

Unfasten your seat belt and get out. You are now in your life as it will be on this date in the future. Where are you? What do you notice about your surroundings? Is anyone with you? Who is there? Who is not there? How are you feeling about being catapulted into the future? As you look at your future, what is your life like? What are *you* like? Are you feeling peaceful, anxious, content, scared, calm, worried, happy, relaxed, resigned, excited, curious, or some other feeling not mentioned? Do you have a combination of feelings?

Before it's time to say good-bye to the future and return to the present, check out anything you feel you need to. Do you want to visit or talk to anyone in particular? Is there something you want to see? Are you curious about anything? Take a few moments to explore your future.

Now it is time to return to the spacecraft and say good-bye to this future. All you need to do is get back inside, close the door, and fasten your seat belt. After the door closes, you will return to the same spot from where the spacecraft launched. As you journey back, what are your thoughts about what you just experienced? Were you surprised? Were you expecting something to be there that wasn't there? Do you feel changed by what you witnessed or felt?

The spacecraft has landed. You are now in present time. Notice what it feels like to be back. Unfasten your seat belt, open the door, and step out. As you walk away from the time machine, it quietly vanishes. Breathe.

Keep your eyes closed while you slowly return to your present environment, allowing a few moments to be with your emotional and physical sensations. Breathe.

When you're ready, slowly open your eyes and begin to write in your journal. Record your immediate thoughts, feelings, insights, and anything else you want to about your experience.

Immediate Writing after the Guided Visualization

Your immediate writing concretizes your experience; those first few moments are precious, and their richness diminishes as you move further away from what just happened. Write now, before you continue reading.

How did it feel to be catapulted into the future without notice? Did you feel anxious not knowing where you were going? Did anything else cause you to worry? Was it exciting? Were you surprised by who was or wasn't there when you arrived? Had anyone been born? Had anyone died? How would you want to change anything you saw?

Whatever you envisioned in this future has meaning even if it's out of your grasp. Some women see a baby or have a *sense* of a son or daughter who has gone off to college. For some it's very clear that there is no child at all. And some see that they're going to be fine no matter what.

How was it to come back to the present? Were you relieved? Sad? Did you feel compelled or inspired to make changes in your current life based on your time travel experience?

This particular guided visualization yields a wide range of feedback, everything from "Not a lot happened" to "Wow! That was powerful!" You certainly aren't alone if you felt uncomfortable visiting your future. The unknown can bring up fear, and that is only natural. Whatever came up for you, remember that you are still turning over puzzle pieces and gathering information. Know that there isn't only *one* possible future or *one* particular way to feel about it.

If you didn't get a clear picture of anything in particular, you can still derive great value from writing about whatever you noticed. What sensations or feelings were you aware of? Did they feel familiar? Allowing yourself to explore fully even the most seemingly unrelated bodily sensations, emerging thoughts, or vague images could very well lead you to your most important discovery. If you feel inspired to work with an emerging thought or image – even if it feels at first like it might be a diversion – trust the impulse.

Here's how using writing as a technique worked for Holly, who initially felt she hadn't done the visualization correctly. "I saw nothing, just total darkness with maybe a hint of light," she wrote. Curious about this state of nothingness, Holly continued to explore her response to the guided visualization until she realized she didn't like to think about her future. She was so afraid to fail that she didn't put herself in situations in which she might fail.

Holly approached life with the attitude of going with the flow rather than making clear decisions. It was easier for her to live her life this way. She intuitively wrote down the statement she lived by: "I go with what is." She investigated the upside and the downside of this statement and came to understand her difficulty of growing up under the burden of tremendously high expectations from her parents. Holly had internalized their implicitly critical message: "You can't do anything right." It was downright scary for her to think about trying and possibly failing, so she typically preempted that possibility altogether by "going with what is." Holly took her writing a step further by describing what failure meant to her. By the time she finished writing, she had gained important information about herself that would have a direct bearing on deciding whether or not to become a mother.

When your writing feels complete, check in with your emotional state. Are your feelings manageable? If you feel overwhelmed, follow these instructions:

Take a deep breath, then exhale as slowly as possible, letting all the air escape your lungs. Allow your body to take in a breath on its own. Continue this several times until you notice a sense of calm. Then tap your feet on the floor. Follow that by tapping the tops of your thighs with your hands. Then tap your arms with your hands. Clench your fists and then release them. These actions help reconnect you to the present and ground you. Doing this is especially important when the emotions you experience feel overwhelming or just too much for you to manage. If you need to take further action to feel reconnected or grounded in the present, stand up and stamp your feet. Then reach your hands up in the air and stretch.

Look around the room and notice objects that bring a gentle smile to your face. Is your focus where you want it to be? Are your emotions manageable? Before you continue, make sure your attention is where you need it to be.

What Happens in Week 9

You've now done a great deal of foundational work, and this week the pace starts to pick up a bit. You'll spend more time with the future you visited, noticing your reactions and the beliefs that inform them. Then you'll explore emotions within you that you might have been avoiding. These emotions might be the best parts of yourself even though they are hidden away. You'll also be introduced to a powerful tool that will help you turn fear or anxiety into a sense of freedom and well-being.

Gaining Perspective

As you imagine your future, do you feel that you're entitled to have things go the way you want them to? Is there anything you wish you could want in your future that you don't feel okay about wanting or that seem impractical or unrealistic to want? Many of us were raised to believe that it's self-indulgent to desire something specific for ourselves. Like Holly, you might have internalized the message that you don't matter and your needs and desires come second, if at all. If that's the case, you likely don't find it easy to project yourself forward in time and allow yourself to think about things you might want. As you become more conscious of how this limiting belief – that you don't deserve to want what you want – might have inhibited many of your life choices to date, you become better able to invite in dreams for your future.

Start small. Allow yourself to dream about some inconsequential pleasure, even if the exact details remain vague or out of focus. Approach dreaming as a daily practice, building to bigger and more elaborate fantasies of what you want. Revisit the suggestion from Week 4 to focus on the *sensation* of wanting and desire. This is a perfect lead-in to dreaming on a larger scale. When you're able to say yes to a big dream or future possibility, whether or not you know how it will come about, you move toward it and life tends to meet you, often filling in the details. Even if you don't yet have any answers, this is a good time to begin to wonder what you want your life to look like going forward.

Uncharted Territory

Think about the future that presented itself during the guided visualization. Did you bump into emotions there that you've been avoiding, either consciously or unconsciously? Did anything come up during the visualization that touched a tender place inside – perhaps something that you don't want to feel or something you didn't even realize existed? This is not at all uncommon.

This happened to Sue when she looked into her future and envisioned a partner she hadn't yet met. She felt inexplicably sad. After she explored this response, she discovered a deeply buried pocket of hurt that she'd been harboring for over thirty years. Sue always thought she hadn't been noticeably affected by her parents' amicable divorce. But even though she'd seen her father regularly after the split, the disruption was traumatic for her. As Sue courageously acknowledged her pain, it finally dissolved into a deep compassion for this younger, wounded part of her. By opening herself to this previously uncharted territory within, Sue developed a greater capacity to trust and take more risks with others. Her determination to heal would impact her choice of whether to become a mother, and it would be important as she continued her search for a partner in life.

Samantha, too, bumped into an emotional response that beckoned deeper exploration. It came up during Week 5 of the program as she delved into better understanding her relationship with her mother. She felt a "fog" of numbness move in and linger. Remember that Samantha's mother struggled with mental illness and was emotionally unavailable to her. Although Samantha's Aunt Bea stepped in often with love and great affection, young Samantha still internalized messages about what a mother is that were limited and inadequate. Over the years Samantha developed a great deal of unconscious shame around the inadvertent negative thoughts she had about motherhood and what it might mean for her to be a mother. By opening to the numbness via the writing assignments in this program, and unraveling the meaning she attached to what it means to be a mother, she became aware that she did, in fact, possess many mothering qualities. Discovering that she knew a lot about being maternal – both how to care for herself and how to nurture others – was a crucial revelation that would inform Samantha's choice about motherhood.

We all have uncharted territories within. The most important reason to explore yours is that, once discovered, they give you direct access to your inner richness, vitality, and freedom. Once mapped out, they free up energy that is available for other pursuits. What do you know of your own as-yet-unexplored tender places? What feels taboo to approach or just too downright painful to try to access? Even if you feel you're not quite ready to jump in and explore these areas inside, it's helpful to be aware that they exist. Acknowledging in advance that you're carrying around something that still needs some attention makes a difference when the time comes to open up to it.

Your uncharted territories are waiting for you. Cast off and set sail toward them.

Reframing Perceptions

Are you someone who sees a half-empty glass or is your glass always half full? Isn't it interesting that the exact same amount of water in this metaphorical glass can be perceived differently even by the same person within a short passage of time? Perceptions are just that: perceptions. They aren't fact or reality. How we come to our perceptions is really,

really important, as it directly affects what and how we feel. You can have more control over your feelings than you might realize. What if, through practice, you could train yourself to move toward thoughts that bring you benefits like enhanced well-being and a more positive frame of mind?

News flash! You actually *can* exert some control over the negative thought patterns that often accompany uncomfortable or painful feelings. While there are still many mysteries about how the brain works, neuroscientists and psychologists have discovered some of the brain's amazing regenerative capabilities. We now know that through practices like self-compassion and meditation we can make positive changes in our neural pathways. These can be measured as changes in brain activity. In essence, we rewire our brains as we heal.

This week we invite you to use your focused attention, or *mindfulness*, to guide you and your thoughts to a more steady inner state of being. As you develop this practice, you help your brain generate better neural connections that allow you to foster hope and positivity with less effort than before. You more easily see the glass as half full!

Most important, *reframing perceptions* can help you tease out negative thought patterns that might be holding you back from making your motherhood decision. The more you can remain in the here and now, feeling good about the positive aspects of your life, the more clear your decision will become.

Let's see how this works: Fast-forward and imagine it's a year from now and you're reviewing the past twelve months. You're especially interested in highlighting thoughts of what felt good. As you take stock of the good that happened, you shape perceptions. Your brain is responsive to such exercise in the same way a muscle is; when you use your brain to redirect your thoughts or shape your perceptions, you move against the tide of old negative thought patterns. It can feel difficult in the beginning, and your brain might even hurt a little. But as you practice this power of positive thinking, your new "muscle" for reframing perceptions strengthens. Your year-in-review might look something like this:

I enrolled in that photography class I've been thinking about for some time and have already attended six classes. I'm inspired by the creativity of the other students and have come up with a great idea for my final project. I've also gained greater clarity around the issue of children and I'm not tormented by it any more. My communication with my sister has become easier, and I can say what I feel more clearly to her.

It's as easy as that. Thoughts redirected and perceptions reframed!

You can also practice reframing perceptions by inching toward feeling good step by step or thought by thought. One thought at a time, gently invite your thoughts toward things that feel good to you. Over time your positive thoughts about the good things, and the corresponding feelings in your body, will change your brain's chemistry. You'll see the glass as half full more frequently. Here's how a thought-by-thought inner monologue might look:

I'm feeling discouraged. I don't like feeling discouraged. I feel sad when I feel discouraged. I'd like to feel something better. I wish I could feel better right now. I look forward to feeling better. I'm remembering that yesterday, when I saw that butterfly hover over those flowers in the garden, it brought a smile to my face. As I remember this, I feel better. I'm also aware that I felt better this morning than I do now. I was happily enjoying my tea with the sun shining in through the window. I felt a sweet freedom as I drank my tea. I'm feeling less discouraged now as I remember this.

The practice of reframing perceptions works in the same way as The Mantra; it gradually eases you away from unhelpful negative thoughts and encourages you to appreciate the present moment. It guides you to the awareness that things are good, or at least okay, right now. It might be a while before you can access the focused attention required to be with what is happening to you at the moment. This *does* take time to achieve, so please be patient. With practice, though, you gain a greater capacity to choose how you want to experience your life, and at the very least have a choice about feeling better sooner than later. You can practice in this week's first writing assignment.

Be Curious: Assignments for Week 9

As you do your assignments, keep in mind that they don't need to be rational, nor do they need to be written in complete, linear sentences. Let your mind and heart free-associate while you let your pen or fingertips take you on an adventure. Unleash your unconscious and let it flow uncensored.

1. My Journal Entry

    Imagine yourself one year into your future and see if you can get a real sense of being there. If it helps, close your eyes so you can sink into the picture more completely. Once you arrive, look back over the last twelve months, visualizing what pleased you. Don't focus on disappointments or longings. Give yourself over to your imagination and focus on what delighted you during this fantasy year. Now describe your year-in-review. There are no shoulds in this writing assignment; if you need to tweak it to make it work for you, do so. It's also fine to write in general terms when being precise doesn't feel beneficial.

Below are five examples of what your journal entry might look like. Notice in each case the positive tone.

> *I love that we finally figured out our decision about children. We saw a couples' therapist for a while and got help with having a more connected relationship. Our life together is better than ever.*

> *My career is taking off and I'm working toward developing myself so I can move into a management position. I know now what my next steps are.*

> *I am now happily pregnant, and we've decided not to learn the sex of the baby.*

> *I'm happily settling into my life without children, and the traveling I did this past year felt great. I'm caring less and less what other people think.*

> *It doesn't feel bad anymore that I don't know. I trust that my desire will become known to me in time. What matters most to me now is that I feel happy inside regardless of whether or not I have children.*

When you're ready, open your journal and begin writing.
Journal entry dated one year from today:

> *As I look back over the past year, I'm pleased to notice…*

2. Time Travel

    Imagine getting back inside the spacecraft from the guided visualization, but this time you program the dial for only five years into the future. Close your eyes and feel the spacecraft move forward in time. After it lands, get out and look around. What do you see? What do you notice in your body? How do you feel?

    Repeat the exercise going ten years into your future. As you compare your five- and ten-year futures, how different are they? How similar?

    Create depictions for your two futures with collage, drawing, or painting, or let yourself write about them and see where your imagination takes you.

3. Body Pie

    Most women have a negative view of their body image at some point in their lives. Advertisers and the media frequently and outrageously target women, especially young women, by conveying an ideal that isn't remotely realistic. Overt and subliminal oppression of women is widespread. Creating a "body pie" can help you identify and uncover negativity about your body you've internalized *(through no fault of your own)* that might be clouding what feels true for you. It's also possible that you are afraid of passing on hurts you received or that you fear the physical aspects of pregnancy. At the very least this exercise shows you what your relationship to your body has been over your life so far.

On the largest piece of paper you can find, draw a circle and divide it into eight pie-shaped sections. Starting at the top, number the outside edge of each pie piece in six-year increments (1–6, 7–12, 13–18, 19–24, 25–30, 31–36, 37–42, and 43–48). If your current age is over forty-eight, number your pie pieces in seven-year increments instead.

Start with the yummy pie piece that holds your current age (for example, if you're thirty-eight now, write in the slice labeled 37–42), and write down any thoughts or feelings you have about your body and your body image. If you run out of space, don't stop yourself. Carry any material that belongs to that pie piece over to a separate sheet of paper. When you finish with your current age slice, move steadily back in time in six-year intervals until you've completed every section of your body pie.

Let your body speak directly for itself as best you can. Include everything that flows out of your consciousness – events such as the onset of menstruation, injuries, and signs of aging in addition to body-image perceptions. Include bodily sensations that brought pleasure and others that caused pain. You might not have body memories for some of the pie pieces, and that's okay. Do your best.

Some women decide to give a title to each of their sections, such as "Anticipation" for 7–12, "Late Dormancy" for 31–36, and "Emergence" for 37–42. Take it a step further and try to imagine what your body might say in the pie piece(s) you haven't yet reached. Earlier program participants have written comments like:

37–42: "My most recent period is one where I felt so in myself. I had the usual premenstrual syndrome, but it didn't make me feel as edgy. If anything, I'd say that my womanliness is maturing nicely. I feel good about my body now. It's been a long haul to get here. I had a dream about eggplants and wonder if it was telling me something."

25–30: "I binged and purged for six years during this time until I was finally able to seek some help. My body was a battleground for all the pain and rage I'd bottled up for too long. I'm grateful that I found the help I needed, and I'm grateful to my body that it functions well even after this treatment."

19–24: "I struggled to like myself, and my body. This was a difficult time, and I found myself pregnant with someone I didn't even really like. My body felt bad. I felt ashamed. I aborted the pregnancy at nine weeks and never told anyone, not even my best friend."

13–18: "My first period arrived without warning on the evening of my eighth grade graduation party. It was confusing to me in that I was happy it finally arrived – I was already fourteen years old – but I wanted to wear my swimsuit because it was a summertime pool party."

13–18: "My first kiss... it was so sweet. I tingled all over."

7–12: "My brother used to sneak into my room and touch me in places I knew he shouldn't have. I felt so alone and so scared, and I never told anyone. He was someone I had looked up to and then my trust was betrayed."

7–12: "I loved how my body felt as I danced around the living room. I felt so strong, so free, and so pretty in my dance clothing."

Further Exploration and Discovery

After you complete this week's assignments, take a day or two to gain perspective, and then go back and reread what you wrote. Use "Your Checklist for Reflection" on page 50 to help amplify themes and gain further insight.

As you read the journal entry from the year-in-review, notice whether you were specific or general. Did you let yourself go there easily? Was the focus on children or was it elsewhere – perhaps on work, travel, or education? Was this exercise fun? Did it feel scary to read out loud and listen to your year-in-review? Were you able to keep the focus on what pleased you? Can you see yourself using this kind of creative journal-writing regularly? Did you practice reframing perceptions?

As you saw yourself five and ten years down the road, was that more difficult than seeing yourself twenty years down the road? How do you feel as you look at your nearest future – five years from now? Some women report that it is sobering. If you are one of them, don't let it worry you. Look on this as an opportunity to think about what might need your attention now. You might also identify in your nearest future some next steps to take. If you created collages, paintings, or drawings, place them where you can view them from time to time. See what develops from the imagery.

As you wrote from the perspective of your body, what connections were made? Were there any big revelations or insights? How have your feelings about your body changed over the course of your lifetime? Are there periods of time that you don't remember well or at all? If you bumped into a body-based memory that still holds pain for you, view this as an opportunity to bring loving attention to that place. You and your body deserve to heal. Keep your pie-shaped diary as a permanent record of your body's timeline. You can refer to it anytime and add to it later.

Be Even More Curious: Optional Exercises

1. Get inside your personal time machine and visit the past. Pick a time in your life that you recall was confusing or painful. Program the dial to that date and go back in time. What do you see? Who's there with you? What do you want to change? Make it so. It's very important that you treat this exercise lightly. It isn't meant to bring up self-judgment or shame. Don't blame yourself for something that was an adult's responsibility. However, if you're going back in time to forgive yourself because you felt responsible for something that wasn't your fault, by all means do so. Then return to the present and write in your journal about that period as if it happened the way you would have wanted.

2. Strengthen your ability to reframe perceptions through writing. Use this incremental method: Write down your current (negative) thought followed by a series of increasingly positive, life-affirming ones.

3. The Honoring Ceremony

If you've had miscarriage(s), stillborn(s) or abortion(s), this week is a good time to work through any unresolved grief, shame, or regret you might still be harboring about this experience. It's not too late for healing, even if many years have passed.

Slowly scan your body to see if there are any places inside that still hurt. What do you notice? Is there an ache in your heart, in your belly, or in your pelvis? Perhaps there is fear blocking the way to a beneficial grieving process. Tears are crucial to your well-being – emotionally and physically. Shedding tears to grieve a lost embryo or baby can bring healing catharsis. Perhaps writing a letter to that part of you that hurts will open up the wound so it can speak and allow the healing to occur. Perhaps you sense that writing a letter to the lost little one will bring resolution and peace.

For many people, holding an honoring ceremony or creating an honoring ritual is the step that makes the difference and helps them move on. If you consider having a ceremony to honor your grief (or other feelings), allow yourself ample time – at least one hour. Begin gathering what you need or want for this ceremony. If you are not sure how to start, here are some suggestions:

Find yourself a candle, a small bouquet of fresh flowers, and either a life-sized doll wrapped in a blanket, a special totem that you already have, or one you make to represent the being(s) that is(are) lost to you. Write a letter to your unborn child telling them everything you need them to know and everything you need to say to release the hurt inside. If there is more than one to grieve, write a letter to each. Place the candle, flowers, doll or totem, and letter(s) in a special, sacred place. This is your healing ceremonial altar.

Begin the ceremony by lighting the candle. If it suits you, have some soft, soothing music playing in the background. Take in the beauty of the fresh flowers. Place your doll or totem on a soft pillow. If you're grieving for more than one loss, set up each on its own pillow. Place each doll or totem's letter next to it.

Sit comfortably, and if it feels right, invite your circle of support that you created in Week 1 to join you. Breathe deeply a couple of times. Relax your shoulders, your heart, and your belly. Imagine the most healing setting surrounding you; it can even be your comfort-within space that you established in Week 1. It can be the most beautiful of natural settings, a field of wildflowers, a tranquil lake, or whatever else brings you a sense of peace and solace. As you picture this setting surrounding you, say these words or other favorite or special words that bring you comfort and support: *I am complete. I have beauty and wisdom, and my heart knows how to heal itself.*

When you're ready – don't rush it – read aloud the letter you've written. Hold your hand over your heart as you do so. After you read the letter, pick up your doll or totem and hold it tenderly, lovingly, in your arms. Hug the being closely and give yourself a hug as well. Say good-bye to this being, closing with sentiments of love and appreciation as you feel them. Sit as long as you want to, taking in the sights, sounds, and feelings of the moment. If you have more than one loss to grieve, repeat the letter-reading and hugging for each. When you feel you have finished, gently blow out the candle and feel appreciation for yourself. If you invited members of your circle of support, thank them for being there for you and say good-bye to them.

Let this ceremony mark the beginning of the opening up of your heart – the opening up of your grief, love, sorrow, shame, and whatever else is harbored there. Allow yourself to open fully to your feelings and self. Trust that your heart will guide you through. It will.

If for any reason this ceremony feels like too much to bear and you want more guidance, find a competent professional to help support you through it. Healing these wounds is well worth it. You are worth it!

What to Hold Inside This Week

This week try to consider yourself as your best friend. Be extra gentle with yourself. See if you can greet an anxious or fearful moment that comes your way with real tenderness – the kind of tenderness you would have if comforting your best friend or a small child who has fallen off her bicycle.

As opportunities arise, practice reframing perceptions. You might even want to go out of your way to find situations that you anticipate will create anxious or scared feelings, and practice turning them into something that feels more hopeful. Place reminder notes in places you visit, and return daily to remind yourself that this technique is available anytime and anywhere.

See if you can let yourself move closer to your uncharted territories this week. Challenge yourself as much as you can without becoming overwhelmed. If you start to feel this happening, use your journal to record your thoughts and feelings. Or, to explore what your territories might look like, draw a map of them. Be as creative as you can. Create a legend or key that identifies various qualities (for example, squiggly lines = anxiety). You might decide to seek professional help to navigate your uncharted territories. Asking for and getting help are signs of strength and courage, not weakness.

Does it help you to learn that most women experience anxiety – sometimes intolerable anxiety – at this stage of the program? If this starts happening to you, hold on, relax, and breathe deeply. You *are* on track. If you feel internal chaos, it means *the healing process is at work*. You are on the road to clarity, and believe it or not, there are benefits in discomfort, because anxiety almost always occurs before some aspect of certainty breaks through. Keep in mind that it's always darkest before the dawn. Discomfort arises when we take risks, and emotional risk-taking means there is positive movement. Try to be gentle, patient, and loving to yourself always, but especially now.

And finally, appreciate yourself for all your tenacity and hard work. You are precious, so treat yourself accordingly.

Self-Care

In the spirit of exploring uncharted territories, we offer you two possibilities for self-care this week. Try one, both, or come up with your own creative alternative.

1. Visiting a Place You Haven't Been Before

    Give yourself permission to visit a place you've always wanted to visit but haven't yet, and make it happen! See if you can let yourself go without planning too much, so that serendipity has a chance to step in. If you feel daring, try using an alternate mode of transportation than what you're accustomed to (train, bus, auto, boat, etc.).

2. A Weekend Excursion

    Before we used cars mainly to get around, some folks used theirs to take leisurely Sunday drives in the country "just because," or perhaps to visit friends or family. Get in your car, pick a destination, or at least a general direction, and start out, giving yourself lots of time to meander. Really take in the landscape as you pass through it. Enjoy!

    The self-care I did for myself this week was...

You Are Not Alone

As you read the stories of Cecilia and Aviva, you'll be struck by their differences. Yet while these two women ended up in very different places, they both followed a consistent inner knowing throughout their lives.

Cecilia's Story

I never really thought to be a mother. It never occurred to me to think I would bear a child myself. I never thought I could physically cope with being pregnant. I always thought in terms of caring for the children of other people. I cannot explain why. I like children, even though in general I am not very warm with them (not playful, engaging, etc.).

My mother lost her husband, my father, in an accident when she was forty-five, after fifteen years of happy marriage and three children. I think she was deeply shocked and quite anxious about our future. She expressed this by how she was nearly always irritated and nervous, especially with me, her eldest child. As I grew older, things became easier between us. I've come to understand that she tried for many years to do her best at playing the two roles, both father and mother. Even so, there have been episodes between us that I cannot forgive.

My father was nice, good tempered, and hard-working. I was fourteen when he died, and I missed him a lot even though I seldom talked about him.

I was my paternal grandmother's favorite, maybe because I looked much like her. She died one year before my father's unexpected death. My brother and sister were *physically similar to my mother's family, and my mother treated them differently from me, or at least I felt there was a difference and I suffered for it. After both my grandmother and father were gone, I felt even lonelier.*

My mother had several miscarriages. From time to time I have a memory come to me where I see my mother terrified of dying because of excessive bleeding. This memory must come from a time when I was quite young, perhaps less than three or four years of age. My mother has never asked me why I have no children myself.

I have never grieved my choice not to have children, not even when my partner died. Everybody told me then, "A pity you have no children," but I never understood the connection between these two events.

I don't see my brother, who is only one year younger than I, very often. He has a son of fifteen now, but as I was busy caring for my husband, who was ill for seven years, I did not closely follow this nephew when he was growing up. Today he is very much like my brother and quite different from myself in character, tastes, and his way of living. With my sister, who is eight years younger than I, the relationship is quite different. She divorced her first husband and is now married to someone else. She suffered a lot emotionally and psychologically before her divorce and sought professional help from a psychologist. Since this period, we speak a lot and have become much more like friends than siblings.

Cecilia is in her late fifties. She has been in a relationship with a seventy-year-old widower for several months and works as a secretary in an urban area. Cecilia always knew that she did not want to be a mother and felt she had permission to take that path. When she was younger she chose not to date men very much, and she was extremely diligent about birth control.

When asked if she would want to be a mother like her mother was (had she decided to have children herself), she said she would have wanted to behave in a way *opposite* from how her mother behaved. This speaks to pain that goes back a long time. As the eldest, Cecilia probably received the brunt of her mother's despair, frustration, grief, anger, or whatever else her mother was going through after being widowed with three young children. At the time, although there was financial support given to widows, there wasn't much in the way of emotional support available.

Would Cecilia feel differently about wanting to have children if her personal story had been easier or happier? Who knows? Only Cecilia knows best what is right for her. She had no role models available to her for the life she has chosen to live, but she did have a couple of girlfriends she could talk to. They were curious about and interested in her choice not to have children.

Cecilia said that her deceased husband was more of a son than an equal. He agreed with her decision to be child-free, but she suspects it is because he liked being the only one competing for her attention. Her current partner has an adult daughter who recently gave birth to a daughter of her own; yet despite this, Cecilia finds that she and her partner are in a different phase of their life, one in which children don't have a big presence anymore. Most enjoyable activities now include spending time in nature and spending time with friends. She likes her life as it is, and strives to live in the present moment without thinking too much about the future or the past.

Aviva's Story

The desire to have children was always there. The choice was more about the timing, the "when to do it" part. I made that choice based on several factors: Having a career that allowed me to support a child. Feeling emotionally ready – because after my difficult childhood I wanted to work on myself long enough so I wouldn't transfer any unresolved baggage to my child; I wanted him to have a better emotional life as a child than I had had. And I wanted a partner. I had my first child at thirty-eight. I waited until the last possible moment to have my child, although it's possible I could have naturally conceived in my forties.

I was twenty-two when I began thinking seriously about becoming a mother. I had been married two years to my first husband at the time. I knew I wasn't ready to become a mother at twenty-two, but I knew I wanted to at some undetermined point in time. Between wanting to become a mother at twenty-two and actually becoming one many years later, the evaluating and reevaluating never stopped. All in all, it took me sixteen years to move through the decision-making process.

I grew up being the caretaker of three younger siblings. I did my best not to resent them for the way my childhood was taken from me, but I emerged from that period exhausted from caring for children and wanting some of my own time. I was married by twenty and divorced at twenty-seven. After that I had some long-term relationships, but none that were going to endure and none that I wanted to bring a child into. During this time I also began having sexual relationships with women. It was not until I was thirty-six that I was in a relationship with a woman that felt suitable to include a child.

My mother left our family when I was four, so my relationship with her was filled with longing and the trauma of being left. I didn't have much contact with her during my growing-up years. The contact I did have was often painful because I knew at the end of the day I had to leave her again. Additionally, my father remarried, and that marriage was not going well; my relationship with my stepmother didn't feel safe. So in summary, I never felt safe around my mothering figure or my actual mother.

After decades of hard work between my stepmother and me, we've carved out some realness and closeness. It still has limitations, but I am okay with us, and I love her a lot. My relationship with my stepmother was good throughout my adult life, but now seems to be growing more distant.

Growing up, I loved my father very much but feared his violence and anger. My father didn't make my life feel safe, and he didn't make taking care of his children a priority. I had many mixed feelings toward him. Those endure to the present day but are far more worked out than they were when I was younger.

I never really shared any of my thoughts with my family. My stepmother once said, when I was twenty-five and talked about my longing for children, "Well, if you haven't had them by now, you never will." I have no idea where that came from, but it stung and stuck. It was a confusing thing to hear. I didn't talk about my desire for children again with my family, and because we were estranged when I became pregnant, I didn't share that news. I am not sure how they learned it, but it must have circulated after I told a beloved cousin that I was expecting a baby. That cousin is gay, and he and a lesbian friend conceived a child and began a family when I did. Their son was born three weeks after mine, and we have remained close.

Nothing stands out regarding making the decision. No regrets or buyer's remorse. I had some anxiety about being a good-enough mother, and this anxiety has persisted. Every mother I know feels the same way. I wouldn't change the decision. If I could change anything about the course of my life, I would have wanted to have started having children earlier and had time for a second one.

I am glad I didn't know back then what I know now: just how labor-intensive, scary, hard, intense, and all-consuming it is to provide for and raise a child. I might not have done it! But I am so glad I did because it's been joyous, hilarious, tender, and awesome. What I like to say about becoming a mother is that it's the very best thing I ever did to totally turn my life upside down. My life got challenged in a beautiful, hard way. I don't think there is any way to explain that beforehand, and if there were, no one would do it; it's that hard. And I had an easy kid! There are families whose kids are ill or have special needs that struggle and work a lot harder than I had to. It is an incredible roll of the dice.

As a parent, I am much more present and available than my parents were. There was no help of any kind in my family, and if I requested help, it was denied. So I learned not to ask. My son knows I am there to help him. I have more attention for him. I am very interested in knowing him for the person he is. I provide more structure, and I don't burden my son with my needs excessively. I probably went too far in the other direction – I could have required more of him and also made him please me. He recently told me, "That ship has sailed" (about pleasing me), but he plans to make sure that his children please him! My stepmother enjoyed her children, and I enjoy my son. We are a fun-loving family and my son and I laugh a lot. I take great delight in my son, and this was modeled by my stepmother.

Having a son cracked my heart open where men were concerned. I began to face the damage in my relationship with my father more, and I began to see men as human again, not just sources of hurt. When my son was seven, my partner and I divorced, and several years later I began a long-term relationship with the man who is now my husband. I would say that having a son was instrumental in healing my pain about men.

I enjoy being at this point in my life. My son is about to leave for college after this last year of high school. He's turned out to be a great human being. I love being around him. I am excited to be an empty nester and to have the extra time that not having a kid around will provide me. I love my work and my friends. My life is really good. I'm sure I'll mourn that the child-raising part of my life is over, but I'm also sure it won't last longer than a few minutes when it does comes up. I have always had a full life, a great profession, and being a mother was not my only identity.

Aviva always felt empowered to choose motherhood. It was an important part of her Jewish culture. While the decision to become a mother had come easily to her, finding the right time to do so was hard. She wanted to be prepared and to provide the best possible environment. Aviva readied herself emotionally, tending to the early childhood emotional pain caused when her mother left and also her unmet needs as the oldest child of her family. She also waited until her career provided the financial stability to support a child, and until she was in a partnership that felt right.

She credited her friends and her partner with providing the support and encouragement she received during pregnancy and birth. Her family disapproved of her choice to be partnered with a woman, and Aviva was estranged from them during the early years of her son's life. Aviva's role models were other women and lesbian friends who had also become parents. She watched how they conceived and how they thought about and talked about becoming parents. It was an exciting time as changes in family structures emerged.

As for negative influences, she said, "I had to come up against the disapproval of my family and some people who thought lesbians shouldn't have babies. But I had strong friendships and a good support system. I also had a strong sense inside that this was a good path, so I can't honestly say I put much stock in the negative things that were said."

Week 10

Wise Woman

"Look well into thyself; there is a source of strength which will always spring up if thou wilt always look there."
–Marcus Aurelius[8]

Welcome to Week 10! How do you feel after last week's work? Were you able to picture yourself clearly five and ten years into the future? As you explored your relationship to the future, did you feel that things could go your way? If you couldn't picture anything, were you okay with that outcome? Did you enjoy the exercise of deliberately moving forward one year in time, then looking back to notice what was satisfying about that year? We hope so. It's a practice you can use anytime you feel out of sorts to help shift your attention away from an immediate concern and gain perspective.

How was it to look into your uncharted territories – the emotional places you might normally avoid? Have you practiced reframing perceptions? Is your glass half full more than it's half empty? Now that you're back in present time, please do your best to continue living in *I don't know* for just a little longer.

Although the end of the program is nearing, there are still some essential activities to complete. We don't say this to overwhelm, but rather to inform you that more puzzle pieces leading the way to your desire are near to hand. If you notice yourself worrying that the program is coming to an end and you don't yet see clarity approaching, try this: Take a deep breath, relax, and review your writings from the beginning. See how far you've come? You've done a tremendous amount of emotional work. Pat yourself on the back! Congratulate yourself aloud. Breathe in deeply with the thought *Answers are coming,* and as you exhale, say out loud, "I *am* one awesome woman!" Repeat this two more times. If *awesome* is not in your vocabulary, choose your own superlative, one that has meaning for you.

Week 10 Guided Visualization

(Adapted from and inspired by "Wise Man" by John O. Stevens in *Awareness: Exploring, Experimenting, Experiencing.* Boulder, Colorado: Real People Press, 1971.)

These visualizations bring information from your unconscious into awareness. Trust that your attentive mind will go where it needs to go. When your eyes are closed, you engage the part of your brain that isn't as easily accessed when your eyes are open. Have someone read the visualization to you or record it for you so you can listen while your eyes are closed, as its power also lies in the element of surprise. If that's not possible, make a recording yourself so you can listen with eyes closed to deepen the experience of where the visualization takes you. If you read the visualization to yourself, read it silently and slowly to give yourself time to savor the experience. Close your eyes now and then to open to the power of your imagination.

Remember that the experience you have is what matters most, and there's no wrong way to do it. Have your journal and writing tool nearby so you can record your impressions and images immediately.

To prepare, choose a quiet place where people and noise won't disturb or distract you, and a time when there's nothing else for you to do and no one who needs your attention; this time is solely for your benefit. Either sit comfortably in a chair or, if you prefer, lie down on the floor.

A Wise Woman Speaks

Now that you're ready, become conscious of your breathing. Let your eyes close gently as you take a deep breath and exhale. Inhale and hold your breath for five counts. Then exhale until most of the air has left your lungs. Inhale again and slowly exhale, letting out an audible sigh through your mouth while you count silently from ten to one. Continue breathing slowly and deeply. As you breathe, you relax. Allow your natural breath to bring a deep sense of peace and well-being. Feel your body relax and let your mind free-associate. Breathe.

By now you're aware that there's a lot more to you than you realized. Feel your inherent goodness, and breathe into that knowledge. Your journey of discovery continues. Breathe into The Mantra: *I don't know. I don't know why I don't know. It's not my fault that I don't know. It's okay that I don't know. I have had clarity before about many things. My true desire matters and no one can know it better than I. I am the definer of me. The answers will come because they never left. Only I can know what's true for me... It's all within me.*

Let your natural breathing return as you imagine yourself walking up a trail in the mountains at night. There's a full moon, which allows you see the trail quite easily. You can see all the details of your surroundings because the moon is full and bright. How would you describe the trail?

What else can you see around you? How do you feel as you walk up this mountain trail? Breathe in the night air. How does it feel?

Just ahead there's a small side trail that leads up higher to a cave that is home to a very wise woman. It happens that she can answer any question you have. You decide to follow this side trail. Notice how your surroundings change as you come closer to her dwelling.

When you arrive in front of her cave, you see a small campfire and you can see the wise woman by the light of its dancing flames. Approach the fire and put some more wood on it. Sit quietly and breathe. Smell the fire. Listen to the wood crackling. How do you feel sitting quietly by the fire? As the fire burns more brightly, you can see the wise woman more clearly. Take a moment to become aware of her body, clothes, face, and eyes. Is there anything about the wise woman that is familiar to you? As you study her, what do you feel? Breathe.

Think about what you want to ask her. Feel your question. Breathe into it. Ask the wise woman your important question. Watch her steadily to see how she reacts to your question. She might choose to answer you with words alone. She might acknowledge you with a gesture or facial expression. She might show you something. What kind of answer does she give you? Notice how you feel about her and how she responds. Do you want to reply to her in any particular way?

Before you depart, observe what it's been like to interact with the wise woman. Is there anything you want to convey before you leave? Just as you are about to say good-bye, the wise woman turns and reaches into an ancient embroidered bag to search for something very special to give you. She removes a gift from the bag and hands it to you to take home. Take a moment to examine this present. How do you feel toward the wise woman now? Let her know and then say anything else you want to add.

Tell her good-bye and listen for her to say good-bye to you. Listen closely when she says, "You are welcome to visit me anytime. I will always be here for you."

Now take your gift and head back down the mountain trail. Carefully observe the trail's landmarks so you'll remember how to find your way back to the wise woman whenever you'd like to visit her again. Be aware of your surroundings and how you feel.

With your eyes still closed, your curiosity inspires you to examine your gift in more detail. What did she give you? Turn it over in your hands and look at it carefully. What does it mean to you? Does it symbolize anything? Gently and safely stow away your gift in your memory, knowing you can retrieve it anytime you choose. Say good-bye to it for now.

Keeping your eyes closed while you slowly return to your present environment, allowing a few moments to be with your emotional and physical sensations. Breathe.

When you're ready, slowly open your eyes and begin to write in your journal. Record your immediate thoughts, feelings, insights, and anything else you want to about your experience.

Immediate Writing after the Guided Visualization

Rather than write, some women prefer to paint or draw what they saw. Regardless of the medium you choose to express your experience of this guided visualization, recording it immediately helps deepen your connection to what occurred. Even if you didn't see any images or you weren't aware of any identifiable feelings, the act of beginning to write, paint, or draw usually encourages something to come forth. Continue to express yourself as best you can. Do this now, before you continue reading.

How did it feel to walk up the mountain trail at night? Scary? Exhilarating? Peaceful? What was familiar about the wise woman? What did you ask her? How did she respond and what did you think of her reply? If she gave you something, how did it feel to receive her gift? How did it feel to say good-bye? Were you left feeling you have access to her anytime you wish? *You and your wise woman*: this is an important relationship, one you should encourage and develop.

When your writing feels complete, check in with your emotional state. Are your feelings manageable? If you feel overwhelmed, follow these instructions:

Take a deep breath, then exhale as slowly as possible, letting all the air escape your lungs. Allow your body to take in a breath on its own. Continue this several times until you notice a sense of calm. Then tap your feet on the floor. Follow that by tapping the tops of your thighs with your hands. Then tap your arms with your hands. Clench your fists and then release them. These actions help reconnect you to the present and ground you. Doing this is especially important when the emotions you experience feel overwhelming or just too much for you to manage. If you need to take further action to feel reconnected or grounded in the present, stand up and stamp your feet. Then reach your hands up in the air and stretch.

Look around the room and notice objects that bring a gentle smile to your face. Is your focus where you want it to be? Are your emotions manageable? Before you continue, make sure your attention is where you need it to be.

What Happens In Week 10

By this time in the program, what you thought had been resolved could be popping up again for you. Or you might feel that there are many competing claims on your attention and that the unfolding is happening too slowly. Perhaps you feel discouraged. Please be gentle and compassionate with yourself. Trust that there's movement in the direction that's right for you.

This week you'll consider *all the wise women* in your life, including yourself. You'll also learn how the *impulse to thrive* is important no matter what choices you make in life. You'll look at what it means to cultivate resilience and how this skill supports your impulse to thrive. And finally you'll consider how shame and self-sabotage might be getting in your way.

Wise Women

There's nothing as nourishing as having a wise woman in your life – a teacher, friend, aunt, grandmother, or another relative who, like Samantha's beloved Aunt Bea, can be there for you with her shining womanly wisdom and love. Is there such a woman in your life right now? Has there been in your past?

Perhaps you grew up wanting your mother to be your wise woman? Did she fulfill this role? If she didn't, maybe it was because her wounds prevented her from being available to you in this capacity. If you don't feel that you've ever had a wise woman of your own to whom you could turn, are you disappointed? You might need to feel the pain of not having the wise woman of your wishes. Grieving what you missed out on can help you move forward to create what you want and need.

If you don't currently have your wise woman, is there someone you can imaging asking for guidance – perhaps from your circle of support? As you're working toward your truth, there could be a woman who has wisdom to share with you. If you don't already have such a person in mind and you want one, it's not too late to get started. One of the optional exercises this week will help you find her.

You can also connect to and foster a relationship with your *inner* wise woman. What inner wisdom or intuition do *you* already possess? What have you gained from your life experiences? Your intuition has always been available to guide and shape your thoughts and actions in your everyday life as well as when you make big decisions. It's a question of knowing how to tap into it. How conscious are you of your intuition? How often do you listen to it? Have you tuned in to it a bit more since you started this journey? The guided visualizations are designed to target the place inside you where intuition dwells. Tap all your inherent resources. Trust and develop them whenever an opportunity arises.

The Impulse to Thrive

We are all born hard-wired to thrive. The impulse to thrive isn't connected so much to what you *do* in life, but rather to how you *feel inside* before and when you do it. It's that uplifting urge that motivates you to appreciate things, move forward in your life, and take your next breath with gusto. It's right there inside, sustaining and inspiring you to shout out from the highest mountain, take a dance class, knit a sweater, run a marathon, parachute out of a plane, write a book, open your own restaurant, volunteer with a local charity, or learn another language.

Depression, trauma, anxiety, and fear of the unknown (all remnants of the past) can generate a kind of misery that weakens or frustrates your impulse to thrive. Fearing regret is another condition that can, in effect, cut off circulation to this natural, life-affirming impulse to thrive. You can suffer enormously if you fear that you'll later miss out on the deeply satisfying experience of motherhood. Conversely, you might fear that you'll look back and wish you'd never given up your treasured freedom and autonomy. Some women actually choose (unconsciously and through no fault of their own) to live with this sustained pain of fearing regret rather than directly face what their fear is really about.

We believe that you deserve to thrive no matter what choices you make or what direction your life takes. Following two paths isn't possible, but you can have a flourishing life with either choice once you arrive at the core of your truth. After discovering what you desire, you can make your conscious decision. Then, at some point, you may look back and say, *I can't believe I almost decided to have a child. I love my child-free life*, or *My life as a mother is so satisfying, I can't imagine it any other way*. Both statements come from well-being and fulfillment rather than regret. Your impulse to thrive is alive and well. You're resilient enough to face any obstacle that blocks your impulse to thrive.

Cultivating Resilience

Resilience is one way we maintain a healthy connection to our natural impulse to thrive, and is more than just a flexible response to life's unfolding events; it's the resulting chemical processes in your brain that positively inform your ability to adapt to change and bounce back from the next challenge that comes your way. This flexibility helps you handle life's natural ups and downs consistently and with minimal effort, and manage the anxiety associated with making difficult decisions.

You can nurture and grow this capacity. In fact, you've been doing this weekly as you've been working through this program. Reframing perceptions strengthens your ability to adapt to evolving circumstances. Every time you encourage an openhearted appreciation for yourself, you are cultivating resilience.

Even if you've been feeling down – or downright miserable – for some time, you still have this capability in your core being. You've only lost your connection to it.

While working the steps in her recovery program, Sue came to understand how she had lost her connection to this resource. The family system she grew up in left her feeling that life's challenges were out to get her. She ended up feeling trapped, and not in control of events. Six months into recovery, Sue understood more deeply the wisdom of these words:

> *Grant me the serenity to accept the things I cannot change,*
> *the courage to change the things I can change,*
> *and the wisdom to know the difference.*
> –Reinhold Niebuhr[9]

Like The Mantra that has helped you remain open to uncertainty, these words became the foundation that helped Sue reconnect to her inner resilience, a connection that continues to inform her daily choices, large and small. Furthermore, as she practices separating the things she can change from those she can't, she strengthens her growing flexibility.

If you've lost your ability to bounce back, you can reconnect to it by learning something new, opening up to one of your uncharted territories, or facing up to one of your fears. Every time you look fear in the face and move toward it, you cultivate resilience. Every time you decide to do something you think you cannot do, you cultivate resilience. We know that you, too, have the inner strength you need to travel well and arrive where you want to be.

Be on the Lookout – Shame and Self-Sabotage

Conscious decision-making occurs when your internal life is just that – conscious. Those inner parts of you that need to be brought into the sunshine and aired out so you can make healthy and considered decisions can be wrecked by the twin perils of shame and self-sabotage.

We all experience and suffer from shame to some degree, and the less we acknowledge or talk about our inner lives, the more shame we are likely to keep under wraps (that is, in our uncharted territories). However, the kind of shame we're talking about here is the toxic kind that carries the message *I don't matter* or *I'm inherently bad*. This kind of shame can distort your perspective on just about everything.

Identifying shame can be tricky because it's an emotion that's tied to other emotions. When shame binds to anger, fear, or disappointment, you have to tease out each of the emotions, separating them in order to heal. If you're not sure if shame is a component of your complex emotions, ask yourself if there's anything you feel like you can't share with those you love and trust the most. If the answer is yes, it's likely that you're carrying some shame that needs to be unearthed and addressed.

Holly's mother's inability to see her daughter as a separate being with her own needs caused Holly to internalize the belief that she was unlovable. In the course of exploring her early attachment wounds, she discovered that she was carrying a tremendous burden of shame. In time, with the help of her counselor, Holly was able to separate the strands of her grief from its by-product of shame. The healing work she did on both of these emotions ultimately allowed her to arrive at the truth: that she is worthy of love.

You've probably already bumped into feelings of shame doing some of the exercises in this program. Maybe you recognized it for what it was; maybe not. If you didn't, perhaps now you can begin to differentiate your feelings and see where shame has either attached itself or is lurking. If this feels too difficult, don't be afraid to ask for help. Sometimes the most efficient way to dismantle and diminish shame is with the assistance of a professional.

Self-sabotage is another obstacle in the way of making conscious decisions for the betterment of your life. It sounds strange on the face of it – why would anyone want to destroy something positive or good in their lives? Self-sabotage is usually an unconscious act, so it's hard to recognize it, let alone to get to the bottom of it. When you can see what lies behind self-sabotaging actions, you discover that the underlying reason is often well-intentioned.

The part of your psyche that responds to crisis and difficulty develops the best strategies it can at any given moment. If these strategies were created when you were very young, they aren't informed by the knowledge and experience that comes later in life. It can make sense to the young one within, who was deeply hurt by someone she trusted, to conclude that being alone is safer than risking being hurt by someone new who could also turn out to be untrustworthy. This strategy can continue to sabotage any developing relationship, usually unconsciously. So even though the original good intention – to keep you safe – is still part of the equation, acting on this strategy can block your path to personal fulfillment and well-being.

Gaining clarity about whether or not to become a mother is so important! You don't need any unnecessary obstacles in your way. Self-sabotage not only slows you down, but it can stop you in your tracks. If you sense that self-sabotage is playing a role in your life, see what the optional exercise this week brings up. If you sense that this is a significant theme for you, consider asking for professional help. It can save you crucial time that can be better spent going after what you truly desire with your heart wide open.

Be Curious: Assignments for Week 10

We hope by now you've developed a nice routine with these exercises and that your stream-of-consciousness writing has brought to the surface plenty of clues and puzzle pieces. Continue to let the unfolding happen, and don't be surprised if fresh feelings and thoughts are evoked this week.

1. Reader's Choice

    This writing assignment allows you to choose your topic. As you read what you wrote immediately following the guided visualization, does the question you asked your wise woman need further exploration or amplification? Can you spot any place in your writing where there's a hint of something trying to break through? Are you aware of any assumptions or outdated beliefs about yourself that you still carry around? Notice if any particular statement keeps circling through your mind, such as:

I never got to be a kid.
I feel inadequate as a human being.
Will I ever matter to someone?
My dreams will never come to fruition.
I've never taken myself seriously.

Maybe you experienced something surprisingly positive about either the question you asked the wise woman or the answer she gave you. Examine your inner world and dive in more deeply to the place that has energy. You know better than anyone else what needs further inquiry. Jump in! Be relentlessly curious and respond to the prompt below. Write until you've said all you want – you can do this on your own now!

To see where it leads me, I need to write about…

2. My Gift

The wise woman gave you a gift. What is it? Describe it. What unique meaning does it have for you? Did the message or symbolism surprise or confuse you? Did you want something else? It's not unusual to have little or no understanding of the gift you received from the wise woman. If your experience of the gift left you with more questions than answers, please don't worry or write off the exercise. The meaning of the gift will reveal itself in due course, often after time is spent sitting quietly, writing, drawing, or painting.

Write, draw, or paint the gift the wise woman gave you.

3. To Thrive

Write about your impulse to thrive. Is it something you notice in your internal world? In your external world? Is anything blocking your impulse to thrive? Do you know what it is? Do you feel you need to have a child to thrive? On the other hand, do you feel that if you have children, it will stifle your impulse to thrive? Take a closer look at what thriving – inside and out – means to you.

To me, thriving means…

When I thrive, my life looks and feels like…

My impulse to thrive feels blocked or diminished. I think this might be caused by…

4. Gratitude

Being in touch with the things you appreciate makes all the difference in how you feel day to day. It strengthens your impulse to thrive and supports your process in this program. If you tend to see your glass as half empty, make a list of all the things and people you are grateful for. Add to your gratitude list daily. At the end of each day, reflect on how it's gone and notice what felt good. If you completed the optional exercise in Week 1 of writing down the highlights of your life, you can refer to it for ideas. Otherwise, start right where you are.

I am grateful to…

I am grateful for _____ because _____.

Further Exploration and Discovery

Take some time away from the Reader's Choice exercise – several hours to a day or two – and then go back to reread what you wrote, considering each of the questions in "Your Checklist for Reflection" on page 50.

How did the Reader's Choice exercise feel? Was it easy to find your starting point? Was it useful to write about it? Are you pleased with where it took you? Were there any surprises? How aware are you of your inner wisdom? This exercise often exposes a *perspective shift*, which can be subtle but powerful.

Birgit shifted perspective in a powerful way while doing the Reader's Choice exercise. The writing began: "To see where it leads me, I need to write about…" She was surprised by the next word that came: "faith." Her primary puzzle pieces in the program had so far included the pressure she felt from her parents who wanted to become grandparents, the support she felt from her husband who was open to either choice, her brush with cancer in her early thirties, and her fulfillment at work. She hadn't realized how supported she was by her belief system. She hadn't counted on her faith to guide her through, although it had supported her while she underwent cancer treatment. Birgit's writing revealed how much her faith supports her. This revelation allowed her to feel confident that her desire will become known. She'll then make her decision, and nature can take its course. She is at peace with the possible consequences, and her worry and urgency have dissolved.

If this particular exercise didn't feel useful or you couldn't come up with something specific to start with, here are three options that might help. (1) Take a look back over all the previous weeks' assignments and repeat any that felt hard to do. Really! It means another puzzle piece is calling out to you. (2) Listen to this week's guided visualization once more to see if your mind takes you to a new place. It might just be where you need to go. (3) Try writing a longer response to the question you posed to the wise woman.

How connected do you feel to the wise woman? How do you feel about your gift? Has anything more come to you about why the wise woman gave you this particular gift? Whatever you're feeling, see if you can take it a bit deeper. Useful information resides in all your feelings and thoughts, so don't underestimate anything.

Is your impulse to thrive in good working order? Assess how resilient you feel in this moment, on a scale from 1 to 10, with 1 being *not very* and 10 being *extremely*. We found that many women tend to under-acknowledge their capabilities and resources; so really take the time to make a fair assessment.

How easy was it to remember what you are grateful for? Just as the practice of reframing perceptions helps you see the glass as half full more than half empty, appreciating the things that matter to you and absorbing how good they make you feel helps cultivate your capacity for gratitude and contributes to your overall sense of well-being.

Be Even More Curious: Optional Exercises

If you have the time and desire to continue your exploration, the following suggestions will help:

1. Think about a woman you deem to be wise. She may be fictional, real, living, or dead. Write to her and tell or ask her anything you wish.

2. If you already know someone who might be able to offer you more access to life's wisdom, consider reaching out to her now. If you feel hesitant to do this, what's in your way? Remember that you deserve to have wholesome connections in your life, and cultivating a connection with a woman you deem wise can bring benefits to both of you. Inviting this woman to join you for coffee or lunch can be a non-threatening way to reach out to her. Share thoughts or feelings with her that feel good to you. If you think she has wisdom in this area – the desire and decision to become a mother or not – respectfully ask her the questions you deem important. Don't hold back. If you need to keep exploring to find just the right wise woman to consult, don't give up until you've found her. And if the timing of this exercise feels premature, wait until it feels like the right time. Trust your instincts on this.

The next two suggestions involve working with shame and the inner saboteur. Intercepting shame with dialogue and talking to the saboteur in you is important introspective work. It exposes your vulnerabilities but also invites tremendous healing.

3. Shame is an uncomfortable feeling. There are many ways to dismantle shame, but here's one way to get you started: Start a letter along the following lines, and then continue to write in your own words.

Dear Shame,
You've been a part of my life for a long time. You came in without ever being invited. You arrived when you did because someone else in my life felt shame and passed it along to me. Now we must part ways. I can

no longer let your toxicity be a part of my life. I know you don't want to go but you must. Rather than carry you around any longer, I choose to thrive [continue in your words]...

4. If you find that good things in your life get sabotaged by something you think or do, make contact with your inner saboteur. Write a letter, or continue the example letter below.

    Dear Saboteur,
    We've been together far too long. It should come as no surprise to you that we'll be parting ways. Our relationship ends here and now. You might have had good intentions to help me when you first started, and for this I thank you; but I have no need for you anymore. I want my life back, and I want to thrive. What this will look like going forward is...

5. The Honoring Ceremony Revisited

    If you held a ceremony last week, reimagine your healing altar. Ask the wise woman to sit with you there and see if she has anything to share with you – words, expressions, or perhaps something in her embroidered bag to add to your altar. Use her in any way that aids in healing the past so that you can move forward free from grief, shame, and regret, and with a sense of ease.

What to Hold Inside This Week

This week be extra gentle with yourself. Move a little more slowly than usual if you can, and give yourself me-time. Feel the courage it takes to look at these issues as you've been doing. Feel the inner wisdom

MOTHERHOOD-IS IT FOR ME?

you carry around day to day. If you find yourself leaning toward yes or no in your desire, try to let the feelings be there without drawing any conclusions.

Connect with your internal wise woman as she follows you around wherever you go this week. Consider the gift she gave you. Be in touch with all the gifts in your life. Let yourself feel what a gift you are to this planet. Think about what little or big shifts might have to occur for you to more fully access your impulse to thrive. If you've been reminded of any shame you carry around or your inner saboteur has made an appearance, make a commitment to deal with it so you can heal more fully.

As you reflect on your current relationships with family and friends, ask yourself if they're where you want them to be. Are there any relationships that need tidying up? Are there any that feel as though they don't suit you anymore? Are there things that you feel need to be said? You don't have to do anything right now; use your journal to note what comes up so you can attend to it later if you prefer.

Self-Care

This week we offer two suggestions for self-care. You can do each of them, separately or together, or choose your own self-care option.

1. Give Yourself a Break from Technology

    If you can, take at least a full twenty-four-hour break from phone, computer, television, car, etc. See if you can rely on simple activities like reading, cooking, walking, and talking in person with others.

Seize the break-from-technology opportunity to connect with sounds, either by making them or listening to them, like Tibetan bells, a tuning fork, chanting, humming, whistling, or singing out loud – in or out of the shower! Some sounds are deeply healing. Explore. Enjoy. Restore. Renew.

2. Experience Nature

Spend a morning, afternoon, or evening in a natural setting. Go hiking. Explore a wilderness area. Walk barefoot at the beach. Watch the birds. Walk barefoot on the grass. Find some huggable trees. Dance in the moonlight. Meet up with your wise woman for a fireside chat. Scientific research has shown that reveling in nature has measureable benefits. If you have to drive to get to a natural setting, pack a snack or a full meal and don't forget to bring along something hot or cold to satisfy your thirst.

The self-care I did for myself this week was...

You Are Not Alone

Sandra and her husband agreed on where to draw the line with fertility treatments. Having been adopted at three weeks old played a role for Lauren. Read their stories when you choose.

Sandra's Story

I would say that infertility was the major reason we decided not to have children, even though I knew from the beginning that in vitro fertilization was not for me, or even intrauterine insemination. I did not want to take hormones or do anything invasive, and my husband felt strongly that it was my body and my decision. While family pressures still weigh on me a bit, the people who wanted it to happen most had all died before this mattered for me. My father would like grandchildren, but he completely understands and is supportive.

The decision was made in a matter of months, but only after trying to get pregnant for over a year. I felt great relief, so of course we shared it. Many people were curious, both friends and family. I didn't feel alone because my husband and I went through it together. I was proud of us for being so conscious.

Yes, I felt relief. And yes, I grieved a bit and sometimes still do. Sometimes I still get a bit envious of friends when they have a new baby or their kid does something totally adorable. But when the kids act up, I feel relieved that I don't have to deal with that. I don't think the grieving will ever fully stop, but I know we chose right for us.

Of course it's very easy to say this as a non-mother, but my mother worried too much and was sometimes too critical. I think I'd probably be the same way, but I like to think I've learned from the things I didn't love about her parenting style. At the same time, there was never a doubt I was the most important thing in her life, and I will always feel gratitude for that. The one issue we fought over in my adult years was that I was never trying hard enough to meet someone. The fact that I was single into my early thirties was very difficult for her to handle, as if it somehow was a poor reflection on her. It drove me crazy, and we fought about it a lot because she didn't know how to hold her tongue in this regard. She died when I was thirty-three, and I met my husband at thirty-five. I sometimes wonder if her wanting it so badly for me somehow impeded it from happening.

I like some of my friends' kids, but not all of them. I'm not one of those child-crazy people. While I love watching my friends' kids getting older, I don't like to spend too much time with the younger ones.

Sandra lives with her husband in an urban area in the western United States. They had been married three years when she stopped trying to get pregnant. Neither was interested in resorting to medical intervention to help Sandra's chances of getting pregnant. Sandra said, "My husband reached his clarity from doing the Parenthood-Is it for me? program with me. His conclusion was that unless we both felt that 'we *must* do this,' it meant a no, and I must say that I agreed with him. I started out ambivalent, and I stayed ambivalent."

Sandra regularly consulted with a close friend of her mother who had struggled unsuccessfully for years to get pregnant. This older woman had pursued infertility treatments and shared with Sandra how awful they were. In the end, this woman and her husband decided not to adopt and to live a child-free life. Sandra's friendship with her continues to provide support and guidance for Sandra. Quite possibly this older woman values the opportunity the friendship provides to mentor the younger woman. Sandra has a role model and another maternal figure in her life. She advises women who are in a similar place, "Seek out other women who haven't had children to talk to them about it, and about how it changes as you get older."

Sandra and her husband value their free and independent lifestyle, a continuing benefit of their decision. "We have a freedom that many of our friends don't. We really love good food, wine, and travel. Obviously our friends' lives and vacations are much more kid-focused." Some of their friends with children tell her that she is brave for having made her decision. She wonders if this means more than it seems to say on the surface. The friends with children are less available to her – sometimes not available at all. Sandra occasionally senses some jealousy directed her way from friends with children who lack the freedom she and her husband have.

Sandra feels close to her father, but remembers a time when she was a teenager when he became distant. She feels that her father didn't know how to respond to her typical adolescent moodiness and lack of communication. He was a professor and would always ask her what she was learning in school. While her grades were perfectly acceptable, she showed no signs of being engaged with what she was learning, and he was troubled by this. Once when she was in college, her excitement about what she was learning became evident to him, and that's when their relationship flourished.

Although Sandra's mother was no longer alive to share their news once they decided, her father has always demonstrated support for the choice she and her husband made. When Sandra was in her twenties she learned that her father's infertility problems might have meant that her parents would never conceive naturally. They were quite surprised when they stopped using birth control to find that they conceived right away, though Sandra was the only child they had.

We never know what the future holds. Sandra shared that she's now dealing with career uncertainty as she juggles between two different careers. Does she prefer one over the other, or should she try something completely different? In our experience, once a woman gains clarity on her choice to be or not to be a mother, she is also able to move forward on other life choices that have been on hold or previously seemed elusive.

Lauren's Story

Although I have been lucky enough to have close, meaningful, honest relationships, there has been this sense I've had – all along – of being alone. Perhaps it is a sensory memory I have of being a newborn baby and then being surrendered for adoption – but probably not. That's too much of an excuse. I have always been a very independent person, but one who had also felt a smattering of separation anxiety when someone left me – even if it was just to say good night after a dinner party. I love people, and I love the feeling of belonging to someone, to a group, or to an ideal. I yearn for the club membership and the secure feeling of being in a committed relationship – the security of knowing someone is there for you.

On one hand I appreciate this part of myself, and on the other hand I know I have seemed needy and clingy in years past. Ironically, if I feel someone has hurt me emotionally, I also have the capacity to completely cut them out of my life – and my heart – with little regret. Up till the time I was in my mid-thirties, this needy feeling was somewhat of a mystery to me.

I was thirty-five, single, and five weeks pregnant when I declared out loud that I wanted to be a mom. I was sitting in the doctor's office, and I was telling the nurse how I wanted to be a mom – but only under the right circumstances. These were not the right circumstances. I had no money, and I wasn't in love with the guy I was dating, if you could even call it that. I was working sporadically, freelancing in television production, and living in a tiny one-bedroom apartment that I struggled to pay rent on each month. I wanted to be able to offer more to a child.

What would that look like? The list started with two parents, steady income, home with a backyard, and a French tutor who visited on Thursdays. Alas, my situation at the time was far from what I held in high regard, and so I had a friend take me to a downtown clinic complete with the classic, conservative, anti-abortion picketers outside. I paid my $20 deductible through my health insurance and terminated a pin-point-sized cluster of cells. No baby and no regrets.

I'm now forty-two and more secure in myself. In the quest to find the other perfect parent for my biological child, I've learned a lot about who I am. I've realized I would make a pretty good parent, even on my own. And I've learned that I don't want to co-parent for the wrong reasons.

Once I decided that I wanted to become a mom, I had to "come out" to my mother about how serious I was about being a mom. This was more difficult than telling *her I was gay when I was twenty-five, which she accepted immediately. The "I want to be a mom" talk was the most intimate conversation I've ever had with my mother. I told her about my abortion and why I intended to break up with my current girlfriend; I wanted to be a mom and she didn't want children. My mother really liked my girlfriend. From my parents' point of view, she and I had an idyllic life, a nice house, money, two dogs, great vacations, and a four-and-a-half-year relationship. My mom tried to reason with me. "Honey, you have two dogs. Dogs are wonderful – you love dogs! Why not just keep getting more dogs?!"*

My parents were both twenty-one years old when they married, and they really wanted children. When they couldn't get pregnant, my mother was devastated. She blamed my father. I know I was not the dream plan, and that adoption was her second choice. They adopted my brother and me when they were in their thirties. I have always believed that our family has a spiritual ancestry that transcends blood. That said, I want to have my own biological child.

My mother and I were very close when I was growing up. She was incredibly encouraging and nurturing. She wanted me to explore the world and the diversity in it. I was interested in music and theater, and she became involved in my school to help my classmates and me explore these areas. My mom took time out from work to spend more time with her children. Both of my parents are extremely bright, and they conveyed that there was a big world out there. They were tolerant and always conveyed in a non-judgmental way that people have differences.

My mother is probably my biggest role model. She has her faults, but she was a great mother. She's now seventy-four. I have a couple of good friends who have become parents, and they are also good role models.

For the most part, I would want to be like my mother was as she mothered me rather than as she mothered my brother, as she did that differently. On the positive side, she gave love unconditionally. She had a curious mind and encouraged me to be the same. She was proactive and involved herself in my activities at school. She exposed me to cultural events. One of my favorite things has always been going to the movies with my mother. I love hearing her opinion after we've seen a movie together. My mom was the main reason I decided to work in the entertainment industry. She is free-spirited, universally spiritual, and culturally Jewish. I would hope to be described similarly.

On the negative side, she doesn't have a lot of patience, and this is something I'd work harder at with my own child. She didn't discipline me a lot, and I recognize that this impacted me in ways I would like to prevent happening to a child of my own. I didn't have a lot of rules, expectations, chores, or responsibilities. I didn't have a spiritual program.

As a mother, I would offer a spiritual program to my child, with an emphasis on meditation and prayer. I would have clear and non-judgmental expectations. In my opinion, my mother contributed to my brother's downward spiral into addiction and continues to enable him. Before he discovered drugs, he and I had a great relationship. I haven't talked to him in ten years.

As I moved toward my choice to become a mom, I felt excited and lonely because I'm not sharing it with someone else. I'm an optimist. I want what my parents had: the white picket fence, to be in love, to be married, and to have a family. At times I also feel overwhelmed, then later sadness, and then I feel empowered again. I move through all of these emotions. I've already tried intrauterine insemination once, and I want to try again.

I've noticed something curious. When I was part of a couple, people always asked us, "When are you going to have kids?" Now that I'm single, they ask me, "Why do you want to be a mother?" When I'm asked why I want my own biological child, I answer, "I want to be a mom because that is what I feel. I want to be a biological parent because I haven't experienced this kind of connection with anyone, and I would like to discover what it feels like to have someone physically related to me." I've always been envious of families who look alike, especially the siblings.

I have often thought, irrationally, that I should have just settled with an old boyfriend because at least by now I'd be a parent. There have been times when I blamed the '70s which empowered young girls to be whatever they wanted to be – "free to be you and me!" By the time I was in my twenties, there was a growing rebellion against just becoming a wife and a mom. I declared, "I'm going to be a professional." A stay-at-home mom was the worst thing you could be. Co-workers and I were judgmental about our high school friends who stayed behind and did nothing but had families. Now that is what I want. If I won the lottery tomorrow, I would be a stay-at-home mom.

When I think of how my dad was when I was growing up, I feel sad because it looks like I'm going miss out on having a male co-parent. My dad represented a cliché father, very strong and always fixing things. I was always safe with him. He was very protective of us. He seems introspective, and is probably a spiritual person, although I don't know this for sure. Although I've never discussed anything personal with him as I have with my mother, I enjoy his company. He was always present and available, and there was great comfort with him. There still is.

There has been a huge shift in my perception of men. It shifted when I made a conscious decision to be a mom, because I started looking at men as father figures or influences in my future child's life. I started studying how

> *they handle anger, how they are with children, how they are with their partners, and how their last name might ring beautifully with any number of my chosen baby names. Oh, come on now, cut me some slack! All single women seeking motherhood do this!*
>
> *I "mother" my dog. I always loved children and have a childlike approach to life myself. I've made a conscious effort to babysit for friends' kids and to be a positive role model. My ex-girlfriend's nieces have a mother who is easily distracted and not interested in parenting, so I became involved in their lives. I took the girls to Chinatown to try dim sum, and got involved in their school projects. I have tried to show them a wider perspective on life than they had been given to date.*

Lauren was adopted when she was three weeks old by a liberal and well-educated couple living in urban northern California. Two years later they adopted a boy. Both Lauren and her brother are biracial, half Afro-American and half Caucasian. Their parents are Caucasian and remain happily married to each other.

Lauren, now in her early forties, is trying to conceive. Her preference is to do so within a love relationship, but she is not waiting for this to happen. She ended her last long-term relationship quite painfully over this issue. She wanted a child and her partner didn't. Lauren identifies as bisexual, but quickly added, "I'm a people person; gender has never been a prerequisite for me. However, I've only ever fallen in love with women." Since the breakup the prior year, Lauren has spent countless hours interviewing prospective fathers as co-parents and has learned that she has what it takes to be a good parent. One of her prerequisites for being a parent is financial security. Not only does she have that now, but her job in the entertainment industry has placed her in a cozy work family in which she feels a sense of belonging.

She wants to have a biological child, something that her adoptive mother could not do. The fact that she can conceive and her mother couldn't makes her feel a bit awkward. That said, Lauren never felt unwanted or unloved – quite the opposite; she and her brother were brought up to feel proud to be exactly who they are. While Lauren always felt that she belonged to the family she grew up in, she did envy other families in which people looked more alike. She said, "One thing about adoption, it's a crap shoot. Temperament comes from genetics. For example, before I met my birth mother at age twenty-three, I guessed that she would be artistic, liberal, mellow, and that she would be happy to see me in a non-emotional way. That turned out to be true. She's an artist, a mother, and a good person."

While Lauren didn't seek professional help while deciding, she used co-parenting groups to educate herself and to learn what qualities are most important for the long-term raising of children. She also has what she calls her "kid committee," her group of women friends who support her emotionally. They will be there for her when she becomes a mother, as she believes it takes a village to raise a child.

She offered this advice to other women who are in the deciding phase: "Listen to yourself. Communicate with others, but ultimately listen to yourself; because at the end of the day it needs to be your decision."

Week 11

Anticipating Arrival

"Just trust yourself, then you will know how to live."
–Johann Wolfgang von Goethe[10]

Welcome to Week 11! You're wiser than when you started this program, and if you already *feel* wiser, that's wonderful! If not, entertain the idea that regardless of whether you perceive it or not, some wisdom has assuredly come your way. You've been engaged in a deep inquiry, exploring territories old and new. You've brought courage to your efforts, allowing new discoveries to arise week after week. You've come face to face with the wise woman who resides within.

How did last week go for you? Were you able to embrace your wise woman as she accompanied you through your weekly activities? Did she give you nuggets of wisdom? Did you bring more attention to your relationships, observing which ones feel satisfying and which ones don't? What did you learn about yourself as you evaluated the strength of your impulse to thrive? How did it feel to be extra kind and gentle with your wonderful self?

Before you embark on this week's material, bring your shoulders up to your ears, hold for a few seconds and then let them drop. Do this a few times to release any tension in your upper body. Then vigorously rub your hands together until you feel some warmth, and place them on your face, cupping your cheeks in your palms. Close your eyes and feel the gentleness and softness of your own hands as you cradle your face. Feel pride in your accomplishments and give yourself a nice big smile. Hold your lovely face in your hands a few moments more, basking in sensations of admiration and delight. Take this in as you say out loud: "I'm very proud of me, and I've accomplished a lot to get to this point in my process."

Week 11 Guided Visualization

Before listening to this week's visualization, review the writing you did following Week 2's guided visualization, "The Journey Begins." What felt important to you at that time? What were your hopes?

These visualizations bring information from your unconscious into awareness. Trust that your attentive mind will go where it needs to go. When your eyes are closed, you engage the part of your brain that isn't as easily accessed when your eyes are open. Have someone read the visualization to you or record it for you so you can listen while your eyes are closed, as its power also lies in the element of surprise. If that's not possible, make a recording yourself so you can listen with eyes closed to deepen the experience of where the visualization takes you. If you read the visualization to yourself, read it silently and slowly to give yourself time to savor the experience. Close your eyes now and then to open to the power of your imagination.

Remember that the experience you have is what matters most, and there's no wrong way to do it. Have your journal and writing tool nearby so you can record your impressions and images immediately.

To prepare, choose a quiet place where people and noise won't disturb or distract you, and a time when there's nothing else for you to do and no one who needs your attention; this time is solely for your benefit. Either sit comfortably in a chair or, if you prefer, lie down on the floor.

The Journey Revisited

Now that you're ready, become conscious of your breathing. Let your eyes close gently as you take a deep breath and exhale. Inhale and hold your breath for five counts. Then exhale until most of the air has left your lungs. Inhale again and slowly exhale, letting out an audible sigh through your mouth while you count silently from ten to one. Continue breathing slowly and deeply. As you breathe, you relax. Allow your natural breath to bring a deep sense of peace and well-being. Feel your body relax and let your mind free-associate. Breathe.

Imagine never knowing inadequacy. Imagine that the concept of doing things wrong doesn't exist. Imagine that living and growing are all about discovery and learning and appreciating yourself. You are wonderful exactly as you are.

Shift your attention to imagining a small carpet in front of you. It is thick and colorful, with a dense and lush weave. Feast your eyes on its beauty. What patterns and colors do you see?

This carpet is calling you to sit comfortably on it, so rest and allow yourself to sink into it. Exhale any tension remaining in your body and mind.

It's time to tell you a little secret. This carpet has magical powers: it is intuitive. As you sit on this carpet, it can sense all that you feel. It holds your thoughts and feelings, the comfortable ones and the uncomfortable ones, the clear ones and the confusing ones. This magic carpet knows what you've been through since you began your journey – this journey of expansion and discovery – and possibly worry, too. This magic carpet is on your side and wants you to be able to see yourself lovingly and accurately.

It can magically go anywhere you wish, including backward or forward in time. And just now, tiny air bubbles are forming under the carpet. The bubbles grow bigger until they are so big that the carpet lifts off into the sky. Let yourself sink into the magic carpet as it safely carries you high above the ground. You are in command as the helmswoman, so go ahead and maneuver the magic carpet as you wish.

You're soon riding high in the sky with a bird's-eye view of all that you have experienced so far in this program. You have come a long way since you began your journey. You might feel weary, or energized; and of course you might feel a combination of both or something else entirely. What do you notice? Are you at peace? Are you relaxed? Do you feel resolved? Do you feel eager or neutral? Are you aware of any anxiety or uneasiness? Are you feeling something else? Whatever you're feeling is just as it should be now. Let your feelings come with you as you explore.

Fly down memory lane from this most wonderful vantage point. In the second week of this journey you were asked to prepare for a trip – for travel that would take you to the place where your desire for wanting children or becoming a mother would become clearer to you. You were encouraged to welcome all your feelings without judgment. What do you remember about this beginning place? If you don't remember anything at all, that is perfectly fine.

Float your magic carpet over the beach where you met and walked with your younger self long ago, and gaze down to see your two selves. What discoveries did you make together? Do you now have a deeper connection with this younger you?

After hanging out on the beach with your younger self, you entertained what happened when saying yes and no. You explored the feelings of wanting and desire. You spoke with your mother and/or your father, and you began to make the internal repairs needed to move toward a more thriving life. What do you see now from this vantage point?

Then you explored the decision to live a child-free life followed by the decision to have a child and become a parent. You had feelings about both scenarios. After that you were catapulted twenty years into your future. What discoveries did you make there?

Take a moment to pause and allow your carpet to hover as you open your eyes to record in your journal *all* thoughts, feelings, and reflections. Write for as long as you want to.

When you finish writing, bring your attention back to your natural breathing. Feel your body relax more with each breath. Close your eyes and continue your journey on the magic carpet.

Feel the softness of the plush carpet under you as you acknowledge some of the inner resources you cultivated along the way. Let your magic carpet amplify your strength and power. You created a safe harbor for nourishment that was called your comfort within. You called forth all the beings you wanted to be in your circle of support. You read The Mantra over and over, with intention and on purpose, to help you relax into not knowing in order to receive more information. You practiced self-care and me-time. You met a wise woman who answered your very important question and gave you a gift that had meaning, whether or not you are yet aware of that meaning. Breathe and take a few moments to fully absorb and acknowledge these inner resources.

Check in with your feelings right now. Do you feel peaceful? Critical? Excited? Disappointed? Relaxed? Or is it something else that you feel? Can you feel your courage?

What has been important to you so far about your overall journey? As the answer comes, breathe into it. What do you *know* now that you didn't before you started? Breathe. What do you *feel* now that you didn't feel before you started? Breathe. Observe your thoughts and feelings. There is nothing more to do and no conclusions to draw just yet.

It's time now to rest, so fly your magic carpet to the Sky Hotel where you already have a reservation. As you settle into the hotel, know that revisiting your journey thus far is done for the time being. Roll up your carpet, stow it away, and feel a deep sense of appreciation for yourself.

Keep your eyes closed while you slowly return to your present environment, allowing a few moments to be with your emotional and physical sensations. Breathe.

When you're ready, slowly open your eyes and begin to write in your journal. Record your immediate thoughts, feelings, insights, and anything else you want to about your experience. Then take a well-earned rest. Good work!

Immediate Writing after the Guided Visualization

Concretize what you saw and what occurred inside you by asking if there's anything else that wants to be said right now. When you finish writing, continue reading.

To help you deepen your experience of the guided visualization, conduct a gentle but thorough physical and emotional check-in with yourself. What do you notice? Comparing and contrasting how you feel now with how you felt during the first week, what's different? What's the same? What do you know now that you didn't back then? What do you still not know? Remember that even a small internal shift can have profound implications. If any new insights have arisen, take a moment now to write about them in your journal.

When your writing feels complete, check in with your emotional state. Are your feelings manageable? If you feel overwhelmed, follow these instructions:

Take a deep breath, then exhale as slowly as possible, letting all the air escape your lungs. Allow your body to take in a breath on its own. Continue this several times until you notice a sense of calm. Then tap your feet on the floor. Follow that by tapping the tops of your thighs with your hands. Then tap your arms with your hands. Clench your fists and then release them. These actions help reconnect you to the present and ground you. Doing this is especially important when the emotions you experience feel overwhelming or just too much for you to manage. If you need to take further action to feel reconnected or grounded in the present, stand up and stamp your feet. Then reach your hands up in the air and stretch.

Look around the room and notice objects that bring a gentle smile to your face. Is your focus where you want it to be? Are your emotions manageable? Before you continue, make sure your attention is where you need it to be.

What Happens in Week 11

With the end of the program nearing, you'll spend this week reviewing some of the key points of your journey. We ask you to pull out your jar and revisit your externals and fears. You'll explore a qualm experienced by many women as they address the question of whether or not to have a child: *the fear of regret*. You'll also take the pulse of your desire, and no matter where you are on the yes-no continuum you'll begin closing one chapter of your life to begin another.

Revisiting Your Externals

Over the past ten weeks or so you've examined to the best of your ability your innermost desires, beliefs, and fears from all angles. You've tended to your inner work with bravery and determination. It's likely that unresolved issues surfaced and some healing has already taken place. Now it's time to review systematically your externals, those circumstances of your life – finances, health, age, relationships, support network, fears, etc. – that you placed in a tightly lidded jar so you could focus on your internal world.

In Week 1 we suggested you put your externals and fears away in a jar for a while. Open that jar now and lay out the items you purposefully set aside. Separate out the fears and place those aside again for now. Spend a few minutes taking a good look at your externals, and notice whatever first comes to mind. Do all of these items still carry weight? Has the emphasis changed for any of them? Do any totally drop out of the picture now? In addition to these externals that you put aside at the beginning, have new ones appeared? Considering each of the earlier externals that are still relevant, do they *feel* somehow different now? Look for any nuanced change between how you felt toward your circumstances then and how you feel now. What do you notice? Take a few minutes to write about your immediate observations.

After you've written, go a bit deeper. Use your journal to list your externals. Note which no longer apply and which have shifted in importance, and particularly note if any new ones have arisen. *The most important thing is to notice what has changed within you and for you.* Maybe you even have clarity now as to what your priorities are going forward.

Personal circumstances – externals – vary tremendously. Your own are, of course, very relevant to you and your life.

One particular woman comes to mind here. She began this program while she was in a relationship with someone who had clearly stated that they did not wish to become a parent. She wasn't yet clear on her desire, but she knew that if her desire turned out to be a yes, she'd have to decide what to do in the relationship. Initially the idea of breaking up frightened her enormously. When she felt her desire leaning toward yes, she could sense that her relationship would possibly come to an end. The shift that occurred for her by Week 11 was the realization that ending the relationship no longer seemed as scary as it had earlier. She now had a good reason to consider ending the relationship, whereas previously the idea of breaking up over this issue seemed impossible.

Another woman, nearing the end of her reproductive years, wanted to know her truth before it was too late to conceive a child of her own. Through her work in the program she intuited her desire not to become a mother but rather to delve more deeply into her creative passion. This, as it happened, was also how she made her living. She reveled in the clarity of desire she felt in her bones, and the false pressure of age fell away.

Another woman, whose desire was leaning toward becoming a single mother, did not have many friends and was estranged from her family of origin. The idea of single motherhood felt quite daunting to her without her fully understanding why. She came to learn that making friends was a bigger challenge for her than the question of becoming a mom. Displaying bravery in her exploration, she came to understand better why she didn't have many friends, and her role in the situation. With her new knowledge she was able to make the changes needed to make friends, which in turn made the idea of becoming a single mom less daunting. She realized it *was* possible to create a support network. Being a single mom would certainly bring its challenges, even with a support network in place, but she was no longer frozen in fear, nor did she feel completely alone.

The most complex and compelling of your externals may well be your relationships with the important people in your life. These relationships can exert powerful forces that pull you away from your inner knowing. Over the past weeks, though, you've been strengthening the muscle that allows you to differentiate yourself from your friends and family members. Take a good look at your relationships with all the key people in your life now. Look at your family map. What new understanding do you have about your family of origin? Is there anything you still want to understand better?

In Week 10, as you brought more scrutiny to your relationships with family and friends, were there any that would benefit from some attention or tender loving care? Do any feel out of balance? Are there things that need to be said? You don't have to do anything about this right now, but record in your journal what comes to mind so you can tend to it later. List the relationships you'd like to see change; they can even include those with deceased or inaccessible people. Note the change you'd like to see happen, if you already know what that is. If you know your next step, make a note of that also.

Let's say, for example, the most complex puzzle piece over the course of the program is your relationship with your mother. It might have been strained while you were growing up; and even today, though you have a friendly rapport, it lacks the ease and depth you long for. You know that an easy fix isn't realistic, but there might be some changes you can make to move the relationship in that direction. Consider writing a series of letters to her, with the final one intended to actually be given to her. In this letter you decide to tell her three things that you appreciate about her and your relationship, followed by three things you wish were different between the two of you. Stay focused on smaller changes that are actually achievable, and remember to write the letter using non-judgmental language. If your mother is deceased, this exercise is still worthy of your time. You can read the final letter to a photo of her.

Perhaps you can identify two relationships with friends that feel out of balance. They need your attention and care. Reflect on what you need from each of these friends, and then what you want to see change between you. Even if you can't predict the outcome, you can begin to take steps to explore these changes with them. A next step might be to consult books on improving relationship skills, or take a workshop on learning healthy communication skills to improve your chances of being able to ask clearly for what you want.

Perhaps, in your relationship list, you identified your estranged sister as someone you'd like to reconnect with. Is there some previous impasse to discuss with her? Did you just grow apart? Consider how you'd like to reach out to her and then take action. Maybe there's a co-worker who always seems quick to criticize your work. What small change can you ask of her? This might involve the risk of being more open and revealing your vulnerability as you let her know how her criticism feels to you. If you need help to ask for this, is there anyone at work or in your network of friends who could support you? Perhaps you have an uncle who hasn't always been respectful to you at family functions. You'd forgotten this until you created your family map. He's deceased, but you decide to write him a letter anyway and let him know exactly how you feel about this poor treatment. Write until you feel you've stood up for yourself fully.

Changing relationships *is* hard work. We won't pretend it isn't. But even difficult communications can become easier with practice. What's more, as you change, the people around you change. So identify the relationships you'd like to be different, create your plan, and start moving in the direction of more nourishing and satisfying connections.

Fears

Just as you did with relationships and externals, gaze back over the landscape of your entire journey to see which of your fears remain. Use your journal to list any fears you put in your jar at the beginning of the program if you didn't do this in the "Further Exploration and Discovery" section of Week 1. Consider each in turn and assess whether or not it is still relevant. What new information do you have? How have your fears changed? Do you feel differently about them? In what ways? Are you aware of any new fears? Read on. You might gain guidance as to how to move forward with them.

At the beginning of the program, Holly's biggest fear revolved around meeting a life partner. She felt anxious whenever she thought about it, and for her, deciding whether or not to have children felt inextricably tied to this relationship that felt out of reach. What Holly discovered as she worked through the program was that she hadn't yet, in fact, developed the interpersonal skills needed to sustain a lasting relationship. This is why the question about having a partner provoked anxiety for her. This new self-awareness allowed Holly to focus her attention on creating and meeting concrete goals within her reach – goals that could help her create more satisfying relationships. This eased her fears somewhat around the urgency of meeting a partner and helped her accept that her decision about becoming a mother needed to be made down the road; first she needed to invest in developing the skills that could help her relate to others in more deeply satisfying ways. Only then, when she was better prepared to meet relationship challenges, would she revisit her desire about parenting a child. For Holly, untangling these two issues released the grip this big fear had on her.

Some women feel that they are powerless to secure their own physical and emotional needs, which translates into a fear of trying to do so. Do you have this fear? If you do, look more closely at your personal circumstances. Is it true that you can't secure what you need? Is it truer to say that you haven't exactly known what your needs have been, or that you don't know *how* to secure your needs and you could use some help figuring it out? If you feel *powerless to ask for help*, this can bind with the feeling that you don't know *how* to secure your needs. Together these feel confusing. Your self-perceptions might need clarifying.

Women who struggle with this particular fear – Can I meet my needs in life? – often tease out along the way that their earliest childhood needs were fraught with complications. For instance, someone else's needs had to be met, or at least came first before their *own* needs were addressed or even acknowledged. Circumstances contributing to this fear can be extreme. Neglect and abuse thwart physical and emotional development, distorting the internal processes that organically identify and inform individual needs. If your needs were not seen or met, you might have an internal (possibly subconscious) voice telling you that you'll never be able to meet your own needs, let alone the needs of another.

This is a big topic, and there are whole books dealing with all the things that can get in the way of securing one's needs in life. If this is one of your fears, here are two important things to consider: Don't assume that you can't secure your needs; and you're not alone in having this fear. It's worth investigating either or both of these misconceptions. Explore it first with a professional, or ask for a reality check from friends, family, or people who know you really well and whom you trust. You might be able to look after yourself better than you imagine. Just understanding what this fear is tied to can be enough to dissolve it. And even if it is true that you need *some* help securing your needs, that's a far cry from saying that you can't manage at all.

Holly wasn't gripped by this particular fear in the way she was about finding a life partner, but it was still one of her fears. During Week 8, when she lived as if she was going to become a mother, she "froze in her tracks" as she wondered how she'd be able to care for both herself and a child. Determined to understand this fear, she discovered a deep resentment toward her mother because of all the emotional caretaking she had to do for her, which only increased after her father died. As a child Holly learned to anticipate and meet the needs of others before even considering her own. She didn't experience having her emotional needs recognized and tended to. She would never want her own child to be burdened as she was. As she worked through this residual anger and got back in touch with what she was actually capable of, Holly was able to see that she *would* be able to take care of herself *and* a child if she decided to have one.

The fear of regret is another fear shared by many women who work the program. In our experience it is also the most misunderstood fear. This fear is described as that of potentially missing out on something meaningful, or sometimes of living in a constant state of shame if a "wrong" decision is made. In the course of helping women unpack their fear of regret over the years, we've identified some common themes.

What many women discover is that they fear *being stuck forever* in a state of regret or misery. The *anticipated* regret becomes a monolithic dread that feels like it's about to move in and park itself – for good. Experiencing a virtually immobilizing anticipation of regret is a good indication that your choice is in fact very important to you. It doesn't, however, imply that the regret will truly remain a static state of heart and mind.

Regret, like all emotions, is temporary *if you can work through the feelings.* You might *or might not* experience some regret once you've made your decision about becoming a mother. But of this you can be sure: When you use your skills to feel and express and then process whatever feelings arise for you, they change over time. *Regret only lingers if you don't grieve the loss that sits underneath it.*

Sue's biggest fear at the outset was that whatever she decided, she'd regret her choice later in life. While it surprised her to admit it, the fear of regret still carried substantial weight for her in Week 11. She felt stuck. To her fellow group participants she described her fear of regret as "potential devastation." It dawned on her that the most caring thing she could do for herself was to see her former psychotherapist to try to get to the bottom of this fear.

Within three meetings Sue was able to uncover an early memory of terror that was connected to her father's drunken rages, which could last for hours. During these times Sue would hide under her bed feeling scared, alone, and unable to comfort herself. Her body held these memories, and her therapist used somatic (body-based) techniques with her that included deep breathing into the terror while being witnessed and supported. What Sue called her "current potential devastation" ended up being tied to trauma from her childhood. It took Sue some time to do the necessary healing work, but afterward these painful family memories that had been hidden away in her body and memory banks gave way to a newfound freedom. After working with her psychotherapist, her fears no longer held the same power over her.

Fear of regret can be rooted in a past experience of being stuck in an acutely unpleasant situation, alone and without help, as it was for Sue. Our bodies remember unresolved trauma. If you sense that you have unresolved trauma or fears that come from an earlier time in your life, working with a therapist specializing in trauma work can help you heal and release your body's remembered experience, freeing you up to make choices based instead on your current circumstances. Healing from trauma also promotes self-confidence so you can better meet the full range of challenges that life inevitably presents, whether you become a mother or not.

Fearing regret need not be a life sentence. It can be a knock on the door indicating an inaccurate belief, an unresolved past event wanting to surface in order to be healed, or a loss needing to be grieved. If working through the program in this book doesn't address this issue for you, seeking help from trusted friends, family members, or professionals to explore these uncharted territories is your best option.

The Pulse of Your Desire

It's time to take the pulse of your desire! This is what you've been working so hard to be able to do. Taking the pulse of your desire touches your truth in the here and now. It's listening to your intuition – sometimes called your gut feeling.

In principle, measuring your desire is simple: We ask you a question, and you offer an immediate, intuitive response. Think of your gut feeling as your friend who will deliver to you your most reliable information.

Sit comfortably in a quiet place where you won't be disturbed. Close your eyes, take two or three deep breaths, and then resume normal breathing. Calm your mind. Relax your shoulders, your neck, and your arms. Allow your belly to soften and your legs to relax. Are you comfortable? Is your mind at ease?

Sit for another minute or two until you feel attentive to yourself. Once you feel ready to proceed, open your eyes and continue reading.

Read the following question out loud:

Do I want to be a mom, a mother, a parent?

Close your eyes and feel the answer.

What's your immediate response – your first feeling, your first thought?

Is there clarity one way or the other?

If it's not completely clear, does your answer have a "Yes, but…" to it? Something like *Yes, but really I want to have a baby more than to be a mom*? Or *Yes, but I want to be pregnant more than anything else*? Or even *Yes, but I just don't want to be pregnant*? Another possibility is *No, but what if I'm making a big mistake*? Don't judge yourself if this happens. Just note it for now.

You might find it helpful to take your pulse a second time while looking into a mirror. This time try addressing yourself in the second person, again out loud:

Do you want to be a mom?

Close your eyes again for a few moments to identify what you're aware of. What do you feel – physically and emotionally? What is the pulse of your desire at this point? Where are you on the yes-no continuum? You might want to open your journal and write. You might also want to compare how you feel now with how you felt when you started the program. If your desire is clear, how does it feel?

If you still don't have a clear answer, perhaps you feel some worry or even a sense of hopelessness. Or perhaps you are feeling neutral about not knowing because *knowing* is not the most pressing issue for you any longer. Some women end up feeling relaxed about not knowing, rather than continuing to feel anxious about it, because their focus has shifted to something else. They know the answer will come as they focus on other issues. Not knowing no longer has a grip on them.

Samantha became completely numb when she took the pulse of her desire. If you remember, she was leaning toward wanting to become a mother. When she took her pulse she was overtaken by a state of numbness that clouded over any yes or no. This surprised and worried her. She explored her numb state initially through free-flow writing. It gave way to another deeper layer of sadness that belonged to the young girl inside who never got the consistent nurturing she had longed to receive from her mother. Adult Samantha mourned for her younger self and the numbness melted away. She came through the experience with the clarity she was seeking.

Some women find, as Samantha did, that hopefulness while moving in the direction of clarity is followed by a general numbness, as though the wind has suddenly disappeared from their sails. This is no accident. A glimmer of hope can be dashed in an instant by a wave of grief as you realize how long you've not felt any hope. It can feel confusing, disorienting, and almost as if you're slipping backward. If this feels like it might be true for you, reconnect with yourself by writing about what you feel. Allowing feelings to arise and change on their own, as they will when you give them space and voice, usually opens the next gateway.

So if you find yourself feeling numb, pause to notice it. Let yourself sit with the numbness, softening to it and allowing it to give way to what's underneath. Be patient. It will change. You might unearth deeply buried feelings of sadness or loss. Have compassion for yourself and allow yourself to grieve. It's not your fault that these feelings are surfacing. It's a natural part of healing. It is, in fact, a necessary step on your path to clarity, even though it can feel like an annoying detour.

Feel free to check the pulse of your desire again and again. Fine-tuning your deep listening to your body and intuition is most rewarding.

Closing One Chapter to Open Another

As you anticipate the end of this program, what chapter is ending for you and what chapter might be opening?

Sue's closing chapter was acknowledging that, for her, life is not about being in service to others, and that saying yes doesn't have to be the automatic response to requests that come her way. She finally felt the deep knowing that she doesn't owe anything to anybody and that what *she* wants in her life does matter. It became clear to her that the unhappiness of others is not her fault and that it isn't her responsibility to fix anything for anyone else unless *she* chooses to. You might recall that Sue's mother had a miscarriage when Sue was three years old. Her mother subsequently withdrew into a depression. While Sue was too young to understand what was going on with her, this experience left her feeling that she had done something to cause her mother's withdrawal. Sue's newly opened chapter gave her permission to say no unapologetically – even to motherhood.

When Samantha opened her jar and laid out her fears and externals, she could already feel the shift that had taken place during the program. While she had been leaning toward wanting to be a mom, she had been fearful of passing on her mother's erratic behavior. She had never known which version of her mom was going to walk through the door. She did not want her child to feel as afraid as she had felt at such times. As a child Samantha would sometimes stay up most of the night cleaning in the hope that her mom would stop crying. At other times her mother would come home from work and want to play games with her and her brother with a frenzy that didn't feel "fun" at all. All this instability left young Samantha feeling shaky. She didn't want a child of her own to have to go through what she'd been through. As her chapter closed and a new one opened, Samantha's fear had dissolved and her self-assessments brought her to recognize that she would be a good-enough mother. With her Aunt Bea metaphorically in her corner, she could trust that her child would have a very different experience than her own.

While taking the pulse of her desire, Birgit found herself still without a clear answer within. However, she did have several key puzzle pieces almost in place. She had more compassion for her parents, who were quite expressive about wanting to be grandparents. She could separate their desire from her own and not feel under any pressure from them. While doing the Week 10 "Reader's Choice" exercise, Birgit moved into trusting that her life would unfold and she'd ultimately be at peace with the unfolding. She felt her faith supporting her in this new trust, and while she still didn't have a clear yes or no as her exploration chapter closed, she felt the opening of a new chapter that brought more clarity of purpose. Birgit would focus on cultivating resilience within and renewing interest in her marriage and her career. She felt that from there her decision about whether to have a child would become crystal clear soon enough.

By now you either know your desire, you are very close to knowing it, or you're aware that there's still something in the way of knowing it. What has changed for you since you began this inquiry? What insights, puzzle pieces, and concrete information have come your way? Are you still looking for a missing piece? If your experience has not yet come together into something you can clearly recognize, describe, or grab hold of, that's perfectly okay. It will come. Trust this. The "Be Curious" assignments this week and next are bound to help.

No matter where you are now on the continuum of yes or no to motherhood, you've participated in a deep unearthing of feelings and possibly new information that is still bringing you to your new place. This new place will reveal itself. Be proud of all the good work you've done and be pleased with where you are right now.

⌐◯⌐

Be Curious: Assignments for Week 11

Unleash your unconscious. Stretch yourself. Give yourself permission to be spontaneous, irrational, and/or inappropriate.

1. It's Collage Time!

    It's now time to bring together the images, photos, and word cutouts you've been saving. If you haven't yet saved any, go on a collection spree now. Ask friends, family, and neighbors for photos, magazines, and other resources. Scan the Internet looking for images that delight, disturb, provoke, evoke, and touch emotions relevant to you and this topic.

    Don't think about the collage. Just make it. Trust your ability to be creative. Feel free to add additional items such as your own drawings, fabrics, painting, or anything else that inspires you. Start with a sturdy background and make it as big or as small as you like. It's for *your* healing. If it feels helpful to have a focus before you make your collage, focus on what you want for yourself going forward. Display your finished collage where it can inform and inspire you. It can reflect aspects of your journey like a mirror.

    Spread the images out and create your collage.

2. Intuition and Desire

    With no one around and no pressure to answer in any particular way, close your eyes, breathe, and think about something totally different from whether or not you want to be a mom. Think about your grocery list, what you're going to have for lunch, or what you're going to wear this evening. Forget that you've been working hard to gain clarity. Let your mind wander as far away as you like.

Then open your eyes, look in a mirror, and ask out loud.

Do you want to be a mother?

Write your answer in your journal *using your non-dominant hand*. Slow down to let the answer flow. What comes? What do you feel in your body? What sensations do you notice? What does your intuition tell you? Continue to write about your experience using your non-dominant hand – you might be surprised by what emerges! If the question doesn't apply to you, tweak it so it does. Some possibilities: Do you want to be a mom? Do you want to be a parent? Do you want to raise a child? Choose or create the question that works for you.

3. Draft Your Current *Accurate* Story

All the puzzle pieces of information you've gathered over the past weeks may have begun to fit together. Perhaps a picture has formed that already has meaning for you, or maybe the picture is still forming. This next activity will help you clarify exactly where you stand.

Below are four stories about the motherhood question. From where you are right now, see if you find aspects of yourself in one, in all, or a little of you in each.

Story I:

I never gave it much thought. I figured one day I'd just know. That day never came, and now I pretty much have to decide or the decision will be made for me. It isn't my fault that I never "just knew," even though lots of women seem to have a strong sense of whether or not they want to become a mother without ever having to agonize over it. At this point I really, really want to know what is right for me.

Story II:

I've always wanted children but never met the right person, and I didn't want to be a single mother. Now I don't know what to do. I'm not so sure I want children at this point even though I did for a long time. I'm finally in a relationship that feels good the way it is. It took me so long to meet the right person that I don't know if I want to rock the boat with a child. I'm sure that I would have wanted children if it had happened sooner. The desire to be a mom was there but the opportunity was not. Now I don't think it's what I want. I feel sad that things didn't happen sooner for me.

Story III:

Having a child was never really on my agenda, but it seems like maybe it should be. My parents want grandchildren, my only brother doesn't want children, my relationship with my partner is good, and we certainly have the finances to have children. I just don't think I want them. I've never wanted to admit that to anyone. Sometimes I wonder if I'll miss out on something important. My partner is okay either way. While I feel okay not wanting children, I just don't feel okay admitting that to the world just yet. I don't want to be criticized for not wanting them when I could provide a good life for a child. I also want to be free from the pressure of "I'm supposed to want them."

Story IV:

I'd always just thought I'd become a parent, and never really considered it wouldn't happen for me. My life hasn't taken the path that I'd imagined would precede this outcome. The relationship I thought I'd be in by now hasn't materialized. I don't feel financially secure on my own, and now I don't know if I could conceive if I tried. I feel the pressure inside me because I don't know what I'll do if I can't conceive. The worry isn't huge, but I am aware that it's there. I really, really, really want to fulfill my dream of becoming a parent. How exactly this will look, I don't yet know. I want to start exploring what options might be available to me.

Since you are the definer of you, no one can know better than you what your truth is. Draft a kind, compassionate story that accurately describes you and where you are right now. To do this, you might take one of the stories above and modify it to make it fit you more accurately, or you can create your own using your own words. The choice is yours. What matters is that your story is completely free from any shaming tones or judgmental words.

Once you've crafted your story, how does it feel to see yourself described accurately in this way? If you feel that you used to view yourself *inaccurately*, or that others have done so up to now, how has this impacted you? Keep your story handy and try to keep it up to date. Change it during the week as more precision comes to you. Next week you'll have the chance to refine it and take it up a level.

4. Unfinished Business: Missing Puzzle Pieces

With one more week to go, now is a good time to review your writing assignments and any added journal entries from the beginning. Turn to your "Things to Revisit Later" section and consider them now. As you reread what you wrote over the weeks, be on the lookout for subtle shifts in your perceptions and attitudes. See if a particular puzzle piece still feels cloudy or emotionally charged. Maybe there's more than one. Review the previous weeks' assignments to see if there were any that didn't feel right to do at the time. Perhaps now is a good time to try them. Are there any other bits of unfinished business you want to tend to at this time?

What still feels unfinished for me?
What exercise(s), if any, would I like to redo – and why?

Further Exploration and Discovery

Take some time – we suggest waiting several hours to a day or two – before considering the exploratory questions in "Your Checklist for Reflection" on page 50 as you review your work. Then continue your discovery work by considering your answers to the next set of questions.

Take a long look at this week's collage. Does it please you? Was it fun to put together? What feelings came up as you created it? What element stands out? Do you see any connections that surprise you? Which image arouses the biggest reaction from you? Are there any pictures that touch a secret fantasy? How would you describe your collage to a stranger? Give it a place of prominence if you can, so it can be a mirror back to you.

What have you learned about the pulse of your desire? How easy is it for you to hear and then listen to your intuition? Did anything about the writing you did with your non-dominant hand surprise you?

Does the way you described your current story in the third assignment above feel pure, in alignment, and accurate? If not, can you identify what still needs refinement? Even if clarity is still out of reach, the draft of your story will help guide you forward. It takes time to get your accurate story just right. Next week you'll have the chance to refine it further.

It's valuable to review your writing. Sometimes what you remember having written can be quite different from what you actually wrote! Did you identify any unfinished business or missing puzzle pieces?

Be Even More Curious: Optional Exercises

If you want to do more, here are this week's suggestions:

1. Pay attention to your dreams. See what the unconscious brings forth. Draw, paint, or write about any images that stand out.

2. Imagine receiving this counsel from your wise woman: "Do whatever makes you happy!" Leaving aside what other people might think about this, what does it mean to you right now? Draw it, paint it, or write about it.

3. Think of a time when you experienced unconditional love from another person or a beloved animal. Now think of a time when you felt unconditional love for another. Savor the memories of how you felt in both scenarios. If you spend a couple of minutes every day practicing this *heart exercise*, it will strengthen your impulse to thrive and grow your self-appreciation.

What to Hold Inside This Week

First and foremost, congratulate yourself! You *wanted* something for yourself and *decided* to go after it. Pat yourself on the back and let yourself spend time this week really feeling the smile of pride on your face. Give yourself full credit for answering some pretty tough questions!

Where to next? What is put to rest and what still needs exploring? As you go about your week, notice what comes to you and record it in your journal.

A *totem* is an object that represents or symbolizes the essence of someone or something. What is the essence of you? What object symbolizes the real truth about who you are? Look for an object, or a symbol or representation of an object, that you can regard as your personal totem. It can be anything. You decide what this *essence of you* is, letting your intuition be your guide. Bring your totem with you when you sit down to begin Week 12. Something special happens from the moment you select your totem, so begin your search now.

Self-Care

Do something fun or nurturing every single day this week. Make me-time for self-nourishment. We hope you've expanded your self-care repertoire over the past weeks. This week we offer more self-care suggestions. Feel free to try them or do something else that appeals to you more. Celebrate the wonder of you.

1. Create Your Magic Flying Carpet

    Okay, now's your chance to have some arts-and-crafts fun! Make a magic flying carpet by drawing, painting, or making a collage. If you know how to weave, you can even make one of your own. Then place on your carpet images of your favorite dreams, poems, or desires, or anything else that suits your fancy. If you want to attach these items to your carpet, do that. Hang it up somewhere special or place it where it will be a changeable stage of items that really make you happy.

2. Your Personal Sky Hotel

    Turn your own bedroom into a luxury hotel experience. Make sure it is after laundry day when the linens are clean and crisp. Place a chocolate or two on your pillow. Send yourself room service on a tray that you've prepped with your favorite beverage and some fruit and cheese. Let yourself linger in bed the next morning.

3. Spa Time at Home

    After a long day of work or outside activity, come home to your own
    personal spa. Draw a special bath, adding essential oils or bath salts.
    Dim the lights or light a candle. Play soft background music. Place a
    "Do Not Disturb" sign on the door and step in for a therapeutic soak.

4. Spend Time with a Beloved Pet or Animal

    Spending time with animals can be very soothing. If you don't
    have a pet yourself, borrow a dog from a friend and head out for
    a walk in the woods, or around the block if you only have a short
    window of time. As you walk, share your thoughts with your four-
    legged companion about how you now feel about motherhood.
    Animals are wonderful listeners ☺.

    The self-care I did for myself this week was…

You Are Not Alone

The final stories belong to Michel and Kate. Michel has decided not
to become a mother. She and her husband are now the proud "parents"
of a very special dog! Kate is still in the process of deciding.

Michel's Story

I always assumed I'd have kids. I kept waiting for my biological alarm clock to go off. It never did. Then I got older and I wanted to want kids. It's what people are supposed to do. So I hoped my husband would start to want kids and I would just go along with it, but he came to the realization he didn't want kids. He said he'd be fine having kids if I wanted to, but he was just as happy (or happier) without them. So time kept ticking, and I started really struggling. At one point I even hoped I was infertile so that the decision would be made for me. I was petrified of the potential regret I might feel when I reached sixty. That paralyzed me, I think. I didn't feel confident in my feelings, and actually wished (maybe still do) I felt differently. I wanted to want children, and I kept waiting for that feeling to come, but it never did.

The reasons I did want kids, though bad reasons for procreating, will never go away:

- *I wanted to name someone after my great aunt. (It's a Jewish tradition to name children after the dead; I've since named my dog for my great aunt Esther.)*

- *I wanted to have someone to whom to pass my family history and my worldly possessions.*

- *I wanted to have someone to spend holidays with and take care of me when I am old.*

- *I wanted to have someone to remember me and carry on my family when I am dead.*

- *I wanted to have someone who would mourn and miss me when I am gone.*

I knew none of these was a good reason to have a child. I have learned that while I'll always be sad I don't have these things, I just have to live with it.

I think the first notion of maybe not being a mother came to me in my late twenties or early thirties; though my mother will tell you it was when I was a teenager and I told her I wasn't going to have children because I didn't want to subject them to her. I wasn't always nice.

My mother says she loved being pregnant. I'm told that I came out kicking and screaming. My mother made me feel valued and supported; I never doubted I was loved. But I was always told how difficult I was. My relationship with my mother was and is close, yet volatile; we fought a lot, but we did enjoy spending time doing things together, such as shopping. Once I went away to college, we became much closer. Once I became exposed to different cultural norms, I began to realize how lucky I am to have a mother who cares about me and supports me so much. We also get along much better when we're not living together. I still feel guilty she's not a grandmother, other than to a dog. My parents want grandchildren, and I have a gay brother who is less likely to become a parent.

I've come to realize that I'd rather live with sadness about them than live with actual children. I just had to accept that sadness and loss will always be with me and that it will be okay somehow.

The twelve-week program was the most pivotal thing in my acceptance. Many of the exercises were extremely helpful to me, including writing a letter to the child I would never have. I had an epiphany in Week 11. It was a guided meditation in which I had to picture an old woman in the woods. I pictured the crone's cottage in Snow White. The old woman gave me a gift, and when Ann (the therapist) asked me what it was, I clearly saw a framed photograph of the daughter I would never have. That's when I realized I had actually already made my decision. I grieved as part of the program. It was an assignment to do so, and I felt better after I had a good cry for the child I wouldn't have.

In some ways I did feel alone. It can be harder to be friends with women who have children unless there exists a really solid history or they're interested in being more than just a mother. I have one good friend who is married and child-free by choice, but she embraced two stepchildren, which, honestly, pissed me off.

I desperately wanted to find a support group, but couldn't. I read every book I could find, most of which, it seemed to me, had a bias toward having children. Most of the child-free people profiled kept making the point that they like children and found ways to have them in their lives, as though it wouldn't be okay if they didn't like kids. Well, I don't like kids, and I really don't want to be around them very much. While I am a very good and willing faux aunt (and godmother to an exceptional eight-year-old), it's not because I have a need to be around children. The book I did find most helpful was written in the '70s and had a very early feminist perspective; though dated, it worked for me!

I like my marriage and the structure of my life. I didn't want to risk negatively affecting either one. And also, I was petrified I would have a child with special needs. Post-decision, I have even less patience for kids and dislike them even more. I resent that everything revolves around families with children, from taxes to boarding airplanes. I prefer that children stay home. That said, I think my dog should be allowed everywhere!

From where Michel is today, if she had the opportunity to revisit deciding, she would've tried to make a final choice earlier. She would then have spared herself ten to fifteen years of angst (her word). She asked everybody she knew or met for personal guidance. Some child-free people she knew seemed unhappy that they didn't have children. Conversely, she has quite a few friends who seem to be unhappy as parents. She felt a great deal of guilt toward her family and also her religion: "I feel a responsibility to keep my religion from dying out, and there is no real place for child-free individuals or couples in the religious structure." After embracing her conscious choice to be child-free, she and her husband adopted a dog that they treat as their "very spoiled only child." The advice she would give to a friend facing indecision: "Read books; go through the Motherhood-Is it for me? program, and give yourself permission to decide."

Kate's Story

I would say that only within the last several months, actually, at the suggestion of a friend (who really wants children) that I have my eggs frozen, did my concern about age and the future possibility of not being able to have children turn to anger. Why do I have to worry about this now? I've decided to eliminate more stress from my life and not have children. But I must be honest and say that this decision stems from a few facts: I am not married, nor do I have a boyfriend at this time. I am not employed, or financially secure at this time. I also do not carry a nagging feeling or urge to have a baby/child whom I would have to be responsible for or care about. I think that bringing another being into this world is a very serious thing. Since I can barely take care of myself, I think that having a child right now would be highly irresponsible, and it pisses me off that somewhere (in my mind?) there is this alarm bell going off telling me that my eggs are aging and I'd better find a career and a man and get to it, soon! This is where I am.

I don't know how this discussion will go with a future husband. I really do want to get married. I think there are just a lot of things that I want to do that would make raising a child – and being truly present for that little being the way that I think parents should be – very difficult.

At some future point, if I become a mother because circumstances are conducive to it, and I want a child and still can reproduce, I would incorporate some of my own mother's elements of mothering. That said, there were definitely things I'd want to do differently. Knowing how sensitive a child I was, I think I would be that much more attuned to a sensitive child's needs.

I had a tough time growing up. I was never the popular kid in school, was a late bloomer (may actually still be blooming), and my mom knew all of this but could only do what she could. The school choices were what they were during that time of 1975 through the '80s and '90s. I was a shy, sensitive girl who grew up in Los Angeles, so my parents put me where I guess they thought it was right for me. I still had social issues, was teased and left out of things (like dance), etc., even though I was in private schools. Regarding my parents' helping me to feel better, my mom was there, but my dad not so much. In any event, my self-esteem was not off to a great start.

I believe that everyone doesn't need to have children, and if I decide it's not right for me, that I am not selfish not to want to give myself completely to another person. This is actually not a selfish thing at all because I would be deciding – through knowing what kind of a mother I would want to be and knowing what children need to grow up happy, healthy, well-adjusted, and confident – that I did not want that responsibility. Furthermore, you never know who or how your child will be, and I just don't know if I would be cut out for parenthood and all it entails. Finally, there are plenty of women like me who have gone through what I went through in my teens and twenties and they also need love, empathy, compassion, nourishment, and nurturing. Who says that I couldn't embrace them, hold them, love and nurture them in order to heal the hurt. This is something that I am still working on: healing the hurt inside.

Kate is still trying to answer the question "What am I going to thrive at?" and describes herself as a late bloomer. She's been slow to find a career that suits her and will also support her independence. She decided not to have children, at least for now; she doesn't want to have to keep it on the back burner. There are already too many pots on that stove: being single and wishing things were different; not working and feeling anxious about it all.

At the time she completed our questionnaire she had recently relocated to another state. She had just celebrated her thirty-sixth birthday. She was struggling to find meaningful employment. While the relocation had been positive from an emotional perspective, as Kate was now living close to a dear friend with a toddler daughter whom Kate enjoyed immensely, the transition called for adjustments that weighed heavily on her time and inner resources.

Kate is close to her mother and can discuss most things with her, including how she feels about not wanting to become a mother herself. She described her mother as easy-going with either choice. However, Kate also senses wishes for grandparenthood. Her relationship with her father is more problematic and nearly always has been. She sees now that her father knew how to raise and nurture a baby and young girl, but that as she grew into an older child and started to struggle in school, he didn't know what to say or do. As a psychiatrist, he had the professional training, but Kate witnessed his personal shortcomings as a human being with his own difficult upbringing to contend with. Her dad also has a short fuse, and this makes her a little fearful of him. She feels residual sadness at what's lacking in their relationship.

Kate has a younger brother who is three years her junior, and an attorney. She often feels like he is the star child in the family – at least that is how her father seems to behave.

Kate pays attention to how she feels around other people's children: "I do notice that when I'm around children, in general, I don't feel my uterus a-thumpin' ☺. Where I have recently moved I have a dear friend who has this one-and-a-half-year-old who is just adorable. I enjoy holding her and watching her try to stand up, walk, etc." Kate's advice to other women facing this issue: "See how you feel around children. Look at your life. Look at what you have done and what you want to do or accomplish. Is there an aching need there for a baby or a huge desire to nurture a child?"

As Kate continues her exploration into the deeper layers of her ambivalence and disconnects from the pressure of time running out, she might discover that she would like to have a child, and could then decide to go ahead and make that happen, or she might decide not to follow through with this desire given her circumstances. She described dreams in which she has just found out that she is pregnant, or in which she is growing bigger, and she finds these to be lovely dreams. Perhaps these dreams mean that Kate wants to have a biological child. Might they be symbolic, as Kate creates her adult self and develops her personal capacity for nurturing? Of course, there could be elements of both interpretations in her dreams. Time will tell.

Week 12

Arriving

ɛ Remember always, you are the helmswoman of your life. ꙮ

You've arrived at the final week of the Motherhood-Is it for me? program. You now have much more information about yourself as you move forward in making your decision. The externals and fears that you identified during Week 1 made their reappearance last week. How was that for you? As you considered them, one by one, which were still relevant? Were any worrisome? Did you deepen your understanding of why regret is nothing to fear?

You took the pulse of your desire. What did it reveal? You also composed a personal story that conveys an up-to-date and accurate picture of where you stand right now. Were you able to write your story objectively, free of any judgmental tone? When you read back what you wrote, did it feel spot-on? If so, could you feel relief? If not, you'll have an opportunity this week to improve on it.

What about your collage? Were you able to have fun with it? Did creating it help you put more pieces of your puzzle together? How inspiring was the search for your totem? Were you able to find an object or symbol that captured the essence of you? If you also took the time to review your writing to date, you probably gained some new insights. Perhaps you even spotted an exercise that you wanted to repeat.

How was it to read about twenty different women (in Weeks 2 through 11), who so generously shared their journeys? They, like you, were seeking clarity. Did you find aspects of yourself in their lives and stories?

You've come so far on your journey! There is just a little bit more to do this week. The guided part of your journey of exploration and discovery comes to a close at the conclusion of this week. Do you notice what's coming together for you while also staying open to the possibility that there are still some nuggets to unearth, all of them contributing to the bigger picture of you?

Wherever you are now on the yes-no continuum, it doesn't mean your discovery process is over. Emotions will continue to surface. The path of self-knowledge is a lifelong journey, ever-changing and evolving. Even though Week 12 marks the end of your journey with the program, the start of a new chapter in your life is just around the corner. Welcome it!

To prepare for this week's guided visualization, take yourself to a place where you'll be undisturbed. Take a few moments to tune in to your breath. As you naturally breathe in and out, allow your mind to settle. Become aware of the miraculous simplicity of your breathing. It's effortless. Then, with your eyes closed, recall the image of something beautiful that you witnessed during the past week. Pause to enjoy this image while taking it in fully.

Week 12 Guided Visualization

As usual, there's nothing to do during this last visualization but let yourself be guided and sink into the images and feelings that emerge. You're aware, by now, that these exercises are in fact jewels, and their function is to bring information from your unconscious into awareness.

Trust that your attentive mind will go where it needs to go. When your eyes are closed, you engage the part of your brain that isn't as easily accessed when your eyes are open. Have someone read the visualization to you or record it for you so you can listen while your eyes are closed, as its power also lies in the element of surprise. If that's not possible, make a recording yourself so you can listen with eyes closed to deepen the experience of where the visualization takes you. If you read the visualization to yourself, read it silently and slowly to give yourself time to savor the experience. Close your eyes now and then to open to the power of your imagination.

Remember that the experience you have is what matters most, and there's no wrong way to do it. Have your journal and writing tool nearby so you can record your impressions and images immediately.

To prepare, choose a quiet place where people and noise won't disturb or distract you, and a time when there's nothing else for you to do and no one who needs your attention; this time is solely for your benefit. Either sit comfortably in a chair or, if you prefer, lie down on the floor.

Coming Home

Now that you're ready, become conscious of your breathing. Let your eyes close gently as you take a deep breath and exhale. Inhale and hold your breath for five counts. Then exhale until most of the air has left your lungs. Inhale again and slowly exhale, letting out an audible sigh through your mouth while you count silently from ten to one. Continue breathing slowly and deeply. As you breathe, you relax. Allow your natural breath to bring a deep sense of peace and well-being. Feel your body relax and let your mind free-associate. Breathe.

Imagine you are blanketed in a cocoon of white light filling you with warmth and love. While you're wrapped in this blanket of white light, go to the place inside where you feel love and appreciation for yourself. That is your birthright. Open fully and breathe into this space within you. By now you're an expert at opening your heart and mind to what presents itself.

Turn your attention back to the Sky Hotel, where your comfort was a top priority. You're back in the lobby of the hotel. It's time to take flight again, as you're ready for more discoveries. Roll out your magic carpet once more and gently settle into its plush support. Feel the tiny air bubbles form under it. The bubbles grow bigger until they are so big that the carpet leaves the hotel and flies into the sky.

As you fly away from the Sky Hotel, look down on the landscape. Breathe. From your vantage point, what do you see? Which puzzle pieces are already in place? As you consider the results of your hard work, which pieces of the puzzle can now also fall into place? What pieces are still missing? Breathe into the feelings that are present right now and let those feelings swirl about in your heart and your body without drawing any conclusions.

Remember that you're in command of your flying magic carpet. Maneuver it as you will. Enjoy this sense of freedom. How does it feel? As you gaze down at the terrain below, can you feel spaciousness within you? What feels crystal clear to you? What is still coming into focus?

As you hover above, what do you see in your future? Do you see any externals that need sorting out? What fears, if any, still lie in wait at the sidelines? Take a moment to *feel* what's there for you. Whether it's relief, joy, sadness, confusion, or something else altogether, let it be.

Fly your carpet over the collage that you created last week. From this vantage point notice what messages are there. What is calling out to you?

Without struggle of any kind, check the pulse of your desire. Do you want to be a mom? Do you want to live a child-free life? Where does your heart go? Where does your mind go?

What comes up when you think about what's next for you? Be mindful of your immediate thoughts and feelings.

Is there a conversation you want to have with anyone? Do you need more time to sit with all that you've experienced? Where are you now in your process? What is your *very next* step going to be? There is no *right* next step, only *your* next step. If your mind draws a blank, that's perfectly fine.

Remember that your magic carpet is intuitive; it remembers all you've experienced to date. Imagine letting *it* be in control now for a few minutes. Where does it want to take you? What does it want you to see? Is there someone the magic carpet wants you to visit? Is there something special it's trying to tell you? Breathe.

After you've allowed the carpet to steer for a while, take back the controls. You've done your work. Feel proud! How does it feel to be closing this chapter? Breathe.

Remember always, you are the helmswoman of your life. Don't underestimate the power of the resources available to you. Don't underestimate what has taken place over these past weeks. You achieved a lot through your sheer determination to uncover your true desire.

Remember also that *you are not alone*. There is and will always be guidance available to you. No matter where this journey of discovery ends for you, a new journey of exploration will begin.

It's time for you to guide the carpet back to where you started. Glide into a soft landing as you come home to yourself. Stand up, step off the carpet, roll it up, and store it away safely in your memory. You can retrieve it later if you want to go for a ride to explore new places or revisit familiar territory. Your intuitive magic carpet will always be waiting for you. Good work!

Keep your eyes closed while you slowly return to your present environment, allowing a few moments to be with your emotional and physical sensations. Breathe.

When you're ready, slowly open your eyes and begin to write in your journal. Record your immediate thoughts, feelings, insights, and anything else you want to about your experience.

Immediate Writing after the Guided Visualization

Trust that there's meaning in all that occurred. When you finish writing, read on.

While on your magic carpet, were you reminded of any earlier experiences you had during the program? Did any new thoughts or ideas emerge? What additional puzzle pieces appeared? Did any pieces come together?

You can experience this final guided visualization as many times as you like. Soaring on your magic carpet above the terrain you covered helps you retain and build on a coherent image of your process.

When your writing feels complete, check in with your emotional state. Are your feelings manageable? If you feel overwhelmed, follow these instructions:

Take a deep breath, then exhale as slowly as possible, letting all the air escape your lungs. Allow your body to take in a breath on its own. Continue this several times until you notice a sense of calm. Then tap your feet on the floor. Follow that by tapping the tops of your thighs with your hands. Then tap your arms with your hands. Clench your fists and then release them. These actions help reconnect you to the present and ground you. Doing this is especially important when the emotions you experience feel overwhelming or just too much for you to manage. If you need to take further action to feel reconnected or grounded in the present, stand up and stamp your feet. Then reach your hands up in the air and stretch.

Look around the room and notice objects that bring a gentle smile to your face. Is your focus where you want it to be? Are your emotions manageable? Before you continue, make sure your attention is where you need it to be.

What Happens in Week 12

Last week you created the first draft of your current story. This week we encourage you to refine and embellish it. A crucial part of this week's work is to deepen your connection with your totem and tune in precisely to your true nature. We wrap up the program by describing scenarios of where this step-by-step guided method has taken other women. You'll gain an insider's view of their journeys. You'll see how their processes unfolded and led to newfound awareness, which in turn informed their decisions and next steps. Reading these women's stories helps you think about *your next steps*. The activities presented in "Be Curious" and "Be Even More Curious" are designed to bring closure and help you embrace the next part of your unique journey. Enjoy!

Refining Your Current Story

We want you to understand why it's so important to have an up-to-date story that describes you and your situation objectively.

When you hold an *accurate, objective, and kind* story of yourself and your journey, you're less likely to be influenced (*or hurt*) by the opinions of others or their projections of what they think is true for you. You've most likely been on the receiving end of emotionally charged opinions and judgments about whether or not you should become a parent. As your life evolves and you develop new insights, continuing to fine-tune your story helps you develop internal spaciousness. This allows you to feel more grounded no matter what your circumstances, while also keeping the judgments of others at a safe distance. Let's see how fine-tuning and embellishing works.

Below is the third sample story from Week 11, followed by its updated version. You can see in the revised version how this woman more clearly conveyed her self-certainty and changed circumstances. She finished her rewrite a few weeks after the program's completion. Sometimes the process needs time to settle. See how you feel about her changes, and as you read, see if you can feel yourself in any part of her story.

Original story, Week 11:

> Having a child was never really on my agenda, but it seems like maybe it should be. My parents want grandchildren, my only brother doesn't want children, my relationship with my partner is good, and we certainly have the finances to have children. I just don't think I want them. I've never wanted to admit that to anyone. Sometimes I wonder if I'll miss out on something important. My partner is okay either way. While I feel okay not wanting children, I just don't feel okay admitting that to the world just yet. I don't want to be criticized for not wanting them when I could provide a good life for a child. I also want to be free from the pressure of "I'm supposed to want them."

Fine-tuned and embellished version:

> I always thought I should want children, and after I found myself in a stable relationship with financial security, I especially thought I was supposed to have them. People told me that I was being selfish for not having children. Saying no to motherhood didn't feel like an option, so whenever I did entertain that possibility, I had to shut it down. I know now that my desire and decision is to have a child-free life – and I know with every fiber of my being that this is not selfish. My partner and I have agreed to have the same answer should we be asked, "Do you have children?" We plan to respond with pride and confidence, "We do not." Depending on who is asking, we may share more details. However, I also know that having good relationships with young people will continue to be important for me since I love having a positive influence in their lives. As time goes on, I feel more internal freedom about both my desire and my decision.

Sue, whose family map was the sample in Week 1, fine-tuned her story this way:

> I had wanted to become a mom years ago. I wish I'd had help back then to gain clarity about my desire. I would have ended sooner the relationship that I was in during my thirties to look for a partner who wanted children. I would've also spent less time taking care of the emotional needs of both my parents. By the time I learned more about boundaries and about how being an adult child of an alcoholic impacted my life, things had changed for me. My life now is different, and I'm older than I wanted to be as a mother. So today it's not my truth to be a parent, even though earlier I did want to be a mom. When people see me without children, I don't want them to assume that I didn't want children. Of course I have no control over their thoughts. I'm still working through my sadness about how it all played out, but the sadness is waning, and I don't blame my parents or myself anymore. The sadness that is still there doesn't get in the way of my moving on with my life. Now I want to focus on creating a healthy relationship in which both my partner and I will thrive. I have nieces and a nephew, and I want to nurture those relationships.

Samantha updated her story this way:

> I never thought I wanted children; and if I did want them, I thought it would be a bad idea because I didn't think I'd be a very good mother given my family background. Now I understand where that thinking comes from. I truly believe with my whole heart that I am capable of being a good-enough mother and will do right by my child. Having a child is what I want to do. I no longer feel the same fear level of being burdened by taking care of a child. I'm excited by my prospects.

Another program participant not featured earlier fine-tuned her story like this:

> Being a mom was never on my top priority list. Even though I leaned toward no on motherhood, it was never a strong no. My focus in life has been my career. I was bothered for a long time when people would question my lack of clarity. I got over that once I participated in the Motherhood program: I knew I'd be a good mother if I decided that I wanted to be one, but an exciting career and a partner were things I wanted to have in place first. When I met a man who really wanted children and would clearly be a great parent, I knew I wanted to join him there. It's the best relationship I've ever had, and I have an emotional maturity that I didn't have in my early thirties. I've decided to become a mother, and I know I'll be the best mother I can be. I feel like I can now really be on board with it. I also feel that if I get stuck or frustrated in any way down the road, there are resources available to me.

In this week's "Be Curious" section, you have the chance to take your story to the next level. The more authentic and informed you can make your self-assessment, the more solid you'll feel within yourself. Your new description of yourself and your circumstances – accurate and compassionate – will lead you to a well-earned boost in confidence and a renewed belief in yourself. It will help you in the face of others' potential judgments or opinions. Stand tall in the truth of your desire. Only *you* know what is true for you.

Your Totem

Last week you were asked to find an object that represents the essence of you. Look at it now before you read on. How does it embody or symbolize the real truth of who you are?

In twenty-five years of guiding women through this program, the same totem has never appeared twice. Imagine that! Some women have proudly described their totems as representing these aspects of themselves: flexible, big-hearted, sharp-thinking, quietly strong, deeply intelligent, connected with nature and animals, fearless, loveable, majestic, sensual, fiercely protective, intuitive, charismatic, a source of energy that gives life to those around, inherent determination, meant to soar, a risk taker… the list goes on and on.

Having a sacred object in physical form allows the wonderful truth of *you* to be symbolically available and readily visible to you – and to others if you so choose. If learning to value your precious self does not come naturally, this representation of you can be very useful. During times when you feel confused, down, or out of sorts, or when you've lost sight of who you really are, having your totem nearby to convey your essence clearly and strongly supports you.

Consider your totem now. Can you see the depth of your inherent beauty and strength reflected back to you? In this week's "Be Curious" exercises, we invite you to explore your totem further.

Wrapping It All Up

This program was born out of a strong commitment to help you discover the crystal-clear truth of your desire so that a conscious decision of saying yes to motherhood or yes to a child-free life can follow. You're *entitled* to know what's right for *you*.

Each of you will end up in a slightly different place at the end of this process. How could it be otherwise? You are unique, and each of you has your own set of circumstances.

Below are the most common outcomes for women who began the program in a state of confusion that ranged from a nagging curiosity to a deep anxiety that plagued every aspect of their lives. You'll see how the program's *process* contributed to each journey's unfolding. You'll find variety in the outcomes. We expect you'll identify with one of the storylines, or at the very least, with parts of them.

The outcomes are ranked from occurring most often to least often. These results are not mutually exclusive, and you'll find a little overlap between them. Longer explanations with illustrations follow the summary.

1. Complete clarity of desire achieved: a decision is clearly in view or emerging; there's a sense of peace and of being free of anxiety, no matter the chosen path.

2. Complete clarity of desire achieved: the decision is not yet known, but there is complete confidence that it will come; again, there's a sense of peace and of being free of anxiety, no matter the chosen path.

3. Clarity of desire achieved: though clarity of *desire* is achieved, and the *decision* is clearly in view, they differ from one another; complete comfort with this paradox; ability to own both the desire and the decision without one overriding the other.

4. A minority of women don't *yet* feel clarity of desire; however, usually there is a sense of being okay with not knowing, since the reason *why* has been discovered. A next step may be apparent; there is awareness

that the process of discovery has concluded and clarity of desire *is* within reach. Some feel worried, anxious, and/or disappointed that clarity is still out of reach.

1. ***Most women who complete the program have their desire come into focus with real clarity.*** With this clarity they feel the burden of indecision fall away and are ready to make their choice. No matter where they end up on the yes-no continuum, the decision that follows feels like the right one. It's conscious. It feels good, solid, and they trust it.

Sue reached the clarity of her desire. Although she wished her earlier life had played out differently, she was now clear that her true desire was no, which was followed by her decision of no. This came quickly and readily once she felt she now had *permission* to say no to motherhood. Sue knew deep inside that having children was not what she wanted anymore. She was ready to let go of that dream and move on to create new dreams.

Sue's friends knew she was going through this intense program and they were eager to hear what it was like for her. After sharing with them what she'd learned about herself, she decided to organize her own No-Baby Shower ceremony, which turned into quite the party. She had worked hard to acknowledge this place of inner knowing, and wanted to celebrate with her closest friends. These friends were delighted for her, applauded her tenacity, and felt honored to participate. Sue, finally, could put herself first; she'd learned how to nurture herself while also giving to others from her heart rather than because it was expected of her. She felt safe. She thoroughly enjoyed being the center of attention. She knew precisely how she wanted her No-Baby Shower to be and did not hold back on any detail.

She created a large banner and painted on it the Serenity Prayer. She asked her friends to write on the banner the strengths they saw in her and anything else to acknowledge what she meant to them. Sue provided colorful markers for this part. She hired two massage therapists who set up two tables in separate quiet rooms in her home, where soothing music was played in the background. Her friends took turns receiving therapeutic massages. After everyone had their massage, they sat down for a meal catered by a local chef. Then Sue brought out her favorite dessert that she had prepared herself earlier. This gave her great pleasure. After being pampered with massage and satiated with nourishing and delicious food, the dance music began. They danced for hours. This was the beginning of a new chapter in Sue's life. She knew what came next to move forward.

After the ceremony, Sue's next step was to bring closure to her process by doing the last bit of grieving over her childhood. She wrote more letters to her young one inside. She also practiced gently acknowledging, rather than overriding, the feelings of hurt that still lived within her heart. She continued to build better boundaries with family and friends. She gained confidence in herself and came to understand that a thriving life – one refocused on her *own* happiness, not on other people's happiness at her expense – was hers to live. Being stuck in an indecision loop had taken a tremendous amount of mental energy, and Sue was relieved when it was over. She didn't feel she had to defend her position. It didn't matter what others thought anymore. For the first time ever, Sue felt inner spaciousness and peace.

Samantha also uncovered her desire and was ready to make her decision. Her partner, Elise, had not gone through the program with her, and Samantha wasn't sure how or where to begin sharing with her such a vulnerable and potentially emotionally charged process. Elise was eager to learn what Samantha had discovered, as her clarity would impact both of them.

With guidance from the "How to Share Your Process" templates in Appendix 1, Samantha was able to share with Elise that she no longer felt afraid of passing on her childhood wounds to a baby. She let Elise know that after confronting her self-doubt she had come to believe that she would be a good-enough mother. Elise was impressed with how much Samantha had been able to heal, and eventually participated in the program herself! Even though Elise herself was already leaning toward motherhood, she wanted to own her yes rather than have it be just a reflection of what Samantha wanted. Samantha was delighted at Elise's wish to be sure of her own desire and decision. She wanted Elise to be fully on board if they were going to raise a child together; then they could navigate with greater ease any obstacles that might come their way.

2. *The second-largest group of women found their desire came into focus while their decision remained unknown.* From gaining greater clarity about their desire, these women now felt they could navigate the journey to making a choice at their own pace without struggle or anxiety. Trying to figure out their desire *and* their decision *at the same time* caused untold anguish. When the two were separated and one was resolved, relief followed. For women who felt tortured by indecision, simply reaching an absence of anxiety felt almost more important and liberating than making the decision itself.

Birgit found herself in this group. She concluded that her true desire was no to motherhood – and she felt fine not making a final decision for a couple of years. One of Birgit's struggles as the middle child of her family was feeling an obligation not to make waves. Her parents wanted grandchildren, and Birgit didn't think her siblings were going to have children. Through working this program and looking under all the stones that were there for her, she came to know *her* truth. Birgit no longer felt it was her responsibility to give her parents grandchildren. She accepted the reality that her desire could be different from theirs.

Although Birgit didn't feel she would eventually choose motherhood, she was open to the possibility of her desire shifting. She felt relaxed and neutral about making a final decision, which was less relevant to her right now. She wanted to enjoy her life with her husband and their dogs while focusing on her career. Her husband supported Birgit in her desire of no. As a couple they were both happy to live life fully and wait a few years before their choice was final. The pressure was gone.

Holly's desire evolved into an unambiguous yes to motherhood. Although she didn't yet know what her ultimate decision would be, the clarity of her desire to be a mother was what she needed to know first. Then she understood what her next steps would be: to heal the psychological wounds that had kept her from developing sustaining relationships in general, and to find a healthy primary intimate relationship.

Even though she was thirty-seven, Holly didn't feel the pressure she had felt before she started the program. She now had a clear picture of what had been in the way of knowing her desire. She could also see what steps she needed to take to have a thriving life, internally and externally. Even if the passage of time she needed for her subsequent grieving and healing might mean that she was no longer able to have children, she was willing to accept that possibility. Holly remained open to the idea of being a mother whether she became pregnant herself, adopted a child, or met a man who already had children. She knew she did not want children of her own at all costs. *To be a mother* was more important to her than figuring out how to have a child. To be in a satisfying and healthy relationship was more important to her than being a mother. The clarity of her desire provided her with relief she had never previously known.

3. *Some women achieved clarity about their desire even though they ultimately decided the opposite.* How can it be possible that someone with a desire of *no* to motherhood ends up choosing *yes*, or that someone with a desire of *yes* makes a *no* decision – without regret

or resentment? This concept is not only hard for some to grasp and fully understand, but it is often the underlying reason for their initial conflict or ambivalence. You'll shortly see how a woman's particular circumstances can lead her to move forward with a yes decision even though her desire is no, and vice versa.

Ending up with a *no* desire and a *yes* decision can arise when one partner wholeheartedly wants to be a parent while the other feels differently but also wants to acknowledge the partner's desire. Becoming a parent is *not* a situation in which one says begrudgingly, "Okay, I'll do it." When this particular woman decides to become a mother, even though her personal desire may be no, she is able and willing to move to another place because of the work she has done. This is her outcome after a thoughtful, heartfelt, and conscious process. Moving forward with the decision, this woman might still need to grieve her loss of the choice not taken as much as a woman grieving the loss of *not* becoming a parent would need to.

If you find yourself in this position, the rationale behind a *no* desire and an ultimate yes choice is your business alone. When you've done your work and are clear on your *no* desire, you are still free to decide yes from a conscious position of power rather than from reactivity or anger. A *no* desire followed by a yes to motherhood ideally comes with the heart and mind working together.

The reverse, a *yes* desire with a *no* decision, is also a very real possibility as a few of the twenty women who shared their stories in this book demonstrate. A woman who becomes clear about her desire of yes only later in life, at a time when her personal situation and circumstance makes this no longer a viable, possible, or realistic choice, also falls into this group. When this happens, the decision generally becomes a no. This woman comes to the painful awareness that if she had been clearer earlier and the conditions supported it, she would have chosen yes. This is what happened to Sue. Part of her refined, accurate story read, "I had wanted to become a mom years ago. Today it's not my truth to be a parent even though earlier I did want to be a mom." This outcome also invites grieving for what has not come to be and for any disappointments that are still being carried.

Two more *yes*-desire and *no*-decision scenarios come from earlier participants in the program. One woman wanted to be a mother but her partner became terminally ill early in their relationship. She decided that quality time together was what was most important to her. The second woman wanted children but also needed to dedicate time to care for her aging parents and her disabled sister. Having a child the way she would have wanted might not have worked given her family commitments. She decided to care for her parents and sibling and to refocus her life on making the difference she wanted to make in the world. While she grieved that her desire never came to fruition, her not becoming a parent didn't carry regret or bitterness.

The truth is that when a woman can *own* her true desire rather than override it, she has more internal freedom to make her decision. When a woman can truly separate out her *desire* from her *decision*, and she fully understands the depth and meaning of all the details that make up and contribute to her desire, she is able not only to make a different choice but to be fully reconciled regarding the difference. It is not easy to make a decision that ultimately differs from one's desire, but it is doable, as many courageous women have shown us.

Once you've arrived at the clarity of your desire, sharing it with others is a very personal experience. Decide for yourself on the timing. Some women want time to be alone with their newfound desire since it's a new feeling. We support this approach. Even if you already have an inkling of your *decision*, bask in the deliciousness of knowing the truth of your *desire* privately for a while. Alternatively you can choose to share the clarity of your *desire* with a partner or other loved one right away, while keeping your ultimate *decision* to yourself for a while. You decide what is right for you.

4. ***Finally, there are women who do not arrive at the clarity of their desire.*** Most of them are comfortable with that outcome because they've reached clarity about what their next step will be and they're eager to take this next step. They are moving *toward* the clarity of their desire. Some feel frustrated because they still lack the clarity they expected would come forth, and they don't fully understand why it hasn't. If this is true for you, *take heart* and don't underestimate what has already happened. You might still be processing. Not knowing what your desire is right this minute doesn't necessarily mean there's a lot more work for you to do. Your truth might be just around the corner.

When a woman completes the program as outlined and comes to the realization that she does not have clarity of her desire but she does finally understand the root of her ambivalence, she is typically quite relieved. She is then liberated and eager to take her next step because she knows in what direction to head. If she felt tortured not knowing, that has gone. The stones she turned over and the healing she experienced as she worked the program prepared her for the next step – likely the last one – that she is now ready to take.

Her one last step to clarity can involve coming to terms with or healing any of the following issues: low self-esteem; blame or resentment toward parent(s) for childhood suffering; a known trauma (such as neglect or physical/emotional/sexual abuse); unresolved grief over the death of a sibling or parent; a personal addiction of any kind; or an early unmet childhood need (such as a need to feel seen, taken care of, or safe) that is frozen in time.

If you relate to the situation in the previous paragraph, rest assured that you are not alone. All the issues listed above have come up before with at least one participant of the program. Next steps, when identified, make movement forward possible. Past feelings you might have carried around unknowingly can fall away.

Perhaps you don't have clarity, but you are truly okay with it because you realize there are more pressing issues that need attention. These are the externals in your life. Through working the program, you took care of unresolved issues that existed. That experience has brought you to the realization that when it's time to face your desire and/or decision, you will do so with ease. You are confident. You earned this strength by doing the work required to get there. Perhaps you are young enough that you feel you have time; you want to travel, change careers, or find the right partner. Perhaps you want to adopt a pet or spend more time with your partner.

Perhaps you turned over all your stones and put your puzzle pieces together only to discover that knowing your desire about motherhood is not such a pressing issue anymore – at least not right now. You experience freedom. You let go and move on. The issue of not knowing disappears. You're okay with it because now isn't the right time to explore this desire or decision. You'll know when it *is* the right time for you.

If you're still struggling even with all the work you've done, *please* recognize that you have made progress. Then breathe. It's okay to feel some disappointment in knowing that there is still more to do. What has come before matters, and so do you!

Sometimes all that's needed to let the entire process bear fruit is a little patience. There's nothing like giving things time, especially when you feel *something* has shifted but you don't quite know what to do about it yet. In the meantime, see if you can allow yourself to relax about not *yet* having arrived at the clarity of your desire, and trust in your internal strength. Either choose to repeat some of the exercises, or simply decide to take a complete break for a while.

It might also be that an unresolved issue needs attention before the clarity of your desire can emerge. These words can come as a surprise and a disappointment to women who reach the end of this program yet still feel ambivalent. "But I've worked on myself; I've healed my old wounds" is a common response. You might indeed have worked through various personal challenges; however, growth is rarely linear, and when a major stressor presents itself, or you bump up against a significant life choice such as deciding whether or not to have children, unexplored layers of an old issue can spiral up to the surface and demand a new level of attention. Even though excavating that painful place *yet again* can open you to more suffering, not doing so brings a different kind of misery – the kind that can deny you access to your most authentic self.

We encourage you to complete the "Be Curious" and "Be Even More Curious" assignments for this week before concluding that you don't know your desire. If you're not satisfied with how you feel after you complete the assignments, we will guide you further with a few more activities that hopefully will help you gain the clarity you're still seeking.

Be Curious: Assignments for Week 12

Many of the women who arrive at this point in the program *still* feeling uncertain suddenly get their clarity while doing these final activities. Often it's just one little insight or one little impulse that turns the tide, and then – voila! Remember that there might be more happening under the surface than you're aware of. These last exercises are also of great value even if you already know what you want. They affirm your truth. Give them your all!

1. Opening the Heart

    Two questions follow. Take them to heart. Remember that your answers don't commit you to anything. This is just another exploration to facilitate the emergence of more information. The answers are for your use only. Be inspired by these words of William Wordsworth: "Fill the paper with the breathings of your heart."[11]

    > *What would have to happen or change inside me to choose motherhood? What would I have to know or believe about myself to decide to become a mom? What would it take to say YES to motherhood and feel good about it?*

    > *What would have to happen or change inside me to choose a child-free life? What would I have to know or believe about myself to choose not to have children? What would it take to say NO to motherhood and feel good about living a child-free life?*

2. Fine-Tuning and Embellishing Your Accurate Story

    You created a version of your accurate story during Week 11. Now take what you wrote and flesh it out. What is your most honest story – factual and without judgment – about yourself? Think about your words carefully, crafting a story that is as kind and gentle as it is accurate. Make sure you touch on all the factors that play a part in your individual situation, including some history about your journey as well as relevant externals, both the positive and the challenging ones. Refine your story until it is such an accurate description that it's a relief to read aloud. If it's helpful, refer to the examples of other women's stories – and keep rewriting your story as often as it feels useful to you.

My refined and fine-tuned accurate story is...

3. Creating an Honoring Ceremony – Bring Along Your Totem

Gaze at your totem. Take in its essence. If you still haven't found one, continue your search. After enjoying some time reveling in the essence of you that your totem embodies, use your journal to describe your totem. Describe how you selected it. Why did you pick this particular totem? How would you describe its nature? How does it represent your essence? Does it surprise you in any way? If so, how? If it could speak to you, what guidance might it have for you?

Now place your totem in a spot you consider safe, even sacred. You are going to create an altar or a *love nest,* a special space to honor *you.* Add a lit candle and perhaps a flower or a full bouquet. Place at least two favorite photos of yourself alongside your totem, one from your childhood and another from adulthood. Give yourself a good fifteen to twenty minutes to sit quietly in your love nest. Breathe deeply into your being, filling in the blanks with the adjectives that describe *you* most accurately:

I am one beautiful, _____, _____, _____, and wonderful woman with integrity. I love who I am and who I've become. I embrace myself wholeheartedly.

4. Assessing Your Process

At the end of any period of self-discovery or learning, it's helpful to look back and evaluate how it went. This review helps provide a greater understanding of what has actually transpired. It deepens your awareness and validates and concretizes what occurred. Take a little time now to do that for yourself. Writing out your answers to the following questions is far more effective than just thinking about them.

> *What do I appreciate about myself for having participated in this program?*
>
> *What did I enjoy about the program?*
>
> *What do I wish had been different about the program?*
>
> *Without being judgmental, is there anything I wish I had done differently?*
>
> *What do I need now to move toward my next step?*

Further Exploration and Discovery

Take as long a break as you need before you go back and read what you wrote. Consider the exploratory questions in "Your Checklist for Reflection" on page 50 to help you dig deeper into your responses and bring any remaining insights to light.

As you worked through the "Opening the Heart" exercise, did your answers come easily or did you have to dig deep? Did any answers feel forced? Were you surprised or delighted? Were the questions thought-provoking? If so, how? Did your writing make you want to learn more? Are you feeling weary from what was uncovered? Your answers to these opening-the-heart questions might change over time. If you do not yet have the clarity you want, these are good questions to revisit on a regular basis.

Keep refining your story until you can breathe an enormous sigh of relief when you finally get it just right. Even if you must face painful truths to write your way into clarity, aligning yourself with what's true gives you a sense of purpose and propels you to whatever healing needs to happen. Then more spaciousness develops.

Visit your totem. Do you feel pleasure or inspiration when you look at it? When you began your search for your totem, did something come to mind immediately? Consider the possibility that what you picked is symbolic or carries an underlying message beyond the obvious and immediate reason you picked it.

We hope you feel proud of yourself! Remind yourself how well you've done with this program and how much courage you brought to it. Pat yourself on the back. If you ended up feeling judgmental or a little disappointed, either about yourself or the program, why not channel these feelings into writing and see where that leads? Consider whether the feelings you have right now are familiar. Explore any disappointment relating to your family of origin or any early childhood events. You could end up discovering that there's some more work to do on a particular issue or event.

Be Even More Curious: Optional Exercises

One or more of these final optional exercises might appeal to you, and who knows? – could give you your voila! moment.

1. Take a large piece of blank paper and list ten things you want to do or experience before you die. Don't overthink it; just have some fun. Once you have your list, see if there are any surprises. Did you feel you couldn't make the list until a final decision was made about children? If you find yourself making assumptions about what you can or cannot do depending on whether or not there are children, see if you can challenge your assumptions. What if you can do parenthood or child-free living *your* way and on *your* terms? How do "having a child" and "living a child-free life" change your list?

2. Revisit your collage, which represents the culmination of your experiences. Tap into your self-awareness. Does anything in particular speak to you? Is there anything you want to add to it to feel inspired when you look at it?

3. Make a list of all the ways you are special and precious. Write about where and how you stretched yourself as you worked this program.

Appreciate yourself for all you've done and all you are.

If you completed all the assignments above and the clarity of your desire isn't as sharp as you would like it to be, here are four further activities to help you accomplish the internal shift you're seeking. You can choose to work through these exercises alone or with the support of a trusted professional.

- Write your future life story as you'd like it to unfold – and err on the side of embellishment.
- If you skipped over any writing assignments during the twelve weeks, go back and do them now. Choose an exercise that seemed just too hard to do back then. Or do one that you've already done that piqued your interest or made you think more was waiting to be unearthed. In either case, you're in a different place now and will likely respond to the suggested assignment differently. Be open to something new emerging. Take your time. Give yourself a chance to continue the exploration.
- Rewrite the letters to your parents (from Week 5) using your non-dominant hand.
- Spend time answering these questions, writing about them for as long as you can:

How long have you been struggling with not being able to decide about motherhood, and how has that been for you? What has it cost you?

How has your ambivalence impacted relationships throughout your life?

What is your first memory of experiencing indecision (about anything)? Were you made to feel ashamed by your indecision? Did you get help with it? (If you didn't get help with it, an unexplored injury could still be lingering.)

Can you articulate (and write about) what pieces of your puzzle are still missing?

For additional suggestions, take a closer look at Appendix II, "I Still Don't Know," in the back of the book. You'll find more helpful activities and advice there.

The strength and power of this program is that at each stage it helps you identify exactly what still needs attention so you can take the next steps. If you don't feel the clarity of your desire in most, if not all, cells of your body, trust that there is a good reason. Chances are you just need more time to either allow the clarity to percolate through or to delve more deeply into the territory of unresolved issues. If you feel it would be helpful to have guidance in this final phase, we recommend seeking a good counselor, psychologist, or psychotherapist. Only you can know what will best support your process. Remember that it doesn't hurt to ask for help. Asking for help is a sign of strength and self-care.

What to Hold Inside Your Sweet Self as You Go Forth

Look what you did! You belong to a special group of bold women. You are a trailblazer. We hope this program reaches more and more women like you. The time and emotional energy you put in took real commitment. You've given yourself the gift of raised consciousness. That alone will help you thrive and positively impact those around you. Feel proud of all your accomplishments. Honor, love, and appreciate yourself.

You might decide to have a ritual or ceremony that spotlights what you just completed. Create your own private ceremony or share your celebration with others. You can refer to some of the weekly self-care suggestions if you need help thinking of something to do. Even if you don't yet know your desire, your achievements are still worthy of a celebration. To start, take your hand now and put it on your heart, smile, and say the words "I'm so proud of myself for being who I am and for being what I am. I am truly a treasure."

Remember the depth and breadth of all your inner resources. Over the course of this program you had the opportunity to create comfort within; you reinforced that you're not alone by establishing your circle of support; and used The Mantra to take a step back when you felt overwhelmed. You now have a spacecraft that can take you forward or back in time as you wish; a wise woman who has answers and gifts to share; a magic flying carpet that you can maneuver or that can transport you; a two-step process – desire, then decision – to use for all requests; the art of reframing perceptions to build resilience; and a future journal entry that helps you regain perspective when you feel you have lost it.

It's important not to underestimate the power of what took place over the weeks you stayed engaged in this process. Don't take any of this lightly.

Nothing is better than allowing enough time to absorb all that you learned. While things continue to settle, you might continue to experience uncomfortable or unexpected feelings. This does not mean that something is wrong at all. You might also find yourself interacting differently with people who are near and dear to you. This is natural as self-discovery continues to percolate from the depths of your psyche. Cut yourself some slack. Be gentle with yourself. If by chance you find yourself in turmoil, please don't be alone with it. Find and get help right away.

We wish you heartfelt warmth and happiness. We honor you and all that you gave to this program. We hope that at the very least you discovered what you wanted or needed. Perhaps you gained even more than you expected.

You are well on your way.

We wish you the very best always.

Acknowledgments

This book's core depends on all the women who have trusted us and the process we shared with them over the years. Many provided valuable feedback that helped the program evolve. We especially want to thank the twenty women (Amy Lynn, Aviva, Cecilia, Cheryl, Danielle, Ghea, Kate, Lauren, Lea, Lesley, Louise, Makayla, Michel, Molly, Nicole, Nina, Sandra, Susie, Sydney, and Tess) who so generously took the time to answer a lengthy questionnaire and then waited years to see the results; their stories add soul to this book and it just wouldn't be the same without them. Their voices help create a necessary dialogue. We are also very grateful to have serendipitously met Jane Waxman, our first editor, who with grace and professionalism, in the midst of herself adopting a five-year-old, managed to meld two voices miraculously into one.

And, from Denise:

If it takes a village to raise a child, then it takes at least a small town to produce a book that is dedicated to helping a woman make the most defining decision of her life. So many friends and colleagues have directly and indirectly supported this project over the years – many more than I can thank here. Let me try. First and foremost, I wish to thank my partner, Ian, who believed in the value of this work and created a conducive environment for several years while it was either cooking or on the back burner. Second, I am indebted to all of the women in my psychotherapy practice who struggled with this question; they were the original inspiration that led to the creation of this program. And then, in no particular order: Gloria Steinem, who has been a principal role model my entire adult life; other women authors who prepared the way for our program; my colleague and collaborator, Ann Davidman; and my ancestors, my family of origin, and those brave enough to marry into it. Every one of the following gave me just what I needed when I needed it the most – and some repeatedly! Ann M., Ann W., Arna, Carin, Carol, Denise, Jacquie, Jessie, Joyce, Kevin, Laura, Linda, Lisa, Louise, Mary, Mia, Minou, Miriam, Nazila, Paula, Peter A., Peter B., Roberta, Ronnie D., Rosa, Sarah, Sharon, Susan, and Val. I wouldn't be the person I am today without the heart workover made possible through my work with foster dogs, in particular Teddy Rey and Pancho, blind since birth, who inspired the title change for Week 4 very late in the day. Finally, I wish to thank everyone who has "mothered" me in oh-so-many ways. Without that, this would not be possible. I bow to each and every one of you in gratitude.

And, from Ann:

The birthing of this book had a longer gestational period than I ever could have imagined, and I'm grateful to everyone who supported me in bringing it to life.

I appreciate particularly the unconditional love of my grandmother, Myrtle Rodbard, who instilled in me the tenacity needed to be able to complete this project. I also want to thank my partner, Nancy Patten, who has cheered me along every step of the way.

I'm grateful to Denise L. Carlini, colleague, co-creator of this program, and co-author, without whom this book never would have seen the light of day. To all the women (too many to count) who honored me with their trust as they journeyed to clarity with this process, thank you for your contribution in enriching this book. I also sincerely appreciate the people who played their parts in helping bring this book to fruition, including Angie, Brenda, Erdmut, Jan S., Jeff C., Kim, Mai L., Mara, Molly H., Nancy C., Patricia, Peter, Shari L., Sharon, Tom, and the entire Cody clan.

My heartfelt appreciation to my parents, Sherry, Bob, Naomi, and Blackie; to my siblings, Linda, Larry, Aaron, and Rachel; and to Alya, my first niece, a special thank you: You have my utmost respect and gratitude for supporting me in numerous ways behind the scenes in writing this book. Many thanks also to the rest of my nieces and nephew, Amy, Elizabeth, Jessica, David, Rebecca, Hannah, Zoe, Autumn, Olimpia, Evelyn, and Josephine, and to all of their partners and my entire extended family. Thank you for loving me the way you do. I also want to thank these three strong, powerful women whom I could always count on for guidance and to help me stay the course: my Auntie Bernice, my Auntie Francine, and my cousin, Nancy M.

And finally, to all the young ones in my life: You inspire me to keep thinking about the next generation – even before you arrive. My love and attention will never wane. And to every woman asking *Is motherhood for me?*: May you only be praised for asking, and never feel alone when your answer or truth isn't immediately known.

Appendix I

Tools for Sharing the Process

A. A Letter to Your Partner Clarifying Recommendations of the Program

To get the most out of *Motherhood – Is It For Me?* it's essential to experience your own uncensored process without sharing your experience and insights with your partner. It's challenging, at best, to try to figure out *your* truth in the face of another person's questions, fears, or ambivalence. If your partner has clarity and you don't, all you'll hear is their sentiments. But it can be helpful to have someone else explain the recommendations of the program that you're about to embark on.

Below are templates for a letter to your partner to communicate the importance of a moratorium on the discussion of children and why it's better to delay sharing details until the completion of all twelve weeks. You can use one of these letters verbatim or use them as guides for writing your own letter. One is from you, and one is from us. You decide which one is more suited to your relationship or circumstances.

If you're not partnered or don't feel you need a letter, disregard this section. Perhaps you are experiencing another situation in which these letters can be useful. Use them as needed. However, please note that we do not make any assumptions about your particular situation, nor do we have an agenda for your relationship. This program and these letters are for all people in all situations regardless of gender, sexuality, or cultural background.

Template for a Letter from the Authors of the Book

Dear *[Other],*

[You] is about to embark on a process that is designed to take about three months. It could take longer and perhaps finish sooner. For *[You]* to be able to have a thoughtful discussion with you about the decision of whether or not to have children, she has decided to participate in the Motherhood-Is it for me?™ program.

[You]'s clarity is essential for her to feel good about making a conscious decision about whether or not to become a mother. Once she knows the truth of her desire, her conversation with you will be far more productive than anything that has occurred to date.

There are two recommendations. The first is that the two of you have a moratorium on discussing whether or not you want children until *[You]* has completed the program. The second is that *[You]* doesn't share with you her feelings, insights, or any of her experience until she has completed all of the suggested steps and is ready to share with you.

Some couples find it a relief to take a break from the topic. As co-authors of the book and co-creators of the program, we highly recommend that for *[You]* to get the most out of the program she take the time and space to have an uncensored private process separate from yours.

It's possible you'll witness some mood or emotional swings while *[You]* is working through the weekly assignments. It's natural to have emotions surface. She might even be surprised by what surfaces. It's fine for her to talk generally about how she's feeling and come to you for support if you're available for that. What we don't recommend is for her to share the details of her self-exploration or why these emotions are surfacing. Throughout the twelve-week program, her emotions and thoughts will be all over the place. Her discoveries might be incomplete. This is natural, as the process is not linear. We don't want her to share with you prematurely because it could lead to her needing to explain herself or possibly getting derailed from her personal journey. We want her to stay connected to herself and to the work she is doing so she can make the discoveries she needs.

If you feel challenged at all by watching *[You]*'s experience, hopefully there'll be room for you to talk generally about it with her. If she isn't available or doesn't feel prepared to discuss your feelings, we encourage you to find a friend or professional to talk to.

Sincerely,
The co-authors of *Motherhood – Is It For Me?* – D. Carlini and A. Davidman

P.S.: If you want to work the program simultaneously, especially if you're both undecided about parenthood, our recommendations are the same. Each of you would work the twelve weeks separately, *not* sharing any details with each other as you go along. After completion of the program, use the guidelines provided to share how the experience unfolded for each of you.

Sharing your process with your partner prematurely can make it more complicated than it needs to be. Discovering your true desire is a deeply personal experience, and it's so very easy to unconsciously censor yourself in the face of your partner's opinions or fears.

(*Motherhood – Is It For Me?* was written for women, so if you are male, the exercises will have to be tailored to fit.)

Template for a Letter from You

Dear *[Other]*,

I am struggling with not knowing if I want to have children or be a mother. I thought this decision would resolve itself by now, and it hasn't. The Motherhood-Is it for me?™ program guides women step by step to gain clarity on this issue. I've decided to work the steps of this program. There are recommendations from the authors of this book that I'd like to share with you so that you understand what I'm about to go through.

The authors of the program point out that it's very difficult to make a decision when trying to figure out a *desire* and a *decision* at the same time. This program consists of a variety of exercises that'll help me become clear on my desire. Once I'm clear on my desire for motherhood, the path to making a decision will be easier than it has been. Afterward, having a conversation with you about becoming parents or choosing a child-free life will be much more productive than it has been.

The reason for this letter is to explain two recommendations that are expressed in the book by the authors, who have been using this program for women (and men, too) since 1991.

The first recommendation is that you and I declare a moratorium on the topic of children. This means we decide to table the discussion and stop trying to make a case for yes or a case for no. It means we stop talking about all the options in front of us. It means we decide to give the topic a rest while I engage in a structured program that will help me develop more clarity about this issue than I have now.

The second recommendation is that while I'm participating in the program, I not share with you any of my experience until I complete it. The program isn't linear, which means I will have many incomplete thoughts and insights throughout the twelve weeks. The authors suggest that if I share incomplete thoughts and ideas with you as a beloved, it leaves too much room for misinterpretation. This could potentially cloud or confuse my exploration.

There are exercises and writing assignments each week. At the completion of the program, I'll share as much detail as I think is helpful.

This process might stir up emotions, so I could be more emotional than usual. If my emotional reactions get in the way of our relating, I'll share with you generally what is happening for me without going into detail. I invite you to talk to me if you feel the connection between us is or becomes distant. I don't want you to feel there is distance between us. Please say something to me if this becomes your experience.

Love,
[You]

B. Templates for Sharing Your Experience with Your Partner

Participants of this program have found it useful to have a template that guides them through a conversation with their partner after they complete the program. If you want to share your experience, you won't want to just blurt out your decision without some preparatory groundwork to both protect yourself and make sure your partner is ready to hear about your newfound awareness and insight.

While you've been on a journey of discovery, it's likely that your partner hasn't and is waiting for the results of your findings. Of course, this isn't always the case; some partners do this program simultaneously or they've been working on their desires using other tools. It's also possible your partner has already made their decision about this issue, and this is one of the reasons you wanted to complete the program.

There are two templates below. One is designed for partners who *have not* been through this or any other guided process, and the other is for those who *have* participated in the program.

We emphasized at the beginning of the book the importance of having your private, uncensored experience. Even if there are still unresolved issues for you, you're certainly in a different place than when you began. We don't have an agenda regarding whether or not you should share your experience. *If* you want to share, *what* you want to share, and *when* you want to share are options. Some women like to share what they've learned right away, and others want to let it simmer more before they share.

Not everyone knows where to begin when it's time to share their experience. The templates below are only guides. Feel free to make them your own. The order of the conversation is only a suggestion.

How to Share Your Process with Your Partner when They Have *Not* Participated in the Program

When you're ready to share, we hope the template provided will assist you. First, find a time when your partner is available and wants to hear about your experience. It makes sense to do this because you want their full attention. You're the one who has had the experience; your partner hasn't been through the self-exploration you've just completed. Although the two of you might have been in similar places when you started, you can be in different places now.

Feel free to make a copy of this template so you can both tweak it to make it work well for your individual communication styles. This is a guide only and won't work for everyone, but it's a good basis to begin from to get the conversation started in a thoughtful way.

When both of you are ready, ask your partner how it has been for them while you've been working the program:

You: *"How has it been for you while I've been engaged in this process?"*

(Listen thoughtfully and respond in such a way that your partner knows you've heard them.)

You: *"This program took courage to complete. A lot of self-exploration was asked of me."*

(Let your partner know how proud of yourself you are. Don't play down the experience. This was a big undertaking. Maybe share what you felt before Week 1 and how you feel post Week 12).

Then let them know in the following order:

You: *"This is what I learned about myself:_____."*

(Listen to see if they want to comment. You can always ask, "How is that for you to hear?")

You: *"These are some of the insights I've gained: _____."*

You: *"I'd like to share some of the writing I've done. Would you like to hear it?"*

(This is only if you want to share your writing. If not, then don't mention it. Also check in with your partner to see if they are ready to hear it or want to.)

You: *"How are you doing? Can I keep sharing or do you need a break or would you like to say anything before I continue?"*

You: *"Do you want to hear my desire at this point, which may not be my ultimate choice?"*

(Wait to see what your partner says.)

You: *"Do you want to hear what my choice would be if it were up to me alone? If you're not ready for that, when would be a good time to share it with you?"*

Pause here for a few moments to check in with each other. Do you both want to continue the dialogue? If either one of you needs a break, honor that need. Continue if/when you both want to.

Ask the following questions of your partner:

You: *"What is your desire and what would you decide if it were up to you alone?"*

"Is there wiggle room in your views?"

"If you haven't made a decision, is there anything you feel you need to tend to before you can make one?"

"Is there anything you need from me?"

How to Share Your Process when Both You and Your Partner Have Completed the Program

First, acknowledge each other's hard work and perseverance. Second, pat yourselves on the back for the courage it took to take a look at uncomfortable feelings and venture to places that many people leave unexplored.

Then ask each other the following questions, in turn:

What did you learn about yourself?

Did you begin to see something about yourself in a new way?

Are you in the same place or a different place?

Do you want to share any of your writing with me? (Read to each other or exchange journals.)

What is your desire at this point? (Not to be confused with your decision.)

Do you want to hear which path I'd choose if it were up to me alone? If you're not ready to hear my decision, when would be a good time to share that with you?

If ready to share:

What is your decision?

Is there wiggle room in it?

Is there anything you feel you need to tend to or address before making a decision is possible?

What else would you like to say or share about your experience?

End with each of you sharing one thing that you appreciate about the other.

Appendix II

"I Still Don't Know!?" – Next Steps

"You won't help the new plants grow by pulling them up higher."
–揠苗助长 (Yà miáo zhù zhǎng)[12]

If you're reading this section it's likely you completed the twelve-week program but feel you still lack the clarity you had hoped for. Or perhaps you feel some anxiety because in fact you do know, but are afraid to face the truth of your knowing. If you finished the program an hour ago or even a day ago, let the program settle a bit inside you. If you still feel uncertain or foggy after a few weeks, consider the options below. At least one is bound to speak out to you.

Remember that you are first trying to identify what you *want* for yourself. The decision part of this equation comes after you know your *desire*. If you attempt to do both simultaneously you will likely remain stuck. First identify your desire. Decision-making feels quite different once you know, feel, and own the clarity of your desire.

Is It Really True?

This happens more frequently than you'd expect: A woman proclaims a certain amount of clarity during Week 9 or 10, but at the end of the program says, "I have no idea what I want. I am in the exact same place I started." Then after a little gentle probing, the clarity comes back.

If you've lived with uncertainty for a very long time, it can become an automatic response even if you don't feel that way anymore.

Think back to how you felt a few weeks ago. Did you feel you had clarity then? It's worth checking in with yourself to see if it's really true that you don't know. Go back and read your answers to the various writing assignments. Even if you think nothing has changed or you are not closer to where you want to be, consider the possibility that you in fact *feel* differently than you did during Week 1. This new feeling might be unfamiliar or uncomfortable, so you don't yet know what to do with it. If you've had discomfort before and you feel some discomfort now, don't assume that the reason is necessarily the same. The cause of your discomfort now might be different.

Some women feel or think that not much happened for them, yet the other participants in her group gave her feedback that indicated they did see changes. Just because you don't *feel* like anything happened for you does not mean that nothing happened. If you worked the program on your own, you don't have the benefit of this kind of feedback.

Rest to Let the Process Happen – Trust

Allow yourself a full three-month gestation or rest period. Nothing takes the place of time and letting things percolate gently on their own. Although this can be easier said than done, doing so allows for a powerful and important validation of trusting your own inner process.

The exercise below could be just what you need to experience the internal shifts that have actually occurred.

Place a note in your diary or on your calendar exactly three months from this date. Then do nothing. Get on with your life. Focus on other activities, especially those that bring you pleasure and joy. Establish a hobby or revive one that has gone dormant. Get on with it. Be happy. Pay attention, of course, if you have a potent dream or you notice things differently while you are getting on with your life, but don't actively engage in trying to clarify your desire.

When the date arrives, sit down in a quiet place. Choose a self-nourishing practice – a special cup of tea, soothing music, a lit candle, or something else that helps make the moment special. Have some writing paper or your journal ready, and respond to the prompt below, without thinking. Just start writing. Fill a page – or better yet, three pages. There is no maximum.

If anything were possible, I'd create a life for myself that looks like...

When the writing has ceased, sit quietly for a few moments, close your eyes, and slow your breathing. Rest comfortably. After pausing for a few moments, read what you wrote out loud. This is important. You might want to read it more than once.

See what you notice in your body and in your heart while you are reading. Do you also see images? Note them. Notice what information you now have. What are you feeling? Is there something new in the mix? What is the key element or theme coming through? Give yourself complete permission to accept all that is there for you. Embrace everything, even if there is some judgment or nagging thought trying to break through. See if you now have something to move forward on.

If you want to take this exercise one step further, you can record what you wrote and then listen to see if you hear something different from when you read it out loud.

Ripple the Waters – A Small Investment Might Just Get You There

If you sense that just a little something else will make all the difference, review the "Be Even More Curious" optional assignments presented each week. Take some time to do one or more of them now. Pick ones that seemed too hard to do at the time (they might be exactly right for you now), or ones that bring up some emotion when you just *consider* doing them.

Why not revisit the guided visualizations, especially the ones in Weeks 3, 7, 8, 9, and 10? Do some writing afterward. This time you could have an entirely new experience.

Revisit the second "My Journal Entry" writing assignment from Week 9 of making a journal entry dated one year from today. It begins: "*As I look back over the past year, I'm pleased to notice….*" See what comes out if you write freely and without inhibition. Then read what you wrote out loud.

Open Up Your Process

Thoughtfully consider women you know (or would like to know) and ask them about their own experience of deciding one way or the other. Choose women you admire either for the choices they've made in their lives or because they appear to live their lives with integrity. Take some time to hear others' stories firsthand.

Read or reread the twenty stories from real women presented in Weeks 2 through 11 and consider how you fit in with their narratives.

Think about putting together your own peer support group and doing the program activities in the company of other women. That would prove to be a very different experience from working on your own.

Check the resources in the back of this book and see if there is a title that piques your interest. Read it from the vantage point of having done all this work. Consider titles that might help you with decision-making. You might find that you know more about your desire than you realize.

If You Discovered Something to Heal

If you've gotten in touch with some unfinished business or unhealed aspect of your life, make an action plan to take care of it and yourself. It can be completely natural and normal to seek professional help to do this piece of work. Your action plan can be time-limited, and could look like one of these:

For the next six months my main focus will be healing the hurt that I don't feel that I matter to anyone.

I'm going to spend time learning how to cope better with the severe anxiety I feel most of the time.

I want to focus on changing my need to control so much of what goes on in my life.

You might not heal these issues completely, but if you make enough of a dent in them it could mean the difference between knowing and not knowing your desire. Just a little bit of work could be enough to allow for an internal shift to take place. Even a slight shift might be enough to know your desire.

Ask for Help

Find a qualified psychotherapist, counselor, or coach to continue the exploration.

Consider working with Ann Davidman, a licensed marriage and family therapist. Check the website www.MotherhoodIsItForMe.com to contact her directly.

Believe in yourself. Trust your abilities. Cultivate self-love and compassion. Take great care of yourself. *You* are your first priority.

References

1. Frost, Robert. "The Road not Taken." *Selected Poems of Robert Frost.* Holt, Rinehart and Winston, 1969. Print.

2. "Lao Tzu". BrainyQuote.com. Xplore Inc., 2016. 5 August 2016. http://www.brainyquote.com/quotes/quotes/l/laotzu386562.html

3. Brontë, Charlotte. *Jane Eyre.* Brainyquote.com. Xplore Inc., 2016. 5 August 2016 http://www.brainyquote.com/quotes/quotes/c/charlotteb388605.html

4. Ziman Tobin, Phyllis O. *Motherhood Optional: A Psychological Journey.* Jason Aronson, 1998. Print.

5. Ibid.

6. Winnicott, D. W. "The capacity to be alone." in *The Maturational Processes and the Facilitating Environment* (pp. 29-36). London: Hogarth Press and the Institute of Psycho-Analysis. 1965. Print.

7. Ireland, Mardy S. *Reconceiving Women: Separating Motherhood from Female Identity.*© Copyright Guilford Press. New York: Guilford, 1993. Print. Reprinted with permission of The Guilford Press.

8. Marcus Aurelius Antoninus. Meditations. *101Sharequotes.com.* 5 August 2016. http://101sharequotes.com/quote/marcus-aurelius-antoninus-look-well-into-thyself-there-is-320576

9. "Reinhold Niebuhr". BrainyQuote.com. Xplore Inc., 2016. 23 February 2016. http://www.brainyquote.com/quotes/quotes/r/reinholdni100884.html

10. "Johann von Goethe Quotes". *Quotes.net*. STANDS4 LLC, 2016. Web. 6 Jun 2016. http://www.quotes.net/quote/1203

11. "William Wordsworth". BrainyQuote.com. Xplore Inc., 2016. 10 June 2016. http://www.brainyquote.com/quotes/quotes/w/williamwor108633.html

12. Proverb, C. (2016). *Chinese Proverb*. China: bestquotestv.com, p. http://www.bestquotestv.com/proverb/chineses-proverb-6375

Resources

A. Books

When we prepared for our very first group in the early '90s, we wanted to put together a resource list for our participants. We eventually found five books that were sufficiently relevant to be worthy of inclusion. Fast-forward twenty-five years, and books, blogs, and websites abound on the topic. With new resources popping up all the time, there are too many to include here. Therefore we selected only those we consider classics (for good reason) or that have helped many women, and those that might not so easily be found through online searches. This book's website includes news about other resources as they're discovered.

Exploring and Redefining Motherhood

Carroll, Laura. *The Baby Matrix: Why Freeing Our Minds from Outmoded Thinking about Parenthood & Reproduction Will Create a Better World.* Live True Books, 2012. Print.

De Marneffe, Daphne. *Maternal Desire: On Children, Love, and the Inner Life.* New York: Back Bay Books, 2005. Print.

Friedan, Betty. *The Feminine Mystique.* New York: W. W. Norton, 2013. Print.

Ireland, Mardy S. *Reconceiving Women: Separating Motherhood from Female Identity.* New York: Guilford, 1993. Print.

Ambivalence and Choosing

Dell, Diana and Erem, Susan. *Do I Want to Be a Mom? A Woman's Guide to the Decision of a Lifetime.* New York: Contemporary Books, McGraw-Hill, 2004. Print.

Engel, Beverly. *The Parenthood Decision: Discovering Whether You Are Ready and Willing to Become a Parent.* New York: Main Street Books, Doubleday, 1998. Print.

Mattes, Jane. *Single Mothers by Choice: A Guidebook for Single Women Who Are Considering or Have Chosen Motherhood.* New York: Harmony, 1994. Print.

Meredith, Ann. *The Baby Dilemma: How to Confidently Decide Whether or Not to Have a Child and Feel Good about It.* San Francisco: Bush Street Press, 2011. Print.

Safer, Jeanne. *Beyond Motherhood: Choosing a Life without Children.* New York: Gallery, 1996. Print.

Scott, Laura S. *Two Is Enough: A Couple's Guide to Living Childless by Choice.* Berkeley: Seal Press, 2009. Print.

Wade, Donna. *I Want a Baby, He Doesn't: How Both Partners Can Make the Right Decision at the Right Time.* Avon, Massachusetts: Adams Media, 2005. Print.

Ziman Tobin, Phyllis O. *Motherhood Optional: A Psychological Journey.* Jason Aronson, 1998. Print.

You Are Not Alone – Others' Stories

Bender, Karen E. and de Gramont, Nina. *Choice: True Stories of Birth, Contraception, Infertility, Adoption, Single Parenthood, and Abortion.* San Francisco: MacAdam/Cage, 2007. Print.

Leibovich, Lori. *Maybe Baby: 28 Writers Tell the Truth about Skepticism, Infertility, Baby Lust, Childlessness, Ambivalence, and How They Made the Biggest Decision of Their Lives.* New York: Harper Collins Publishers, 2007. Print.

Mantel, Henriette. *No Kidding: Women Writers on Bypassing Parenthood.* Berkeley, California: Seal Press, 2013. Print.

Walker, Rebecca. *Baby Love: Choosing Motherhood after a Lifetime of Ambivalence.* New York: Riverhead Books, the Penguin Group, 2007. Print.

Healing and Self-Care

Baraz, James and Alexander, Shoshana. *Awakening Joy: 10 Steps to Happiness.* Berkeley, California: Parallax Press, 2012. Print.

Beattie, Melody. *The New Codependency: Help and Guidance for Today's Generation.* New York: Simon & Schuster, 2009. Print.

Borysenko, Joan. *A Woman's Book of Life: The Biology, Psychology, and Spirituality of the Feminine Life Cycle.* New York: Riverhead Trade, 1998. Print.

Boston Women's Health Book Collective. *The New Our Bodies, Ourselves: A Health Book for and by Women*. New York: Touchstone, 2011. Print.

Brown, Brene. *The Gifts of Imperfection: Let Go of Who You Think You're Supposed to Be and Embrace Who You Are*. Center City, Minnesota: Hazelden, 2010. Print.

Cameron, Julia. *The Artist's Way: A Spiritual Path to Higher Creativity*. New York: Jeremy P. Tarcher/Putnam, 1992. Print.

Day, Jody. *Living the Life Unexpected: 12 Weeks to Your Plan B for a Meaningful and Fulfilling Future without Children*. London: Bluebird, an imprint of Pan Macmillan, 2016. Print.

Graham, Linda. *Bouncing Back: Rewiring Your Brain for Maximum Resilience and Well-Being*. New World Library, 2013. Print.

Napier, Nancy. *Getting Through the Day: Strategies for Adults Hurt as Children*. New York: W. W. Norton & Company, 1993. Print.

Neff, Kristen. *Self-Compassion: Stop Beating Yourself Up and Leave Insecurity Behind*. New York: William Morrow, an imprint of Harper Collins, 2011. Print.

Northrup, Christiane. *Women's Bodies, Women's Wisdom: The Complete Guide to Women's Health and Wellbeing*. New York: Bantam, 2010. Print.

Parnell, Laurel. *Tapping In: A Step by Step Guide to Activating Your Healing Resources through Bilateral Stimulation*. Boulder, Colorado: Sounds True, 2008. Print.

Payne, Niravi B. *The Language of Fertility: The Revolutionary Mind-Body Program for Conscious Conception*. New York: Harmony, 1997. Print.

B. Online

www.calm.com

www.babycenter.com

www.ourbodiesourselves.org

www.handinhandparenting.org

www.aa.org

www.al-anon.org

www.coda.org

www.adultchildren.org

www.againstthestream.org

About the Authors

Denise L. Carlini, M.A., Marriage and Family Therapist

From her earliest days as a licensed psychotherapist, Denise heard many of her female clients say they felt utterly alone while considering whether or not they wanted to become a mother. She came to realize this feeling was actually quite common, and it inspired her to create with a colleague and the co-author of this book the Motherhood-Is it for me?™ program. The two went on to lead groups with women for many years, and a bit later added an adapted version for men. Now retired as a psychotherapist, Denise, who chose not to have children, shares a home with her partner, whom she met while making a walking pilgrimage. She spends time writing, creating art, cooking, being in nature, tending to her garden, and fostering dogs. A portion of her profits from the sale of *Motherhood – Is It For Me?* benefit women and children throughout the world.

Ann Davidman, M.S., Licensed Marriage and Family Therapist

Ann Davidman has been helping women find clarity about whether or not to become a mother for twenty-five years. As a *motherhood clarity mentor*, Ann believes every woman has the right to explore this question and find a truthful answer. Her passion for this work continues to grow and has been sustained since 1991 when she and Denise L. Carlini created the Motherhood-Is it for me? program. Ann's expertise lies in helping both women and men rid themselves of self-limiting beliefs and rigid patterns, expand their capacity to think outside the box, resolve internal challenges, and discover their true desire about whether or not to become a parent. Her only agenda is for her clients to be free from confusion and achieve peace of mind. Ann offers the Motherhood Clarity Course™ privately and online to reach women in any time zone who are struggling with this issue. Ann received her graduate degree from San Francisco State University and is a member of the California Association of Marriage and Family Therapists (CAMFT). She maintains a successful psychotherapy practice in Oakland, California, USA, where she helps clients with a variety of concerns, always bringing the utmost respect and compassion to her work.

Index

A

Abortion, 39, 56, 106, 110-111, 294, 335-336, 441

Accurate Story, 365, 369, 402, 407-408

Addiction, 338, 404

Adoption, 13, 166, 243, 248, 256, 334, 336, 341, 441

Alcohol, 38-39, 199

Ambivalence, 5-7, 71, 179, 195, 219-220, 225-227, 240, 255, 258-260, 381, 401, 404, 413, 421, 440-441

Ambivalent, 193, 230, 332, 406

Attachment Wound, 195-197, 319

B

Being Decisive, 252-254

Birgit, 40-41, 104, 165, 235, 259, 324, 362-363, 399

Birth Order, 32, 34, 39

Birth Story, 263-265

Body-Mind Approach, 12

Boundaries, 71, 125, 198-201, 220, 273, 392, 397

C

Ceremony, 225, 230-231, 233, 257-258, 294-296, 327, 396-397, 408, 414

Collage, 28, 103, 170-171, 206, 231, 289, 292, 364, 368-369, 371, 383, 387, 411

Coming Home, 385-388

Conscious Choice, 6, 77, 194, 261, 377

Conscious Decision-Making, 225, 251, 319

Contain, 15, 77, 237, 266

Containment, 14-15

Containment Wall, 15

Counseling, 9, 110, 270

Creating Comfort Within, 45-46

Creating Your Circle Of Support, 54-55

D

Decision-Making, 11, 30, 121, 130-133, 148, 151, 179, 201, 223, 225, 246, 251, 262, 270, 303, 319, 431, 435

Dialogue, The, 155-157

Disappointment, 127, 130-131, 137, 171, 287, 319, 402, 405-406, 411

Dreams, 28, 56, 76, 235, 265, 369, 371, 381

Dwelling, 100, 151, 160-161

E

Empowerment, 129, 136-137, 261

Expectation, 69, 104, 150, 163-164, 200, 244, 273, 280, 337-338

Externals, 13-14, 27, 42, 52, 62, 177, 183, 193, 256, 350-354, 362, 383, 404, 408

F

Family Map, 27, 29-40, 57, 61, 75, 101, 136, 164-165, 172-173, 198, 352, 354, 392

Family Of Origin, 29, 35, 37, 40-41, 159, 259, 352, 411

Fears, 6, 11, 27, 42, 47-48, 51-52, 56, 62, 115, 212, 256, 260, 318, 350, 354-358, 362, 383, 421, 424

G

Generational Inheritance, 163-165, 171, 193, 259

Genogram, 29

Good-Enough Mother, 196, 202, 208, 304, 362, 392, 398

Grief, 94, 177-178, 181, 226, 231, 233, 259, 261, 272, 294, 296, 301, 320, 327, 361, 404

Grieving Process, 259, 294

Guided Visualizations, 2, 18, 20, 27, 43-44, 62, 72, 121, 125, 208, 316, 434

H

Having Children, 13, 36, 40-41, 84, 112, 142, 146, 165, 200, 210, 227, 256, 274, 305, 376, 391, 396

Healing Process, 167, 186, 297

Holly, 40-41, 133, 195-197, 264-265, 280, 282, 319, 354-356, 400

Honoring Ceremony, 294-296, 327, 408

Honoring Your Process, 14

I

Indecision, 5, 182, 225, 258, 377, 396, 398-399, 413
Infertility, 227, 330, 332-333, 441
Inner Child, 96, 170, 257
Inner Freedom, 96-97
Inner Resources, 44, 53, 380, 414
Intuition, 86, 275, 316, 359, 361, 364-365, 369-370

J

Journey Begins, The, 63-65, 344
Journey Revisited, The, 345-348
Judgments, 6, 164, 189, 225, 232, 234-235, 390, 393

M

Mantra, The, 66-72, 120, 140, 237, 267, 276, 414
MeGSS, 13
Mindfulness, 285
Miscarriage, 30, 56, 240, 245-246, 248-249, 294, 300, 362
Mother And Daughter, 189-190

N

Negative Thought Patterns, 239, 285-286
No-Baby Shower, 231, 396-397
Nurture, 96, 208, 284, 318, 379-381, 396

O

Object-Relations Theory, 196
Old Wounds, 159-160, 406
Overwhelming, 13, 17, 38, 40, 94, 125, 158-159, 170, 224, 231

P

Pace, 9, 17, 25, 172, 281, 399

Parenthood, 411, 423, 439-441

Parenting, 202, 211, 261, 263, 331, 340-341, 355

Partner, 11, 14-15, 26, 52, 62, 104, 132, 161-163, 227, 237, 354-356, 366, 401-403, 405, 421-430

Pregnancy, 35, 52, 56, 85, 106, 109, 111, 117, 149, 240, 242-243, 245, 271, 289, 291, 307

Psychotherapy, 40, 162, 201

Pulse Of Your Desire, 350, 359-361, 369, 383, 387

Puzzle Pieces, 16, 25, 95, 280, 310, 321, 324, 362-363, 365, 388, 405

R

Reactions, 51, 96-97, 101, 104, 119, 226, 228-229, 281, 425

Reframing Perceptions, 284-287, 292, 296, 309, 318, 325, 414

Remember a Time When, 122-124

Resilience, 44, 315, 317-319, 363, 414, 442

Responses, 96-97, 104, 119

Rite of Passage, 201-202, 230

Ritual, 59, 77, 141, 225, 230-231, 233, 257-258, 294-296, 327, 396-397, 414

S

Saboteur, 326-328

Samantha, 40-41, 98, 103-104, 162, 197, 233-234, 257, 283-284, 315, 360-362, 392, 398

Self-Facilitated Group, 10

Self-Imposed Pressure, 227

Self-Sabotage, 315, 319-321

Sexual Abuse, 38, 404

Shame, 6, 50, 68, 127, 139, 173, 189, 222, 228, 234, 260, 284, 293-294, 296, 315, 319-320, 326-328, 357

Sibling, 32-37, 39, 206, 399, 402, 404

Single Mother, 113, 118, 273, 352, 366, 440

Sue, 30-35, 39-40, 98, 130-131, 194-195, 199-200, 256, 259, 283, 318, 357-358, 361-362, 392, 396-398, 402

Sue's Family Map, 31
Surprise Detour, A, 277-279
Surprise Encounter, A, 89-92

T

Things To Revisit Later, 27, 368
Thrive, 120, 200, 206, 315-317, 323, 325, 327-328, 343, 347, 370, 392, 397, 400, 414
Time Travel, 279, 289
Totem, 370, 383, 389, 394, 408, 410
Trauma, 161, 260, 303, 316, 358, 404
Two-Step Decision, 131-134

U

Uncertainty, 6, 26, 66, 142, 219, 227, 318, 432
Uncharted Territory(ies), 283-284, 297, 309, 318-319, 358
Uncomfortable Feelings, 15, 49, 76, 151, 429
Unmet Need, 95, 97, 161-163, 307
Unresolved Issues, 154, 159-160, 164, 220, 350, 404, 413, 426

V

Vulnerability, 169, 326, 354
Vulnerable, 197, 208, 398

W

Winnicott, 195, 437
Wise Woman, 315-316, 321-322, 325-329, 343, 347, 369, 414
Wise Woman Speaks, A, 311-313

Y

Yes-No Continuum, 7, 350, 360, 384, 396
Yes? No? Maybe?, 221-223
Younger Self, 96, 100, 102-103, 105, 120, 159, 163, 170, 208, 360
Your Checklist For Reflection, 50